Henry Cabot Lodge

The war with Spain

Henry Cabot Lodge

The war with Spain

ISBN/EAN: 9783337231934

Printed in Europe, USA, Canada, Australia, Japan

Cover: Foto ©ninafisch / pixelio.de

More available books at **www.hansebooks.com**

THE
WAR WITH SPAIN

BY

HENRY CABOT LODGE

ILLUSTRATED

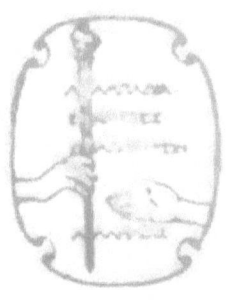

CONTENTS

ILLUSTRATIONS

ILLUSTRATIONS

ILLUSTRATIONS

ix

THE WAR WITH SPAIN

CHAPTER I

THE UNSETTLED QUESTION

THREE hundred and fifty years ago the empire of Charles V circled the globe, and was the greatest military and political power among civilized men. Of that mighty fabric, the year 1898 has witnessed the unlamented end. We of to-day have thus beheld the closing scene of one of the great dramas of history. The colonies planted in America by the English and the Dutch have risen to be a great nation, and that nation has finished the work begun by the followers of William of Orange, when, amid the dikes of Holland and upon the stormy waters of the English Channel, they struck at the power of Philip II even in its pitch of pride. Such events as these are not accidents, nor are they things of yesterday. The final expulsion of Spain from the Americas and from the Philippines is the fit conclusion of the long strife between the people who stood for civil and religious freedom, and those who stood for bigotry and tyranny as hideous in their action as any which have ever cursed humanity. The work has been a long one, but Spain at last is confined practically to her peninsula, where her people can do as they please with each other, but whence they can trouble the world no more. Spain has ceased to rule; her once vast empire has gone, because she has proved herself unfit to govern, and for the unfit among nations there is no pity in the relentless world-forces which shape the destinies of mankind.

The irrepressible conflict between Spain on the one side and England and Holland on the other, after the former had been crippled in Europe, was transferred from the Old World to the New. They seemed at first very remote from each other in the vast regions of the American continents, but nevertheless the two opposing forces, the two irrevocably hostile systems, were always drawing steadily together, with the certainty that when they met one of them must go down before the other. The Seven Years' War drove France from eastern North America, and fixed forever the fate of that region. It was to be English, not French:

The lilies withered where the lion trod.

The expulsion of France not only removed the long standing northern peril to the English colonies, but swept away the last barrier between them and Spain. In the American Revolution, France, seeking her revenge for the conquests of Pitt, forced Spain to become her ally against England; but Spain had no love for the rebellious colonists. A treacherous, nominal friend, she tried to wrest advantage from their weakness, and to secure to herself in final possession the Mississippi valley and the great Northwest. Failing in this, she sought, after American independence had been won, by false and insolent diplomacy and by corrupting intrigues among the Western settlers, to check the American advance across the continent. It was all in vain. Through woodland and savanna, over mountain and stream, came the steady tramp of the American pioneer. He was an adventurer, but he was also a settler, and what he took he held. He carried a rifle in one hand, he bore an axe in the other, and where he camped he made a clearing and built a home. The two inevitable antagonists were nearing each other at last, for they were face to face now all along the western and southern borders of the United States. The time had come for one to stop, or for the other to give way. But there was no stopping possible to the Americans, and through the medium of French ownership the Louisiana purchase was made, the Mississippi became a river of the United States, and their possessions were stretched across the continent even to the slopes of the Rocky Mountains. Still not content, the Americans pressed upon the southern boundary until, in 1819, they forced Spain, in order to avoid war, to sell them Florida and the northern coast of the Gulf of Mexico as far as Louisiana. Meantime, inspired by the example of the United States in rejecting foreign dominion, and borne forward by the great democratic movement which, originating in America, had swept over Europe, the Spanish colonies rose in arms and drove Spain from Central and South America.

A few years passed by, and then the restless American advance pressed on into Texas, took it from Mexico, and a territory larger than any European state except Russia was added to the United States. Still the

American march went on, and then war came with Mexico, and another vast region, stretching from Oregon to Arizona, became an American possession. All the lands of North America which had once called Spain master, which Cortez and De Soto, Ponce de Leon and Coronado, had bestowed upon the Spanish crown, had passed from the hands of the men who could not use them into those of the men who could. The expulsion of Spain from the Antilles is merely the last and final step of the inexorable movement in which the United States has been engaged for nearly a century. By influence and example, or more directly by arms and by the pressure of ever-advancing settlements, the United States drove Spain from all her continental possessions in the Western Hemisphere, until nothing was left to the successors of Charles and Philip but Cuba and Puerto Rico.

How did it happen that this great movement, at once racial, political, and economic, governed as it was by forces which rule men even in their own despite—how did it happen to stop when it came to the ocean's edge? The movement against Spain was at once natural and organic, while the pause on the sea-coast was artificial and in contravention of the laws of political evolution in the Americas. The conditions in Cuba and Puerto Rico did not differ from those which had gone down in ruin wherever the flag of Spain waved upon the mainland. The Cubans desired freedom, and Bolivar would fain have gone to their aid. Mexico and Colombia, in 1825, planned to invade the island, and at that time invasion was sure to be successful. What power stayed the oncoming tide which had swept over a continent? Not

Cuban loyalty, for the expression "Faithful Cuba" was a lie from the beginning, like many other Spanish statements. The power which prevented the liberation of Cuba was the United States; and more than seventy years later this republic has had to fight a war because at the appointed time she set herself against her own teachings, and brought to a halt the movement she had herself started to free the New World from the oppression of the Old. The United States held back Mexico and Colombia and Bolivar, used her influence at home and abroad to that end, and, in the opinion of contemporary mankind, succeeded, according to her desires, in keeping Cuba under the dominion of Spain.

The reason for this action on the part of the United States is worse than the fact itself. The Latin mind is severely logical in politics, which accounts in a measure for its many failures in establishing and managing free governments. Being of this cast of mind, the Spanish-American states, when they rose to free themselves from Spain, also freed their own slaves, and in this instance they were not only logical, but right. The people of the United States, on the other hand, were at once illogical and wrong, for they held just then that white men should be free and black men slaves. So they regarded with great disfavor this highly logical outcome of South-American independence, and from this cause Southern hostility brought the Panama Congress, fraught with many high hopes of American solidarity, to naught. The sinister influence of slavery led the United States to hold Cuba under the yoke of Spain, because free negroes were not to be permitted to exist upon an island so near their Atlantic seaboard. It

was a cruel policy which fastened upon Cuba slavery to
Spain as well as the slavery of black men to white,
when both might have been swept away without cost to
America. Those who are curious in the doctrine of
compensations can find here a fresh example. Lincoln,
in the second inaugural, declared once for all that our
awful Civil War was the price we paid for the sin of
slavery; and the war of 1898 was the price paid at last,
as such debts always are paid by nations, for having
kept Cuba in bondage at the dictates of our own slave
power.

The United States had thus undertaken to stop the
movement for the liberation of Spanish colonies at the
point selected by itself, and had deliberately entered
upon the policy of maintaining Spanish rule in its own
neighborhood. This policy meant the assumption of a
heavy responsibility, as well as a continuous effort to
put to rest an unsettled question, by asserting stoutly,
and in defiance of facts, that it really was settled if people would only agree pleasantly to think so. But in
this, as in all like cases, the effort was vain. Cuba was
held under Spanish rule, and the question which had
received the wrong answer began almost at once to
make itself heard, after the awkward fashion of questions which men pretend to have disposed of, but which
are still restlessly seeking the right and final answer,
and, without respect for policies or vested interests,
keep knocking and crying at the door. Some American
statesmen saw that there was a real question in Cuba
demanding a real settlement, and declared, like John
Quincy Adams and Henry Clay, that Cuba must be an-
nexed, and that it would become indispensable to the

integrity of the Union. Even then did Adams also assert that the transfer of Cuba to some other power was a danger obtruding itself upon our councils. But the plan of leaving the island with Spain prevailed. Cuba had come near to both independence and annexation, but both gave way before the slave power, and for twenty years the policy of 1825 had sway. As late as 1843, indeed, Webster said that negro emancipation in Cuba would strike a death-blow to slavery in the United States, thus giving cynically and frankly the bad and true reason for the policy steadily pressed since 1825. Never at rest, however, the slave power itself, a few years after Webster's lucid definition of its Cuban policy, changed its own attitude completely. From desiring to keep Cuba in the hands of Spain, in order that the Cuban negroes might remain slaves, it passed, as dangers thickened round it at home, to the determination to secure Cuba, in order that more slave territory might be added to the United States. Hence a continuous effort to get the island by annexation, and various projects, all fallen into more or less oblivion now, to bring that result about, were devised by American slaveholders and their allies. Their schemes ranged from Buchanan's offer to purchase, rejected with deep scorn by Spain the intelligent, to the Ostend Manifesto —a barefaced argument for conquest—and included attempts to bring about Cuban independence by exciting insurrections and landing filibustering expeditions. But the time was fast drawing near, even while the American slaveholders were thus seeking new territory, when the slave power would be thinking not of extension, but of existence. In 1861 American slavery invoked the ordeal of battle, and perished utterly. With it died its political power, and the policies, foreign and domestic, which it had so long imposed upon the United States. But slavery also left a number of debts to humanity which were not buried with it, but which required payment at the hands of the American people, who had been responsible for slavery living, and could not avoid settling its debts when it was dead. Among these debts was Cuba. Nobody had thought of it much since the Ostend Manifesto. If anybody chanced to remember it during or after the Civil War, the thought probably was that Cuba at last was well out of the way, together with the slave power which had been forever meddling with it, and talking about it, and casting covetous eyes upon its rich lands and forests.

None the less, although the slave power of America had undertaken to fix the destiny of Cuba, and, spurred by its own sense of weakness to eternal restlessness, had kept the question constantly alive, it was not the question itself. Cuba and Spain and Spanish oppression remained, even if American slavery was dead. Moreover, the slaveholders who had caused the United States to force Cuba back under Spanish rule had gone a step beyond this, and had warned off all other nations. In a word, the United States had become responsible for Cuba, and had drawn a ring-fence around the island to exclude all other nations. In this way we undertook and sought to maintain a wrong settlement of a great question, and wrong settlements are equivalent to none at all. So, after the inconsiderate fashion of unsettled problems, the Cuban question would not stay quiet. The slave power kept stirring it; and when the slave power perished and men thought it was all over, the ancient wrong reared its head again, and turning to the power responsible for its existence, demanded redress.

This time the movement came from the island itself. Cuba, although uninvaded, had not been untouched by the revolutionary movement in the first quarter of the century. Societies were formed to support Bolivar and the Mexicans; and after the movement was checked, Spain, acting in her usual fashion, instead of ignoring the indications of revolutionary sympathy, proceeded to give the Captain-General the powers of the governors of besieged towns, or, in other words, put the whole island under martial law. With this piece of sweeping and needless tyranny, resistance to Spain began in Cuba, and has continued at intervals to the present day, each successive outbreak becoming more formidable and more desperate than the one which preceded it.

The first rising came at once. In 1826, only a year after the intervention of the United States, an insurrection broke out, and its two chiefs were executed. Soon after came another, known as the "Conspiracy of the Black Eagle," which was also harshly repressed, and those engaged in it were imprisoned, banished, or executed. In 1837 the representatives of Cuba and Puerto Rico were excluded from the Cortes, on the ground that the colonies were to be governed by special law. In 1850 and 1851 occurred an expedition for the liberation of Cuba, and the death of its leader, Narciso Lopez. There were also expeditions under General Quitman and others, and in 1855 Ramon Pinto was put

to death, and many other patriots banished. These last
raids were part of the slaveholders' movement intended to bring about the independence of the island, and
subsequent annexation to the United States, but they
failed like their predecessors. After this, for a number of years, the Cubans attempted by peaceful methods
to secure from the government at Madrid some relief
from the oppression which weighed upon them, and
some redress for their many wrongs. All their efforts
came to naught, and such changes as were made were
for the worse rather than for the better.

The result of all this was that in 1869 a revolution
broke out under the leadership of Carlos Manuel de
Céspedes, and the United States was aroused to the
fact that the Cuban question was as unsettled as ever.
The existence of slavery in Cuba dulled the edge of
American sympathy, for the bitterness of our own conflict was still upon us. Still there was much interest in
the United States, and a strong feeling in behalf of
men struggling for freedom. The old American sentiment against the domination of Europe in the New
World, which slavery for its own objects had for a time
suppressed, woke again and found active and ardent
expression. The revolutionists, it is true, did not suc-
ceed in getting beyond the eastern part of the island,
but they were successful in many engagements, they
crippled still further the already broken power of Spain,
and they could not be put down by force of arms. At
first the United States held carefully aloof; but the war
went on; Spain was in the throes of revolution at home;
and the administration of President Grant, however reluctant, was compelled to take notice of the fire burning

at our very doors. Mr. Fish, Secretary of State, reverted to the old idea of purchase, and informally brought the proposition to the attention of the Spanish government. General Prim, the one very able man Spain has produced in recent times, saw at once the sense and advantage of this solution, but the scheme got noised about prematurely, there was an outbreak of silly passion which the Spaniards call pride, and Prim was obliged to declare vehemently against any alienation of the national territory. Then in 1873 came what was certain to come sooner or later, an outrage by Spain against the United States. The *Virginius*, a vessel of American register, was captured on the high seas, taken to a Cuban port, and some fifty of her officers and crew, Americans for the most part, summarily shot. The wrath of the American people flamed out; President Grant could have had war and ended everything in a moment; but the forces which cared nothing for humanity and a great deal for an undisturbed money market prevailed. The register of the *Virginius* was opportunely proved to be fraudulent, we took money for our dead, and peace was preserved. The unsettled question had come very near a solution, and had shown, to all who cared to think, that Spanish tyranny was capable of dangerous crimes against others than its own subjects.

Still the war dragged on. It was very annoying, especially to those who were afraid of being disturbed in their daily business, and the administration was forced to intimate, in 1875, that if Spain did not stop the war, the intervention of other powers might become necessary. The hint was not without effect, and, coupled with Spain's increasing exhaustion, hastened the end. In two years more, after the insurrection had lasted ten years, peace was made with the insurgents, but only by a treaty in which Martinez Campos, in the name of Spain, promised to the Cubans certain reforms for which they had taken up arms. In consideration of these reforms the insurgents were to abandon their fight for independence, lay down their arms, and receive a complete amnesty. The insurgents kept their word. They laid down their arms and abandoned their struggle for independence. Spain unhesitatingly violated the agreement. With a cynical disregard of good faith, her promise of amnesty was only partially kept, and she imprisoned or executed many who had been engaged in the insurgent cause, while the promised reforms were either totally neglected or carried out by some mockery which had neither reality nor value. The result of this treachery, of the bloodshed which accompanied it, and of the increased abuses in government which followed, was that the Cubans again prepared for revolt, and in February, 1895, José Martí landed in eastern Cuba and another revolution broke out. The unsettled question had again appeared, still demanding the right answer.

There is no need to trace here the history of this last insurrection. The insurgents formed a government, carried on a vigorous guerrilla warfare, swept over the island from Santiago to the outskirts of Havana and into Pinar del Rio, and soon held sway over most of the provinces outside the towns. They fought better, and were better led, by partisan chiefs like Maceo and Garcia, than ever before. But the head and front of the

Rebellion was Maximo Gomez, a man of marked ability
and singular tenacity of purpose. His plan was to refuse all compromises, to distribute his followers in detached bands, to fight no pitched battles, but incessant
skirmishes, to ravage the country, destroy the possibility of revenue, and win in the end either through the
financial exhaustion of Spain or by the intervention of
the United States, one of which results he believed must
come if he could only hold on long enough. His wisdom, persistence, and courage have all been justified,
for the results have come as he expected, and the rest
of the story is to be found in the course of events in the
United States.

When the insurrection of 1895 broke out it excited,
at first, but a languid interest among the people of the
United States, who are only too well accustomed to
revolutions in Spanish-American countries. It soon
was apparent, however, that this was not an ordinary
South-American revolution, that the Cubans were fighting the old fight of America to be free from Europe,
that they were in desperate earnest, would accept no
compromises, and would hold on to the bitter end.
Then, too, a few months sufficed to show that this time
the Cubans were well led, that their forces were united,
that they were not torn with factional strife, and that
they were pursuing an intelligent and well-considered
plan. Interest in the United States began to awaken,
and grew rapidly as the success of the Cuban arms became manifest. In the Ten Years' War the insurrection
never spread beyond the hill country of the extreme
east. Now, in six months, the province of Santiago,
except for the seaports, had fallen into Cuban control,

and the Cuban forces marched westward, taking possession of all the rural districts as far as Havana.

This brave fight for liberty and against Spain presently aroused the sympathy of the American people, which showed itself in the newspaper press and in public meetings, always with gathering strength. When Congress met, the popular sentiment sought expression in both branches. A minority desired the immediate recognition of Cuban independence, a large number wished to recognize belligerency, an overwhelming majority wanted to do something, while the naturally conservative elements were led by a few determined men who were opposed to any interference of the remotest kind, and a few of whom, even if they did not openly avow it, were bent on leaving Spain a free hand in the island. Out of this confusion came, as might have been expected, a compromise, in which the men in the small minority, who knew just what they wanted, got the substance, and the large, divided, and undecided majority, who vaguely desired "to do something for Cuba," obtained nothing but a collection of sympathetic words. The compromise took the form of a concurrent resolution, which, after much debate, delay, and conference, finally passed both Houses.

This resolution merely declared that a state of war existed in Cuba, that the United States would observe strict neutrality, and that the President should offer the good offices of the United States with the Spanish government to secure the recognition of the independence of the island. As the resolution was concurrent, it did not require the President's assent, and was nothing but an expression of the opinion of Congress. It therefore had little weight with Mr. Cleveland, and none at all with Spain. Whatever was done by the administration in offering our good offices to secure the recognition of Cuban independence, there was no result, and the only part of the resolution which was scrupulously carried out was in observing neutrality, which was done by the President with a severity that bore heavily upon the Cuban side alone.

The administration was in fact opposed to any interference in Cuba, and the action of Congress left it free to follow its policy of holding rigidly aloof. Spain relied with entire confidence on the friendly attitude of Mr. Cleveland, and this confidence was not misplaced. But the unsettled question could not be put down in this fashion, or pushed into a corner. It kept on proclaiming its ugly existence. The war did not die out, as the opponents of Cuba confidently predicted that it would, in the course of a month. On the contrary, it continued; the insurgents were successful in their plan of campaign; they kept gaining ground and getting a more and more complete control of the interior of the island. On July 13, 1895, the battle of Bayamo was fought—the only considerable action of the war, for Gomez avoided steadily all stricken fields. At Bayamo, however, they won a decisive victory, and Martinez Campos, who barely escaped, was forced to resign, and was recalled, six months later. The retirement of Martinez Campos was an important advantage to the Cuban cause, for he was the wisest and most humane of the Spanish Captain-Generals. He had settled the last revolt, and by diplomacy and good management there was always danger that he would divide the insurgents again and bring about another compromise. He was, however, neither successful enough nor sufficiently ferocious to satisfy Spain, and hence his removal. The man who succeeded him, if, as events proved, equally unsuccessful in war, left nothing to be desired in the way of ferocity. Valeriano Weyler came to Cuba February 10, 1896, with an evil reputation for cruelty and corruption earned in the Philippines and in the suppression of the disorders at Barcelona, a reputation which he not only maintained, but enhanced in his new government. His military movements were farcical, consisting in marching columns out here and there from garrisoned posts, having an ineffective brush with the Cubans, and then and there withdrawing the troops, with as little effect as the proverbial King of France who marched up the hill. The insurgents continued their operations without serious check; they broke through the trochas, swarmed into Pinar del Rio, wandered at will about the country, and carried their raids even into the suburbs of Havana. Weyler, who seems never to have exposed himself to fire, but to have confined his operations in the field to building more trochas, made his few military progresses by sea, and preferred to stay in Havana, where he could amass a fortune by blackmailing the business interests, and levying heavy tribute on all the money appropriated to public uses by the bankrupt and broken treasury of Spain. If, however, Weyler was ineffective as a commander in the field and no lover of battle, he showed that he was energy itself in carrying out a campaign of another kind, which was intended to destroy the people of the island, and which had the great merit of be-

SEÑOR CÁNOVAS DEL CASTILLO

Late Prime Minister of Spain

ing attended with no risk to the person of the Captain-General. A large portion of the Cuban population in the country were peasants taking no part in the war, and known as "pacificos." They were quiet people, as a rule, and gave no cause for offence, but it was well known that their sympathies were with the insurgents, and it was believed that they furnished both supplies and recruits to the rebel forces. Unable to suppress or defeat the armed insurgents, the Spanish government characteristically determined to destroy these helpless "pacificos." Accordingly an edict, suggested apparently by Weyler, was issued on October 21, 1896, which applied to Pinar del Rio, and was afterwards extended to all the island, and which ordered the army to concentrate all the pacificos, practically all the rural population, in the garrisoned towns. These wretched people were to be driven in this way from their little farms, which were their only means of support, and herded in the towns and in the suburbs of Havana, where they had nothing before them but starvation, or massacre at the hands of Spanish soldiers and guerrillas. Whether the idea of this infamous order originated in Havana or Madrid is not of much consequence. The Queen-Regent, for whom some persons feel great sympathy, because she is an intelligent woman and the mother of a little boy, set her hand to the decree which sent thousands of women and children to a lingering death, and the whole government of Spain is just as responsible for all the ensuing atrocities as Weyler, who issued the concentration edict and carried it out with pitiless thoroughness and genuine pleasure in the task.

By March, 1896, Spain had sent 121,000 soldiers to

the island, which gave her, at that time with the forces already in Cuba, 150,000 men. Her debt was piling up with frightful rapidity; the insurgent policy of preventing the grinding of the sugar-cane was largely successful, had paralyzed business, and wellnigh extinguished the revenues. It was apparent to all but the most prejudiced that even if the insurgents could not drive the Spaniards from Cuba, the island was lost to Spain. With 200,000 soldiers in 1897 Spain had utterly and miserably failed to put down the rebels, who never had in arms, in all parts of the island, over 35,000 men. The Spanish government could give protection neither to its own citizens nor to those of foreign nations, nor could it even offer security to business, agriculture, or property. So Spain, impotent and broken, but as savage and cruel as she had ever been in her most prosperous days, turned deliberately from the armed men she could not overcome to the work of starving to death the unarmed people, old and young, men and women, whom she could surely reach.

These facts began to grow very clear to the people of the United States in the spring of 1896, and the two great political parties, at their national conventions, passed resolutions of strong sympathy with Cuba, and demanded action. Even the excitement of the most bitterly fought election ever known in the United States could not wholly shut out Cuba, and when the election was over, the Cuban question came to the front again as soon as Congress met. Even the all-absorbing financial question could neither obscure nor hide it. There it was again, under discussion, and the reason for its reappearance was simply that the feeling of the

American people was growing constantly keener and stronger, and forced the subject forward in Congress. Among those who sympathized with Cuba there was a general belief that it was not merely right to recognize the independence of the island, but that such action would enable the insurgents to raise money, fly the flag of the republic on ships of war, and open ports, and that they would then secure their independence without involving the United States in war with Spain. Subsequent events have shown that even recognition would not probably have strengthened the insurgents to such a degree that they could drive out the Spaniards. But it is equally clear now that recognition was the only chance of saving the United States from ultimate intervention and war. A majority of the Senate Committee on Foreign Relations holding this opinion, Senator Cameron reported from that committee on December 21, 1896, a brief resolution recognizing the Republic of Cuba, and setting forth the reasons for doing so in a very able and elaborate report.

This resolution of the Foreign Relations Committee caused much excitement. Stocks fell, and the financial interests of the great Eastern cities rose in wrathful opposition. They declared, without any reservation, that war "would unsettle values"—a horrid possibility not to be contemplated with calmness by any right-thinking man. The error of the financial interests was in thinking that war would "unsettle values." That which "unsettled values" was the Cuban question, and so long as that remained unsettled, "values" would follow suit. There was but one way to remove this disturbing element, and that was for the United States to bring the Cuban War to an end. So long as it was permitted to go on, the damaging uncertainty and suspense were sure to continue, and sooner or later, out of the fighting in Cuba and the agitation in the United States, would come the overt act which would bring the sword from its scabbard. Nevertheless, financial interests had their way. Mr. Olney announced, in an interview in the Washington *Star*, that no attention would be paid to the joint resolution even if it passed both Houses over the veto, because the right of recognition pertained solely to the Executive, and the resolution would only be the opinion of certain eminent gentlemen. This was quite conclusive at the moment in regard to the Cuban war, for nothing can be plainer than that under our system of government no serious measures can be wisely undertaken, or indeed undertaken at all, against a foreign nation unless the Executive and Congress act together. This was entirely obvious to the Foreign Relations Committee of the Senate. It was doubtful if they could carry the resolution for recognition of the Cuban Republic through the Senate, and quite certain that it would be useless if they did. So the resolution slumbered on the calendar and was never called up, the wise financial interests prevailed, Cuban independence was not to be recognized, and we were to go on pretending that the war was not there, and that we had answered the unsettled question, when we really had simply turned our heads aside and refused to look.

And then when the troublesome matter had been so nicely laid to sleep, the result followed which is usual when Congressmen and Presidents and nations are trying to make shams pass for realities. Only a few weeks went by, and the Cuban question was up again. It could not be kept out of the newspapers, or the minds of men, or the debates in Congress. We were engaged in enforcing the neutrality laws and preventing filibustering expeditions. If an expedition got out of our ports it was a success in almost every instance, for the Spanish were so inefficient that they could hardly ever prevent a landing, and the upshot was that the United States did the main work in checking the insurgents. In other words, the enforcement of neutrality meant in practice our being the ally of Spain. This fact came gradually into public view and gained general appreciation, with a consequent increase of feeling among the American people, who, horrified by the reports of the starvation of the "reconcentrados," did not at all relish being made even indirect participants in that odious crime against humanity. A still deeper source of irritation was in the treatment accorded to Americans by the Spaniards. Cases were continually arising in which American citizens were seized, thrown into prison, kept in solitary confinement, and subjected to every kind of cruelty, in total disregard of both treaty and international rights. So long as these unfortunate men were of Cuban birth and had Spanish names, the opponents of Cuba felt that they had in these facts a complete answer, and that the additional fact that they held the naturalization papers of the United States could be entirely disregarded. Still the cases kept on coming to the surface, gave rise to sharp debates in Congress, and stimulated popular feeling. The Spaniards, however, emboldened by our government's apparent indifference to the rights and the protection of

American citizens, soon ceased to confine their outrages to naturalized citizens of Cuban extraction, and proceeded to extend the same treatment to men whose names were as American as their birth-place. The administration could not plead ignorance of the situation, for General Lee, who had taken charge of the Consul-General's office in Havana on June 3, 1896, informed the State Department three weeks after his arrival that while the insurgents could not drive the Spaniards from the island, it was equally impossible for Spain to subdue the insurrection. The President therefore knew that without decided measures on our part there was nothing possible in Cuba but bloodshed, pillage, the wholesale destruction of life and property, and the gradual extermination of the inhabitants by starvation and massacre, but he remained entirely unmoved in his determination not to interfere even to the extent of putting pressure on Spain. As the winter of 1896-7 wore away it also became generally understood that General Lee, whose good sense and firm courage had steadily won the confidence of the country, was not sustained by the administration as he should have been in some of the cases of American prisoners. The manner in which the consular reports were withheld, or only grudgingly or partially given out, augmented the popular distrust, for the secrecy observed convinced every one that the publication of the official truth was feared by those who wished to hold aloof from Cuba and to pretend that there was no question there demanding settlement. The American people are justly sensitive in regard to the protection of American citizens, and the imprisonment of Scott, the murder of Ruiz, and

GENERAL FITZHUGH LEE
United States Consul-General in Havana

the treatment of the *Competitor* prisoners, together with many other cases, especially when there were added to them the ill-concealed differences between the administration and General Lee, stirred popular feeling and excited popular anger to a high degree. The situation growing out of the Spanish treatment of Americans was fast bringing on a crisis which threatened to prove not only acute, but decisive.

Just at this moment, when the unrighted wrong seemed about to force the inevitable decision, Mr. Cleveland went out of office, and with the interest awakened by a new administration, and the hopes of a changed policy, the immediate excitement subsided, and men who realized that however absorbing the tariff might be, the real and great question lay south of Florida, were content to wait and give to the new authority every possible opportunity and assistance. The Republican party, which now returned to power, had taken very strong ground at its convention in regard to Cuba, asserting practically that it would charge itself with the duty of compelling a final settlement of the question. President McKinley not only sympathized with the declaration of his party, but he felt profoundly the gravity of the Cuban situation, and cherished a deep desire to meet it successfully and conclusively. The question had been left in such an acute state, and so near to extreme action, by neglect of the cases of American prisoners, that it was plain that something must be done at once or the new administration would find itself plunged into hostilities before it had fairly taken the reins of power into its hands. The crucial point was the American prisoners, and President McKinley,

less sensitive than his predecessor in regard to injuring
the feelings of Spain, immediately demanded prompt
release and redress in every case. His tone was so
firm that the Spaniards at once gave way, and by the
end of April every American prisoner had been released. With the removal of the immediate and crying
evil the situation grew quieter, the crisis passed by, and
the impending peril of war rolled back again into the
distance. The cause of war would not come from
Spanish outrages upon American citizens. So much
was fixed by the President's decided action. But the
question was still there, still moving and pressing, never at rest. And just when every one who was against
doing anything was saying again contentedly that all
was nicely over, and that the sham was a reality, and
that there was no Cuban question, out the question
would break in a new quarter. May 20, 1897, the Senate, without division, passed a joint resolution recognizing Cuban belligerency. This resolution, taking its
usual course, had scarcely had time to reach the House
and be sent by the Speaker to slumber in the Committee on Foreign Affairs, because there was not and ought
not to be a Cuban question, when in came a message
from the President on that very subject. It appeared
oddly enough, that war was still going on, and that
under the reconcentration system American citizens, as
well as natives of the island, were being starved to death
in Cuba. This the President, thoroughly informed
by the consular reports, thought that he could not
permit, and he therefore asked Congress for $50,000
to purchase and send supplies to these Americans who
were being put to death by the methods of war em-

GENERAL STEWART L. WOODFORD

United States Minister to Spain

ployed by Spain. Congress gave the money at once, and the act was approved May 24, 1897. We demanded and received the assent of Spain, and thereupon ships were chartered and food sent to all the American consuls, in order to feed starving Americans. The Americans were fed, and many others not Americans also, and the United States by this action had at last interfered in Cuba; for no more complete act of intervention than this, which tended to cripple the military measures and check the starvation campaign of the Spaniards, could be imagined. It was not admitted, certainly not generally realized, that the United States had finally broken from the old policy of holding aloof, and had entered on the new policy of intervention in Cuba; but, nevertheless, the true answer to the unsettled question was beginning to draw visibly nearer.

Meantime the President, after careful consideration, selected General Stewart L. Woodford for minister to Spain—the most important diplomatic post to be filled at this juncture. No one could have been chosen who was more conciliatory than General Woodford, or more desirous to obtain a peaceful solution of the ever-increasing differences with Spain. With such a minister at Madrid it was certain that no effort would be spared to soothe Spain and bring about an agreement calculated to gratify everybody, if such a thing were possible under the circumstances, which seemed unlikely, for it looked as if the question had gone beyond the stage when it could be dealt with by soft and gentle handling. Nevertheless, until the new administration and the new President, through the freshly appointed minister, could take up the thread of the negotiations with Spain, there came a pause in the controversy between the two nations. There was no pause in Cuba, no pause in starving to death the miserable "reconcentrados," or in the desolating raids of both combatants, which were fast making the island a desert waste. There was no pause in the agitation in the United States, or in the growth of the popular feeling about Cuba and the horrid scenes there existent. The unsettled question kept moving on, even though negotiations paused. Then came another delay, for before General Woodford reached Spain on September 1, Senor Canovas, the Prime Minister, was murdered, on Sunday, August 8, 1897, by an Italian anarchist. There was much alarm, a ministerial crisis, and then Senor Sagasta came in and formed a Liberal ministry. At last General Woodford was able to open his negotiations, and the demands of the United States were seriously pressed. We asked for the recall of Weyler, and, above all, for the revocation of the reconcentration edict. The new ministry made haste to comply in appearance with every request, and to promise everything we demanded. Then they asked in turn that we should give them opportunity to try autonomy in Cuba —another wrong answer to the old question, absolutely useless, and quite gone by in the autumn of 1897. But after all the ostensible compliance of the Sagasta ministry with our requests, the opportunity to try autonomy could not well be refused. The trouble was that, with the exception of the recall of Weyler, on October 9, 1897, about which no deception or postponement was possible, not one of these Spanish promises was worth the paper upon which it was written. It was all

entirely characteristic of Spanish diplomacy, much vaunted by Spaniards, and much admired in Europe, and consisted simply of lying, evading, and making promises which there was no intention of performing. As the representatives of the United States tried to tell the truth, they laid themselves open to much European criticism for their rude diplomacy, and for not understanding the refined methods of older nations; but they had one grave disadvantage in a failure to realize that Spanish diplomacy consisted chiefly of falsehood, as it had done for some centuries, and that no faith could be put in anything they alleged or promised.

Meantime all agitation in the United States was restrained on the ground that after the Spanish concessions we were bound to give them a reasonable time to try autonomy, which was an entirely just view if the concessions had been real and autonomy either honest or practical. But as the weeks passed by it became apparent that autonomy was neither practical nor genuine; the atrocities and starvation went on despite the withdrawal of Weyler and the coming of the less brutal Blanco, and both Congress and people again began to grow restless.

The situation of the Americans in Havana also began to cause uneasiness, and there was so much disquiet that the administration very wisely determined to send a ship of war to that port. The battle-ship *Maine* was selected for this duty, and reached Havana on the morning of January 24, 1898. We were at peace with Spain, and we had an entire right to send a ship to any Cuban port. If it had been done, as it ought to have been done, at the beginning of the Cuban troubles, it would have excited no comment; but at this late date in the war it assumed an importance which did not rightfully belong to such an accident. The Spanish minister, Senor Dupuy de Lome, blustered in private and talked about war, but being informed quietly and decidedly by Mr. Day that the ship was going in any event, he quieted down in public, and the Spanish cruiser *Vizcaya* came to New York to demonstrate that the presence of the *Maine* at Havana was only a friendly visit. The sending of the *Maine* was received by the country with a sense of relief, and the action of the President was universally approved. Public attention, however, was soon distracted from this subject by an incident which in a flash revealed the utter worthlessness of all the Spanish concessions and promises. A letter of Senor Dupuy de Lome, dated December 25, 1897, and addressed to a friend, Senor Canalejas, had been stolen in Havana by some one in the Cuban interest, and sent to the Cuban Junta in New York, which gave it to the press on February 9, 1898. This letter contained a coarse and vulgar attack upon President McKinley, which led to the immediate resignation and recall of the writer, who had served Spain well and unscrupulously. But far more important in its wider bearings than this disclosure of the character of Dupuy de Lome was the fact that the letter revealed the utter hollowness of all the Spanish professions, and showed that the negotiations in regard to autonomy and commercial relations were only intended to amuse and deceive the United States. The effect of this revelation was just beginning to make itself felt when the American people were stunned by an event which

THE MAINE OFF MORRO CASTLE

drove everything else from their minds. On the morning of February 16 came the news that on the previous evening the battle-ship *Maine* had been blown up and totally destroyed in the harbor of Havana. The explosion occurred under the forward part of the ship, and 264 men and two officers were killed. The overt act had come. This gigantic murder of sleeping men in the fancied security of a friendly harbor was the direct outcome and the perfect expression of Spanish rule, the appropriate action of a corrupt system struggling in its last agony. At last in very truth the unsettled question had come home to the United States, and it spoke this time in awful tones, which rang loud and could not be silenced. A wave of fierce wrath swept over the American people. But a word was needed, and war would have come then in response to this foul and treacherous act of war, for such in truth it was. But the words of Captain Sigsbee, the commander of the *Maine*, whose coolness, self-restraint, and high courage were beyond praise, asking, even in the midst of the slaughter, that judgment should be suspended, were heeded alike by government and people.

Scarcely a word was said in either House or Senate, and for forty days the American people and the American Congress waited in silence for the verdict of the board of naval officers who had been appointed to report on the destruction of the *Maine*. To those who understood the American people this grim silence, this stern self-control, were more threatening than any words of sorrow or of anger could possibly have been. Spain, rushing ignorantly, arrogantly, on her doom, understood nothing. A generous sympathy, a prompt offer to make every reparation, while she disclaimed all guilt, and she could have turned the current of feeling and gone far to save herself and her colonies. Instead of that, with incredible stupidity and utter meanness of soul, she announced, before any one had even looked at the wreck, that the ship was blown up from the inside, owing to the carelessness of the American officers. Her ambassadors abroad reiterated this ministerial falsehood, and, not content with that, insulted the brave men who had the *Maine* in charge, while official Spaniards everywhere insinuated or declared that lack of discipline was what blew up the battleship. There was much anger, mostly of the very silent sort, in the United States as these charges flew on wires and cables about the world; but the American reply to them was not given until some months later on May 1 and July 3 when certain proofs were given of the discipline and quality of American sailors which even Spain could not overlook. Still the Spanish attitude in regard to the *Maine* had one undoubted merit —it moved the unsettled question forward, and made a wrong answer more difficult than ever.

CHAPTER II

THE COMING OF WAR

As the weary days went by after the destruction of the *Maine*, public feeling grew tenser every instant, and the waiting became more intolerable, until at last the report of the American board appeared, closely followed by that of the Spaniards, which told the lie agreed upon forty days before, and which they had not even taken the trouble to back up with any substantial evidence, or with more than a perfunctory examination of the wreck. No one heeded the Spanish report; public men, of course, read it, but the people knew Spain at last, and their instinct told them with entire certainty that here was a sham and an untruth, very patent and flagrant, upon which time was not to be wasted. The American report was based upon a most elaborate examination of the wreck and of witnesses, and upon the most carefully sifted testimony. It was honest and cool, and said that the *Maine* had been blown up from outside. There was no mortal doubt after reading the report, and Captain Sigsbee's evidence before the Senate committee, that the outside engine of destruction was a government submarine mine, and had been exploded without the authority or knowledge of the Spanish government, by men who wore the uniform of Spain.

The President transmitted the report of the board to Congress without comment. It was perhaps needless to make any, for Senate and House and country supplied all that was necessary. Moreover, the President, as became a chief magistrate, had been and still was using every possible effort to avert war by peaceful and diplomatic methods, and continued to hope against hope for a successful result. The American people likewise were averse to war. An overwhelming majority would have so declared even after the report on the *Maine* had been submitted to Congress. On the other hand, an equally overwhelming majority were determined that there should be atonement for the *Maine*, and that Spanish rule in Cuba—which had caused the destruction of the ship—and the horrors of the "reconcentrados" should end. These demands meant war even if those who made them did not realize it, and it was this public sentiment that drove Congress forward to meet the popular will, which members and Senators very well knew could be fulfilled by war and in no other way. Against the sentiment springing from the popular instinct which at the great crisis of American history has always been true and right, an opposition strong in purpose although in large measure concealed, was arrayed. The naturally timid and conservative elements of the community shrank from war, and the powerful financial interests of the Eastern cities, too short-sighted to see that their selfish advantage was in the certainty of action and not in suspense, exerted their great force to stop every forward step along the inevitable path. For the result now was inevitable; had been so, in reality, since the fatal 15th of February,

CAPTAIN CHARLES D. SIGSBEE
United States Battle-ship *Maine*

although men did not understand it at the moment, and still thought that they could stay the current of events which had been gathering strength for seventy years and broken loose at last.

The *Maine* message was sent in on March 28, and as men everywhere discussed the evidence, it became clear that although the President was reluctant to abandon hope, the resources of diplomacy had failed. What the exact course of the negotiations conducted by the President and the able Assistant Secretary of State, Judge Day, had been was unknown then, is not known now, and will not be thoroughly known until the time comes when the secret correspondence between Washington and Madrid is open to the historian. But it was perfectly well understood that Spain would not grant independence to Cuba, and that whether our minister had made the fact plain to the Spanish government or not, no peaceful settlement was possible on any other basis. Diplomats might plan, and twist, and devise, and exchange notes, and deal in all the forms so futile at a great crisis, but the American people had made up their minds that the only real and possible solution was the end of Spanish rule in Cuba. They had determined that the unsettled question must receive this time a right answer, that it should knock at their door no longer, and the American people were right.

Meantime the tension and excitement steadily increased. The peace-at-any-price people fought hard but in vain against the sweeping tide of public sentiment. It was understood that a message would come to Congress on Monday, April 4. Then it was given out that it would be sent in on Wednesday, April 6, and the Capitol was thronged in expectation of the great event. When the House met, there was delay, and then the leaders of the House and three Senators of the Foreign Relations Committee were summoned suddenly to the White House. There the President showed them a despatch from General Lee, saying that if the message went in that day he could not answer for the lives of the Americans in Havana, and that he ought to have until Saturday at least to get them out of Cuba. To this appeal there could be but one answer. The message must be held back, and the Senators and members returned and made the announcement to their respective Houses.

Thereupon the tension, the excited suspense, the doubts, the rumors, were all renewed and intensified. It was generally believed that Spain would take advantage of this respite to make some new proposition, even if she had not already done so, and Saturday proved the correctness of the anticipation. On that day word came that Spain proposed an armistice with the insurgents, and that her council had voted $600,000 for the relief of the "reconcentrados." Those who wished to be deceived by these offers were so deceived, but no one else. An armistice was impossible without the assent of both parties to the war, and the Cubans, on the eve of victory, of course would not consent. Moreover, the armistice, as soon appeared, consisted merely in an invitation to the insurgents to come in and lay down their arms. The proposition was not even a well-framed or judicious lie. As to the money for the "reconcentrados," it was an empty sham. There is no proof that a peseta was ever

really appropriated; and if it had been, as General Lee justly said, it would all have been absorbed by Spanish officials before it reached its destination. The Spanish case closed fittingly with these false and fraudulent promises.

Anxious as the President was for peace, he could not and would not accept as realities such shams as these, and on Monday, April 11, the fateful message on Cuban affairs at last came in, and was referred to the Foreign Relations Committees of both Houses. The reading of the message was listened to with intense interest and in profound silence, broken only by a wave of applause when the sentence was read which said, "In the name of humanity, in the name of civilization, in behalf of endangered American interests which give us the right and duty to speak and to act, the war in Cuba must stop." The President led up to this declaration by a dispassionate review of the Cuban question, and by a strong and moving description of the conditions of the island, which he characterized as a wilderness and a grave. He asked Congress to empower him to end hostilities in Cuba, and to secure the establishment of a stable government, capable of maintaining order and observing its international obligations." He said that he had exhausted diplomacy, and therefore left the issue with Congress, while he referred to Congress for its consideration the statement that the Queen-Regent had ordered a suspension of hostilities. In the deep excitement of the moment many persons felt that the message was too gentle, and that the President really did not desire as yet decided measures. But it was pointed out that when he asked Congress for authority to establish a government in Cuba "capable of observing international relations," he requested power to make Cuba independent, because only an independent people can maintain relations of that character. More decisive still, indeed absolutely conclusive, was the simple fact that the President, having declared that he had exhausted diplomacy, had remitted the question to Congress. Congress has no diplomatic functions or attributes. With a foreign nation it has but one weapon —the war power; and when a President calls in Congress in a controversy with another nation, his action means that Congress, if it sees fit, must exercise its single power, and declare war. On this sound ground, which is constitutionally the only ground possible under such conditions, Congress proceeded to act.

For more than a week a draft of a resolution to be passed by Congress had been in existence, and had been seen by some Senators and a few others, which provided that the President should be authorized to intervene in order to stop the war in Cuba, to secure their peace, order, and a stable government established by the free action of the people, and to use the army and navy of the United States for these purposes. Whence this resolution came, or who drafted it, was not known, but some of those to whom it was submitted pointed out that it was utterly vague, that under its carefully loose terms the forces of the United States could be used to crush the insurgents, and that the government to be set up might be Spanish just as well as independent. Whether this resolution emanated from those opposed at all hazards to Cuba and to war, or not, it sank out of sight for a time, and then reappeared in the report

SEÑOR PRAXEDES MATEO SAGASTA
Prime Minister of Spain

of the Committee on Foreign Affairs made in the House on April 13. It read as follows:

Resolved, That the President is hereby authorized and directed to intervene at once to stop the war in Cuba, to the end and with the purpose of securing permanent peace and order there, and establishing by the free action of the people thereof a stable and independent government of their own in the island of Cuba; and the President is hereby authorized and empowered to use the land and naval forces of the United States to execute the purpose of this resolution.

One very important change had been made in the original draft, without which, it is safe to say, it could not have passed the House committee. The alteration was the insertion after the word "stable" of the words "and independent." This greatly improved the resolution, but it still remained dangerously loose and vague, and had the cardinal defect of not saying squarely and honestly what the American people and Congress intended, which was the expulsion of Spain from Cuba. Nevertheless, after the Republican majority had voted down the Democratic proposition to recognize the insurgent government, the resolution as reported by the committee passed by a vote of 324 to 19, and was sent to the Senate.

The situation in the Senate was quite different. For a week before the message of April 11 came in, the Committee of Foreign Relations had been at work upon a resolution based upon one introduced by Senator Foraker of Ohio. The committee were determined that any resolution reported by them should be perfectly clear on the point that the object of the United States was to put an absolute end to Spanish rule in Cuba. With a preamble setting forth the treatment of the

"reconcentrados" and the destruction of the *Maine*
as the grounds of intervention, a resolution of this
character was agreed to tentatively, and Senator Davis
of Minnesota, the chairman of the committee, drafted
a report to accompany it.   Both the resolutions and the
report were sent to the President for such suggestion
and comment as he might see fit to make.   After the
message of April 11 came in, these resolutions were
taken up for immediate action.   There was a desire
on the part of some members of the committee to come
as near as might be to the general line taken in the
House resolution, but the chief point of difference
arose upon the question of recognizing the government
of the insurgents.   The President, with wisdom and
foresight, had declared in his message against any
such recognition.   A majority of the Senate committee
sustained the President's position; and while the whole
committee supported the main and essential resolution
as to the withdrawal of Spain, a minority reported, as
an amendment, a clause recognizing the insurgent government.   Senator Davis made the report for the committee, and in that report the case of the United States
against Spain and the grounds of armed intervention
were stated not only in the best way, but with a force
and power, both legally and historically, which left
nothing to be desired.   The resolutions of the committee and the minority amendment submitted to the
Senate on April 13 were as follows:

REPORT OF COMMITTEE ON FOREIGN RELATIONS.

Whereas the abhorrent conditions which have existed for more
than three years in the island of Cuba, so near our own borders,
have shocked the moral sense of the people of the United States,

THE UNITED STATES SENATE COMMITTEE ON FOREIGN AFFAIRS

have been a disgrace to Christian civilization culminating as they have, in the destruction of a United States battle-ship, with 266 of its officers and crew, while on a friendly visit in the harbor of Havana, and cannot longer be endured, as has been set forth by the President of the United States in his message to Congress of April 11th, 1898, upon which the action of Congress was invited; Therefore,

Resolved, by the Senate and House of Representatives of the United States of America in Congress assembled,

First. That the people of the island of Cuba are, and of right ought to be, free and independent.

Second. That it is the duty of the United States to demand, and the government of the United States does hereby demand, that the government of Spain at once relinquish its authority and government in the Island of Cuba, and withdraw its land and naval forces from Cuba and Cuban waters.

Third. That the President of the United States be, and he hereby is, directed and empowered to use the entire land and naval forces of the United States, and to call into the actual service of the United States the militia of the several States, to such extent as may be necessary to carry these resolutions into effect.

VIEWS OF THE MINORITY.

The undersigned members of said committee cordially concur in the report made upon the Cuban resolutions, but favor the immediate recognition of the Republic of Cuba, as organized in the island, as a free, independent, and sovereign power among the nations of the world.

DAVID TURPIE.
R. Q. MILLS.
JNO. W. DANIEL.
J. B. FORAKER.

The amendment reported by the minority committee was to amend the first paragraph, by inserting, in line 4, after the word "independent," the following:

And that the government of the United States hereby recognize the Republic of Cuba as the true and lawful government of that island.

On the presentation of the resolutions to the Senate a very earnest and very able debate ensued, which turned almost entirely upon the question of recognizing the insurgent government, and scarcely touched at all the second resolution, which was the one really effective and essential portion of the measure, which meant war, and could mean nothing else. The discussion lasted until Saturday evening, and then the Senate, with only one absentee, voted in the presence of crowded galleries and in the midst of intense excitement. The amendment of the minority of the Committee on Foreign Relations was adopted by a vote of 51 to 37, thirty-three Republicans and four Democrats constituting the minority, and ten Republicans voting with the Democrats and the Populists in the majority. The amendment of Senator Teller of Colorado, disclaiming any intention of seeking sovereignty or dominion over Cuba, was accepted by the committee and agreed to without division. All other amendments were voted down, a few short speeches were made, chiefly by those opposed to the resolutions, the Senate resolutions were substituted for those of the House, and then the resolutions as amended were passed by a vote of 67 to 21, nineteen Republicans and two Democrats forming the minority, and twenty-four Republicans voting with the Democrats and Populists in the majority. The resolutions were then sent to the House without a request for a conference, and the Senate adjourned until Monday.

The Sunday which intervened was a day of rumors and excitement. There was a well-founded apprehension that enough Republicans would break away and unite with the Democrats to carry concurrence in the Senate resolutions as they stood, including the

REDFIELD PROCTOR

Whose report of his observations of the results of Spanish rule in Cuba
profoundly influenced public feeling in America

recognition of the Cuban Republic. To prevent this the Republican leaders of the House put forth all their power, and made every exertion, with entire success, as the event proved, so far as recognition was concerned. When the House met on Monday, Mr. Dingley of Maine moved to concur in the Senate resolutions, with an amendment striking out the words "are and" in the first resolution, and the entire clause embodying the recognition of the insurgent government. This motion prevailed by a majority of 22. Thus did it come about that in the struggle over the question of recognition, forced into the resolutions by the action of the ten radical Republican Senators, everything else had been lost sight of, and in "everything else" was the one essential, vital resolution which demanded the withdrawal of Spain from Cuba. This second resolution was the effective one, for it meant war, and to this the leaders of the House, in their eagerness to defeat recognition of the republic, had been forced to agree, and the House accepted it without debate. With the two Houses agreed on this resolution, the real issue was settled, but much remained to be done in order to end the controversy under which had been carried the one absolutely vital clause in the entire measure.

So the amended resolutions came back to the Senate, the crowd rushed over from the House, pouring into the deserted galleries, there was a short debate, and then the motion of Senator Davis to concur was voted down by 46 to 32, and the resolutions went back to the House with the Senate's insistence and without a request for a conference. The excited crowds of onlookers swept over to the House, the resolutions were at once taken up, and the House, by a majority of 26, voted to insist on its amendments, and asked for a committee of conference. Again the crowds passed from the House to the Senate, and the resolutions were once more taken up. There was another debate, the ten dissenting Republicans announced that they would no longer insist upon recognition of the Cuban Republic, a conference was agreed to, and both Houses took a recess until eight o'clock.

It was generally understood that on the Senate's receding from its position in regard to recognition the House would recede from its first amendment striking out the words "are and," and personal assurances were said to have been given to that effect. When Senators and members returned to the Capitol, therefore, they expected an agreement to be reported from the conference, an immediate acceptance of the report, and an adjournment in a few minutes. To every one's surprise, and to the great indignation of the Senate, a disagreement was reported from the committee, because the House refused to recede on its amendment to the first line striking out the words "are and." The point was not worth a contest on either side, for the whole phrase was purely rhetorical. It was rhetoric when Richard Henry Lee first read it to the Continental Congress, it was rhetoric still, hallowed by time and association, when applied to Cuba. At the most it was merely a declaration of intention, which it was proposed to make good by converting the intention into a fact. But personal feelings had been aroused, and now began to run high. The Senate, justly or un-

justly, believed that it had been unfairly dealt with, while the House felt that the Senate was unreasonable. In this mood the House, by a majority of 32, voted to insist and asked for a further conference, which was agreed to by the Senate. Again the conferees withdrew and the two Houses waited. The hours wore drearily away, and rumors came thickly that there would be another disagreement and a deadlock. Senator Morgan of Alabama sent a plain declaration of war up to the desk, and announced that at the proper time he would call it up. The hint was not without its effect. Senators hostile to Cuba crossed the Capitol and urged upon the Speaker that the House should give way. At this juncture the House conferees asked to withdraw from the conference and hold a consultation apart. They then saw the Speaker, returned, and receded on the words "are and." After this an agreement was immediately reached, and reported to both Houses. Midnight had passed and a new day* begun. It was the 19th of April, a date very memorable in the history of the United States, when the Senate, by a vote of 42 to 35, and the House, by a vote of 311 to 6, accepted the conference report. The resolutions as finally agreed upon were precisely word for word those reported by the majority of the Senate Committee on Foreign Relations, with the single addition of Senator Teller's amendment, which the committee had accepted. The Congress of the United States had gone clear of all pitfalls, and had declared just what the American people meant it to declare, that Spanish rule in Cuba

---

*The legislative day was still the 18th of April.

43

must cease. In fact, if not in terms, it was a declaration of war.

The resolutions thus adopted went at once to the President, who held them over one day and then signed them. He sent a copy, early on the morning of the 21st, to the Spanish minister, Senor Polo y Bernabé, who thereupon asked for his passports and left the country. Before this, the resolutions had been cabled to our minister at Madrid, but the despatch was there held back long enough to enable the Spanish ministry to send General Woodford his passports before he could present the resolutions, a feat which called forth much admiration on the Continent among those who love diplomatic futilities, but which was as silly as shams usually are in the presence of realities. For the reality was war, and the precise manner in which it was brought into existence was of trifling consequence except to the arid diplomatic mind of Europe.

As soon as Spain severed her relations with the United States, on April 21, the American fleet, under the command of Admiral Sampson, was ordered to Havana, and the President proclaimed a blockade of that and certain other Cuban ports. On April 23, the guns of the *Nashville* cracked across the bows of the *Buena Ventura*, a Spanish merchantman; and Congress, on April 25, formally declared that war with the kingdom of Spain had existed since April 21. The pretences were over, the wrong which had lived on, for three-quarters of a century was now to be redressed, the restless unsettled question was to get its true and right answer at last.

CHAPTER III

MANILA

FERNAO DA MAGALHAENS, or Magalhães, was a boy when the discovery of Columbus fired the imagination of western Europe, but he was also one of those whose adventurous spirit was kindled and roused by this wonder tale of new lands beyond the Atlantic. He was still young when, in 1505, he made one in an expedition from Portugal, his native land, which, coming from the West, discovered some of the famous Spice Islands. Not long after, wounded by an insult from the Portuguese government, which impugned his honor as a man and a soldier, he left his country, solemnly and publicly renounced his allegiance to Portugal, was naturalized as a Spaniard, and took service with Charles V, who had the instinct of greatness in picking out able and effective men to do his work. Magellan, as we call him, was imbued with the Columbian ideas, and also held that, despite the Columbian discoveries, a short route by water to the East could be found by sailing westward. It was a great conception, and a true one, except that the route was longer than that round the Cape of Good Hope. With an expedition splendidly equipped by the Emperor, Magellan set sail on August 10, 1519. He crossed the Atlantic, touched at the bay of Rio de Janeiro, made his way southward, repressed

45

savagely a dangerous mutiny, and on October 21 entered the strait which bears his name. On November 28 he passed out of it with only three of his five vessels left, and found himself and his rejoicing crews in the Pacific. He felt that he had succeeded, but he had miscalculated the vast extent of the new ocean; and sailing on for days and days, in some fashion missed the countless islands of the Pacific, and did not see land until he reached the little group which he called the Ladrones, because the inhabitants stole a boat from him. There he lingered a short time, either at Rota or in the curious harbor of Guahan, destined, nearly four hundred years later, to receive the war-ships of a nation of whose future existence even those old believers in El Dorado never dreamed. From the Ladrones, which were discovered March 6, 1521, the weary voyage was continued until a new archipelago was reached, on the fifth Sunday in Lent. Gradually the magnitude of this new discovery became apparent, and Magellan named the new group in honor of St. Lazarus, on whose day it was discovered. They landed on Mindanao, made their way to Cebu, flattered themselves that they had converted and subdued the inhabitants, and then becoming involved in a tribal war, Magellan was killed, and his chosen successor, Serrano, was left behind to death and torture. Two ships escaped, one going east, and one, the *Victoria*, under Elcano, which left Timor on February 11, sailing still to the westward. On September 6, 1522, after many hardships and perils, the *Victoria* reached Spain, and a great voyage, the first which circled the globe, second only to that of Columbus in conception, and beyond all in the daring displayed and the distance traversed, came to an end.

Thus was a new possession added to the dominion of Spain; yet, although her navigators discovered it, a fraud finally made it hers. By the treaty of 1494, as afterwards expounded, all the world beyond the meridian 1,080 miles west of the Azores was divided between Spain and Portugal, the eastern half going to Spain. The Spaniards, however, made the maps, and putting Magellan's discovery twenty-five degrees east of its true position, brought it within the Spanish half, when it really belonged to the portion allotted to Portugal. Twenty years later Villalobos, sailing from South America, visited the islands of Magellan, and named them the Philippines, in honor of the Prince of Asturias, afterwards Philip II. Again twenty years passed, and in 1565 a great expedition went from Mexico, and Spanish rule was established by Legaspi in the Philippines—first in Cebu, and later in Luzon—which was destined to continue unbroken for more than three hundred years.

Even in its last stage of decay, an empire which had once thus arrogated to itself the possession of half the world outside Europe still showed traces of its former grandeur in scattered fragments lying far apart on either side of the globe. When war came, and the United States looked out to see where to strike its foe, it found Spain present not only at its own doors, but far away across the Pacific, and there in the distant East the first blow fell.

The Navy Department, with watchful prevision, as the relations with Spain grew more strained, began to

send out orders which would make all ready in case of
war. Even in January the commander-in-chief of the
European squadron was ordered to retain all men
whose enlistments had expired; the *Helena* was stopped
at Funchal, the *Wilmington* in the West Indies, and at
the end of the month orders were sent to assemble the
European squadron at Lisbon. A month later orders
went to all the squadrons to fill their bunkers with coal,
and to be ready to move on the click of the wire. As
early as January 27 the Asiatic squadron also had been
directed to retain all men whose enlistments had expired, and on February 25 a cable message was sent to
Commodore Dewey by Mr. Roosevelt directing him to
assemble his squadron at Kong-kong, retain the *Olympia*, which had been ordered back to San Francisco, and
be prepared in case of war for offensive operations in
the Philippines. On the 3d of March the *Mohican* was
sent with ammunition to Honolulu, there to await the
Baltimore, which was to take the ammunition on board
and proceed at once to join the Asiatic squadron. No
wiser or more far-sighted precautions were ever taken
by an administration than these, and it was all done so
quietly that no one on the outside knew what was happening. While the country was stirring to its depths
with the events which were fast bringing our relations
with Spain to the breaking point, while the air was
filled with rumors and debates and the strife of con-
tending forces, the *Baltimore* was speeding across the
Pacific carrying ammunition to the Asiatic squadron,
and Commodore Dewey was preparing very carefully
and accurately for certain work which he saw before
him. The order directing the Asiatic squadron to as-

semble at Hong-kong had gone on February 25, and on
the following day another went telling the commodore
to fill all the bunkers with the best coal to be had. By
March 28 the squadron had assembled, and then came
a period of waiting. Very dreary and very hot this
waiting was, long drawn by constant strain and listening. With much anxiety, and always on the alert all
through the trying time of suspense, the commodore
was constantly making ready. First he sent the fleet
paymaster over to the consignees of the English steamship *Nanshan* and bought her as she was, with 3,300
tons of good Cardiff coal on board. Then he bought the
Zafiro, a steamship of the Manila-Hong-kong line,
just as she was, with all her fuel and provisions, and on
her was placed all the spare ammunition, so that she
became the magazine of the fleet. On April 18 the
McCulloch came in and joined the squadron. She was
only a revenue cutter, it is true, but she was as good as
a gunboat, being built of steel, having 1,500 tons displacement, and carrying four 4-inch guns and a crew
of 130 men all ready to fight. The news coming now
from the United States was fast removing every doubt
as to the future, and on the 19th of April, the day of
Concord, when the two Houses were passing the war
resolution, the American sailors in Hong-kong went
over the sides with their paint brushes, and in a few
hours the white was gone, and the ships looked leaden
and sombre in the dull dark drab of the war-paint. On
the 21st, when General Woodford was leaving Madrid
and Señor Polo was slipping out of Washington, the
Baltimore appeared, a powerful addition to the fleet,
and bringing also her load of ammunition so that she

was doubly welcome. Hardly had the new-comer found time to put on her war-paint when news came of the declaration of war, and then of the English proclamation of neutrality. This compelled a departure from Hong-kong on April 25 to the Chinese harbor of Mirs bay, a few miles to the north; but there was not to be much more of the dreary waiting at this new anchorage. On the following day the *McCulloch*, left behind at Hong-kong, came rushing up the bay bringing a despatch dated at Washington, April 24, and worth reading just as it was written, for it opened a new page in history, and has become famous from its results—

Dewey, Asiatic Squadron:

War has commenced between the United States and Spain. Proceed at once to Philippine Islands. Commence operations at once, particularly against the Spanish fleet. You must capture vessels or destroy. Use utmost endeavors. LONG.

It is a great thing to be ready and to be without doubts, and Commodore Dewey was both. Before the day closed the captains had all been called to consultation on the flag-ship, and at two o'clock on April 27 the sailing-pennant went up, and the fleet steamed out of Mirs bay and steered southward across the 620 miles of one of the roughest seas in the world which lay between them and the Philippines. On the morning of April 30 the fleet was off Bolinao bay, and looked in carefully. Nothing there. Then came Subig bay. More care here, for the last report from Manila—a report that had flown on the cables all over the world —was that the Spanish admiral had brought his fleet to Subig bay, and meant to give battle there. The *Boston* and *Concord* went ahead as scouts and examined the harbor. No enemy here either. Only two little fishing-boats, from which not even information could be obtained. Quite clear now that the Spaniards had determined to make their stand at the gates of their capital, and thither the fleet must go. So, on Saturday afternoon, April 30, the fleet started slowly along the thirty miles which lay between it and Manila. The tropical sun sank red across the land, and the great yellow moon rose, on the other hand, out of the sea to light them on their way.

Let us look at the squadron for a moment as it forges onward past the Luzon coast. There are nine ships in all, of which two the *Nanshan*, a collier, and the *Zafiro*, a supply-ship, are non-combatants. Then there is the *McCulloch*, a revenue-cutter, but, as has been said, well enough built and armed to pass as a gunboat. Next is the *Petrel*, a true gunboat, but very small, only 892 tons, and carrying four 4-inch and four small machine guns. The *Concord*, also a steel gunboat, but with a displacement of 1,710 tons, carries six 6-inch guns, and a secondary battery of eleven machine-guns, and has her deck and conning-tower protected. The next step is a marked advance in power, and brings us to the *Raleigh*, a second-rate steel cruiser of 3,213 tons. Her armament consists of one rapid-fire 6-inch, and ten rapid-fire 5-inch guns, with a secondary battery of eight 6-pounders, four 1-pounders, and two Gatlings. Her deck and conning-tower are protected with armor; she has a cellulose belt and steel sponsons. The *Boston* is another cruiser of the second rate, of 3,000 tons, a partially protected deck, two 8-inch, and six slow-fire 6-inch guns, two 6-pounders, two 3-pound, two

1-pound rapid-fire, and four machine guns. The *Baltimore* is a third steel cruiser of the second rate, with a displacement of 4,413 tons, and a protection of steel deck-plates and shields for all the guns and conning-tower. Her armament is heavy, and consists of four 8-inch and six 6-inch guns, with two 6, two 3, and two 1 pounders, all rapid-fire, and six machine guns. Last in the list comes the *Olympia*, the flag-ship, a first-class steel cruiser of 5,870 tons, protected by steel deck-plates, steel-covered barbettes, gun-shields, and conning-tower, and a cellulose belt thirty-three inches thick and eight feet broad. Her main battery is composed of four 8-inch guns, her secondary battery of ten quick-fire fives, and in addition fourteen 6-pounders, six 1-pounders, all rapid-fire, and four Gatlings.

The speed of the ships varied from 21.5 knots for the *Olympia*, to 13.7 knots for the *Petrel*, the latter, or less, being of course the highest speed of the fleet. Speed, however, played no part in the action, and need not, therefore, be considered. From this summary it will be observed that although the American ships were all modern, and armed, as a rule, with the best modern guns, there was not a single armor-clad among them. They were all practically unarmored, and they were going through channels which were said to be filled with torpedoes, to encounter, so far as they knew, a more numerous fleet, composed of old ships, it is true, but armed with modern guns, and backed, as was understood, by forts mounted with the finest and heaviest modern rifles. The prospect was serious, and it was faced by officers and men alike with quiet confidence. The night was still, and the fleet, as it drew near to Ma-

nila, waited until the moon set, and then rounding the
last point, saw the entrance to the great bay, which
runs nearly thirty miles into the land, open before it.
A very splendid bay indeed it is—one of the finest harbors, and one of the greatest of roadsteads; as a harbor, in fact, one of the prizes of the world, quite unde-
veloped, because it has been in feeble, incompetent, and
corrupt hands ever since it was taken from its original
owners. Twenty-six miles from the mouth is Manila.
Some 250,000 people there, the vague Spanish statistics
tell us. It is an interesting town, low-lying, and called
the Venice of the East, because rivers intersect it. There
is a new and also an old town, the latter beautifully
walled in the manner of three hundred years ago, with
moats, drawbridges, and portcullises, altogether very
picturesque, and worthy of preservation. Ten miles
nearer the bay's mouth, and on the same side, lies Cavité, a suburb of Manila, with some 5,000 people, a
navy-yard, arsenal, and fortifications. At the entrance
of the harbor lie two islands pretty well in the middle
—one large, over 600 feet high, called Corregidor, one
small, but over 400 feet in height. Between the islands
is a narrow channel with eight fathoms of water at
the narrowest part. Between Caballo and the little island of El Fraile three miles width of channel with
eighteen fathoms of water, and known as the Boca
Grande. On the other side, between Corregidor and
San José point, a channel known as the Boca Chica,
two miles wide and of ample depth. Taken together,
they are very fit and stately entrances to the great bay
beyond. There are forts on Corregidor and Caballo,
as well as light-houses, and batteries also on El Fraile,

which lies to the southward. More forts are on Limbones and San José points, heavily armed with the best Krupp guns, according to the information brought to Hong-kong. Nevertheless, they all were to be passed, and as the ships headed for the bay they saw the great light, the guardian of peaceful commerce, burning bright upon Corregidor. There was no light on the ships, but the throb of the engines shook the still air as they entered the Boca Grande, expecting each moment a shot from the batteries. On they went, well into the channel now, and still no sign of life from the shore. The war-ships had all passed, when some enthusiast on the *McCulloch* flung coals upon the fires, there was a rush of sparks and black smoke from her funnel, and the Spaniards waked up. A shot from the south side of the channel broke the stillness, and then two more, the shells dropping into the water. The reply came from the *Concord*, and one of her 4-inch shells struck the fort with a crash, followed by a cry in the darkness. A shot from the El Fraile batteries was answered by the *Raleigh*. Then an 8-inch gun boomed out from the *Boston*, and the *McCulloch* snapped away with her 4-pounders; there was more firing from the batteries, and then the islands and the mainland relapsed into profound quiet, and it was all as if nothing had happened. The American fleet had passed the dreaded forts at the entrance, and was in the bay of Manila. On glided the ships, ever more slowly and quietly, until it seemed as if they hardly moved at all, and then with the sudden dawn of the tropics came day, and there ahead lay the Spanish fleet, close under the forts and batteries of Cavité. The moment had come.

WRECK OF THE CRUISER *ISLA DE CUBA*

It came, fortunately, to a man who knew exactly what he meant to do—a most victorious quality, and one all too rare in a world given overmuch to uncertainty and stumbling. Commodore Dewey had his plan thoroughly laid out, and now proceeded to carry it into execution. Making a wide detour to the east to drop the supply-ships out of range, the fleet swept slowly along. As it passed, the batteries and ships at Cavité opened fire, the sharp crack of the modern rifle mingling with the heavier roar of the older guns. The American fleet made no answer.

As the ships turned and passed in front of Manila the sight-seers on the walls and the cathedral towers could be seen with a glass, and the guns of the Luneta flung some heavy shells far out and wide of the ships, and a steady and useless fire continued from these batteries throughout the engagement. The *Concord* replied, and up went the signal on the flag-ship, "Hold your fire until close in." So the fleet moved silently and steadily down toward Cavité. Suddenly, just ahead of the flag-ship, there came a quivering shock, and a great column of water leaped into the air; another quiver and another burst of mud and water followed, again too far away for harm. The dreaded mines were really there, then, and the fleet was upon them; but no ship swerved, no man stirred, and, as sometimes happens, the brave were favored, and this was the last of the Spanish torpedoes. If there were others, they failed to explode, and those which had exploded failed to check the American ships for an instant. On they went, still silently, holding their fire, the Spanish batteries and ships now beginning to pour out shot and shell as their enemy drew near. Closer and closer they came, until at last the distance was but little over five thousand yards. "If you are ready, Gridley, you may fire," said the commodore to the captain of the *Olympia*. It seemed that the captain was ready. The port 8-inch gun of the forward turret rang out, and the great shell sped over the water to the Spanish flag-ship. Up went the signal "Fire as convenient," and the ships behind the *Olympia* opened at once. The Spaniards were not behindhand. From ships and forts there was a continuous roar, and the shells began to strike all about the American squadron. One burst so near the *Olympia* that its fragments cut the rigging, ploughed a furrow in the deck, and tore the bridge where the commodore stood. Still, none were hit, and on the order to "Open with all the guns," the American ships poured forth a fire which in volume, rapidity, and accuracy could not have been surpassed. Back they came from the second round, within four thousand yards this time, pouring in the same volume of concentrated fire from the starboard as before from the port batteries. The *Boston* and *Baltimore* were both hit, but not materially injured, and again they swung round in front of Manila, and again, nearer than before, steamed steadily down toward Cavité. On each turn they drew nearer to the Spanish fleet, and the heavy, well-aimed American broadsides became more and more deadly. The Spaniards were suffering severely, and at seven o'clock the flag-ship, *Reina Cristina*, left her moorings and steamed bravely out, directing her course toward the *Olympia*. What the purpose of the Spanish admiral may have been no one

WEST BATTERY, CAVITÉ, AFTER DESTRUCTION

knows, but word was at once passed to concentrate all
fire on his advancing flag-ship. As she drew nearer,
the storm of the American fire thickened about her.
Her sides were torn, her bridge shot away; she could
not stand the awful battering, and turned about to return to her anchorage. As she swung round, an 8-inch
gun of the *Olympia* sent a shell which struck her opponent squarely in the stern. The great projectile raked
the *Reina Cristina*, tore up her decks, and exploded her
after boiler, so that she could barely reel back to the
shelter of the forts, with one hundred and fifty of the
crew dead and ninety wounded on board. While the
flag-ship was thus engaged, two gunboats equipped as
torpedo-boats slipped out from Cavité, one making for
the supply-ships. The *Petrel* rushed after the latter,
opened with the 4-pounders, drove her ashore, and then
blew her to pieces with her rapid-fire guns, which was
the end of the first Spanish torpedo-boat. The second
headed for the *Olympia*, kept on despite the fire of the
secondary battery, and began to get ominously near,
men thought, but coming under the fierce storm of the
machine-guns in the tops, turned to fly. So her end
came. A well-directed shell struck her fairly inside
the stern railing. There was an explosion, the gunboat
seemed to break in the middle, and down she went.
Meantime the *Baltimore* had set the *Castilla*, the only
wooden ship in the Spanish squadron, on fire, and she
was soon a mass of flames.

Five times in all did the American ships turn and
move past their opponents, each time closer, and each
time with a more deadly broadside. There had been
now two hours' hot work under the rising tropical sun,

and at a quarter before eight the commodore, erroneously informed that ammunition for the 5-inch guns was running short, ran up the signals to cease firing and follow the flag-ship, so that he might consult with his captains, and if needful redistribute the ammunition. Something quite new and unheard-of, this stopping in the middle of a great naval action for any purpose. It is said that the American sailors, before they understood the meaning of it all, began to grumble at not being allowed to go on and finish up their task. The Spaniards, battered as they were, set up a cheer as they saw their foe withdraw to the other side of the bay, and sundry telegrams flew over the cable to Madrid saying that the Spanish fire had "forced the American ships to manœuvre" (the Spanish version of the skillful evolutions which had helped so much the American fighting), and that the enemy had now retreated to land their dead and wounded. Very characteristic and worthy of note these messages to Spain—no longer able to recognize facts, living among lies and delusions, and quite lost to that veracity of mind so essential, as Carlyle has pointed out, to the successful existence of men and nations. The evolutions of the American fleet were all planned beforehand; there were no dead and wounded, as the Americans found, not a little to their own astonishment, when the reports were made after this first round, and although several of the ships had been hit, no injury in the least serious had been done to any of them. Moreover, Commodore Dewey, as at the start, knew just what he meant to do. The Spanish fleet could not possibly escape. It had been disabled and crippled in the first round, but it still held the har-

WRECK OF THE FLAG-SHIP, THE CRUISER *REINA CRISTINA*

bor, and the land batteries remained to be dealt with. The orders were to "capture or destroy." There must be none left; none must escape to harass future operations, or to try to cross the Pacific and alarm and perhaps attack the western coast of the United States. The work demanded could be most surely finished and made perfect if the men upon whom everything depended were kept in the best possible condition. So, after the withdrawal to the other side of the bay, there was a good rest for all the crews, a hearty breakfast eaten quite at leisure, a cleaning of decks and turrets, an examination of all the guns, a fresh supply of ammunition brought up, and then, at a quarter before eleven, after three hours thus occupied, up went the signals, the shrill whistles of the boatswains rang out, and off the fleet went for the second and last assault.

This time the work was to be more direct. Again the fleet swung round in front of Manila, and again it steamed down toward Cavité, the *Baltimore* in the lead. On it went, and first one Spanish shell, then another, struck the *Baltimore*, and men were wounded by the splinters. Still silence on the American ship, and no reply to the Spanish fire until at last the range was less than three thousand yards. Then the *Baltimore* poured her broadside into the *Reina Cristina*, whence the admiral had transferred his flag to the *Isla de Cuba*, and the former flag-ship, fatally wounded in the duel with the *Olympia*, went to pieces under the fierce fire of her new antagonist. Her magazines blew up, and she sank. Then the *Baltimore* turned on the *Don Juan de Austria*, and was joined by the *Olympia* and *Raleigh*. While the Spanish ship quivered under the heavy fire, a shell from the Raleigh pierced her magazine and she blew up, tearing off also the upper works of a gunboat, which was then destroyed by the *Petrel*. The *General Lezo*, another gunboat, was driven ashore by the *Concord* and burned, the *Velasco* went down before the *Boston*, the burning *Castilla* was scuttled, and the *Don Antonio de Ulloa*, the last ship which was able to fight, sank under the fire of the *Baltimore* with her flag nailed to the mast. Meantime the *Petrel*, running into shoal water, set on fire and destroyed the *Marques del Duero*, *Don Juan de Austria*, *Isla de Cuba*, *Isla de Luzon*, and *General Lezo*. Just before this, Admiral Montojo, on his new flag-ship, the *Isla de Cuba*, with his guns silenced and his fleet gone, had run the gunboat ashore, hauled down his flag, left his vessel to its fate, and escaped to Manila. Thus the Spanish fleet was completely destroyed; but the shore batteries continued to fire, and one after another of them had to be silenced, which was done as fast as the American ships could close in upon them. They held out longest at Cavité, but a last and well-placed shell entered the arsenal magazine, a terrific explosion followed, the batteries all fell silent, and the white flag went up on the citadel. The battle of Manila had been fought and won.

The next day the fleet went into Cavité, and a landing party destroyed the batteries. On May 3 the forts on Corregidor, at the entrance of the harbor, surrendered to the *Raleigh* and *Baltimore*. At Cavité there was an effort to pretend that no white flag had been run up, and some cheap falsehood was indulged in, but facts were a little too strong even for Spaniards. The Spanish commander ran up the white flag again before

WRECK OF THE CRUISER *ISLA DE LUZON*

eleven o'clock, and departed with his men, whereupon
the American marines landed, and having assured the
priests and nuns that they were not going to massacre
the wounded in hospitals, as the Spanish had stated,
established a guard, and took possession of the arsenal and dock-yards of Cavité. Commodore Dewey,
through the British consul, announced the blockade of
Manila; and as the Spaniards, still unable to recognize
more than one or two facts at a time, refused to let him
control the cable, he promptly cut it, and thus held the
great harbor and city firmly in his grasp, stripped of all
means of communication with the outside world which
he did not allow.

The rapidity, brilliancy, and completeness of the
American victory at Manila riveted the attention of
the world. In Europe, where hostility to the United
States was everywhere felt and expressed, the news was
received either in the silence which is sometimes the
sincerest flattery, or with surprised expressions of wonder and grudging admiration. England, which from
the beginning manifested a genuine and cordial friendship, praised Dewey's work generously and freely. Yet
both on the Continent and in England, after the first
shock had passed, critics appeared who sneered at the
battle, called it a butchery, exaggerated the American
force and diminished that of Spain. One English critic
called it marvellously easy, and a well-known English
journal said Dewey had merely destroyed a few old
wooden ships. The last allegation was, of course,
merely a wilful falsehood, for there was only one wood-
en ship, the *Castilla*, in the Spanish fleet, and the fact
that the others also burned proved nothing, for all Cer-

vera's ships, the very latest productions of European dock-yards, took fire, in the Santiago fight, just like the older types at Manila. As to "its being so easy," it certainly looked easy after it was all done, and so did setting an egg on end seem easy after Columbus had shown how to do it. Such criticisms are really beneath contempt, but it is important to bring the facts clearly together and examine them, for on those facts Dewey's victory can stand without fear, and take its place in history.

The greatest naval action in which the victor came down upon his enemy anchored in a harbor was Aboukir. Of the splendor of Nelson's performance, and of the victory which he won, there can be no question. Let us try Dewey by that high standard.

The Bay of Aboukir is an almost open roadstead. All that was necessary was to keep clear of the shoals which make out from Aboukir point and island, and then, if the wind were fair, as Nelson's was, to bear down on the hostile fleet. The French fleet was anchored at Aboukir, and so were the Spaniards at Manila, with the additional protection of a boom at Cavité. The distance to be traversed by Nelson from the open sea to the French fleet was trifling. He had no channels to come through, no entrance-forts to pass, no mines to fear. Dewey had to pass through a wide channel, with powerful forts armed with modern guns on either side, in order to enter the bay. He then had to steam sixteen miles before he came opposite Cavité, while, from the best information received, he expected mines to be all about him, and two actually exploded in his near neighborhood. Nelson's fleet was numerically

A Comparative View of the American and the Spanish Fleets engaged at Manila.

AMERICAN FLEET.

NAME.	Class.	Armament.	Men and Officers.	Built in
Olympia	Protected Cruiser	Four 8-in., ten 5-in., 24 R. F.	466	1892
Baltimore	Protected Cruiser	Four 8-in., six 6-in., 10 R. F.	386	1888
Boston	Par. Protected Cruiser	Two 8-in., six 6-in., 10 R. F.	272	1884
Raleigh	Protected Cruiser	One 6-in., ten 5-in., 14 R. F.	295	1892
Concord	Gunboat	Six 6-in., 9 R. F.	150	1891
Petrel	Gunboat	Four 6-in., 7 R. F.	100	1888
McCulloch (not in action)	Revenue-Cutter	Four 4-in.	130	1888
			1,808	

SPANISH FLEET.*

NAME.	Class.	Armament.	Men and Officers.	Built in
Reina Cristina	Steel Cruiser	Six 6.2-in., two 2.7, 13 R. F.	352	1887
Castilla	Wooden Cruiser	Four 5.9, two 4.7, two 3.4, two 2.9, 12 R. F.	349	1881
Don Antonio de Ulloa	Iron Cruiser	Four 4.7, 5 R. F.	150	1875
Don Juan de Austria	Iron Cruiser	Four 4.7, two 2.7, 21 R. F.	179	1887
Isla de Luzon	Steel Protected Cruiser	Six 4.7, 8 R. F.	150	1887
Isla de Cuba	Steel Protected Cruiser	Six 4.7, 8 R. F.	156	1887
Velasco	Iron Cruiser	Three 6-in., two 2.7, 2 R. F.	147	1881
Marques del Duero	Gunboat	One 6.2, two 4.7, 1 R. F.	96	1875
General Lezo	Gunboat	One 3.5, 3 R. F.)	115	1885
Argos			82	
Two torpedo-boats and two transports, practically not in action.			1,706	

* El Correo is mentioned in Admiral Dewey's list of May 4, but is omitted in that given in his despatch of July 2, which is followed here.

the same as that of his opponent, but all the English fighting-ships were seventy-fours, while the French had three heavier, one of 120 guns and two of 80 each. It has been said freely and frequently that the Spanish were so hopelessly inferior that they could only hope to die, and that Dewey's sole glory was in the rapidity with which he and his captains and men did their work without injury to themselves. There is scarcely more foundation for this statement than for the wholesale falsehood of the English weekly that all the Spanish ships were made of wood. The statistics on this point are worth consideration and study.

Commodore Dewey had six fighting-ships, and the revenue-cutter *McCulloch*, acting as convoy to the supply-ships, and not taking part in the action. These six ships have already been described, but for a better understanding, their tonnage, armament and state of construction are given in the table on page 63.

Numerically the Spaniards had ten fighting-ships and two torpedo-boats against the American six. Commodore Dewey had no armored ships at all, and no more protection against shell than his opponent. The Spanish ships, compared to the American, were older and of inferior types, but as they fought from an anchorage, speed and engines did not count, and they were armed with modern guns, which was by far the most important qualification. The Spaniards had 52 classified big guns* and 72 rapid-fire and machine guns; the Americans 57 classified big guns, and 74 rapid-fire and machine guns. The Americans had 10 eight-inch guns, while the largest Spanish guns were 6.2 inches.

Argos guns estimated at three.

RESIDENCE OF AGUINALDO

Commodore Dewey therefore had the advantage in weight of metal and in heavy guns, and his flag-ship, the *Olympia,* far outclassed anything opposed to him. Nelson at Aboukir was slightly inferior to his antagonist in weight of metal and number of guns, and had no ship as powerful as *L'Orient.* On the other hand, he equalled his foe in number of ships, while the Spaniards outnumbered Dewey two to one, and had 1,796 men against the American 1,678 engaged in action. A far more important difference was that, while Nelson had only the French fleet to deal with, the Spaniards at Manila were supported by powerful, strongly manned shore batteries mounted with modern rifled guns, some of very large calibre. This last fact, too much overlooked, made the odds against Dewey very heavy, even after the two mines had exploded without result.

Both Dewey and Nelson hunted down the enemy, and engaged them at anchor where they found them. Nelson entered an open roadstead by daylight, began his action at sunset, and fought on in the darkness. Dewey ran past powerful entrance-forts and up a deep bay in the darkness, and fought his battle in daylight. Neither took the enemy by surprise, for Admiral Montojo's report shows that he had tried Subig bay and given it up, and that he then made every preparation possible to meet the Americans at Cavité under the shelter of the batteries. Nelson practically destroyed the French fleet, but Admiral Villeneuve escaped the next morning, with two ships of the line and two frigates, and there was only one English ship, the *Zealous,* not enough for the purpose, in condition to follow them. Dewey absolutely destroyed every Spanish ship, including the transport *Mindanao*, and captured the other transport, the *Manila*. He silenced all the land batteries and took Cavité. Aboukir had its messengers of death in the escaping French ships; Manila had none. Absolute completeness like this cannot be surpassed. The Spaniards admitted a loss of 634 killed and wounded in ships and forts, while the Americans had none killed and only eight wounded, all on the *Baltimore*. The American ships were hit several times, but not one was seriously injured, much less disabled. This has been attributed to the extremely bad marksmanship of the Spaniards, and has been used to explain Dewey's victory. It is easy to exaggerate the badness of the Spanish gunnery. They seem, as a matter of fact, to have shot well enough until the Americans opened upon them. The shells which struck the *Baltimore* effectively were both fired before that ship replied in the second round. But when the American fire began, it was delivered with such volume, precision, and concentration that the Spanish fire was actually smothered, and became wholly wild and ineffective. The great secret of the victory was in the accuracy and rapidity of the American gunners, which have always been characteristic of the American navy, as was shown in the frigate duels of 1812, of which the United States won against England eleven out of thirteen. This great quality was not accidental, but due to skill, practice, and national aptitude. In addition to this traditional skill was the genius of the commander, backed by the fighting capacity of his captains and his crews. True to the great principle of Nelson and Farragut, Dewey went straight

after his enemy, to fight the hostile fleet wherever
found. In the darkness he went boldly into an unfa-
miliar harbor, past powerful batteries the strength of
which his best information had magnified, over mine
fields the extent and danger of which he did not and
could not know. As soon as dawn came he fell upon the
Spanish fleet, supported as it was by shore batteries,
and utterly destroyed it. The Spanish empire in the
East crumbled before his guns, and the great city and
harbor of Manila fell helplessly into his hands. All this
was done without the loss of a man or serious injury
to a ship. The most rigid inspection fails to discover a
mistake. There can be nothing better than perfection
of workmanship, and this Dewey and his officers and
men showed. The completeness of the result, which
is the final test, gives Manila a great place in the history of naval battles, and writes the name of George
Dewey high up among the greatest of victorious admirals.

CHAPTER IV

THE BLOCKADE OF CUBA

To THE American fleet which through many weary weeks had been waiting for action in grim impatience at Key West the news of the resolution of Congress and of the President's order to sail brought great relief. The order came in the late afternoon of April 21, but there were still some ships to coal, some more detailed instructions to be received from Washington, and it was not until the next morning at half past six o'clock that they got under way and steamed slowly off toward Havana. The blockade proclaimed by the President covered Havana and all ports east and west between Cardenas and Bahia Honda, as well as Cienfuegos on the south coast, from which a railroad ran to the capital city. It was generally believed at the outbreak of the war that Havana, which drew most of its supplies from the United States, would soon be starved into surrender when cut off from the continent and with nothing but a desolated country behind it to turn to for relief. Events showed that this conception, a perfectly natural one at the time, was absolutely unfounded. Either Havana had vast stores on hand, or the surrounding country and the blockade-running through the southern ports were able to supply the city, or all three sources combined were sufficient for that object. Whatever the ex-

planation, certain it is that although there was a great deal of suffering in the capital, there is no indication that at the end of the war it was, as a military position, much nearer to surrender on account of starvation than at the beginning of hostilities. Nevertheless, with the theory then prevalent as to the desperate condition of the city whose fall meant the end of Spanish rule in Cuba, the American blockade closed tightly over Havana, and in the opening days of the war Spanish vessels and steamships plying to the blockaded port fell rapidly into the hands of the Americans, until this commerce was practically stopped or destroyed.

Blockading and prize-taking were not, however, the sole duties of the American fleet. It was obvious that any attempt to get into the harbor of Havana through its narrow channel crammed with mines would be at once mad and useless. But it was at the same time very desirable to keep open and unprotected, so far as possible, the other harbors, because at that moment the theory was that we should either land a large army to proceed against Havana, or important expeditions to co-operate with the insurgents in a movement to cut off the capital from the interior. This theory, whether strongly or lightly held, was soon set aside by events and never acted upon—a very fortunate thing, for it rested upon a gross underestimate of the strength of Havana and of the Spanish forces, and upon an equally gross over-estimate of the numbers and efficiency of the insurgents. In the early days of the war, however, it had sufficient strength to affect the naval operations near Havana, but very luckily led, practically, only to work which it would have been well to do in any event.

The first affair growing out of these conditions, and the first action of the war, occurred at Matanzas. It was discovered that the Spaniards were establishing batteries and raising new fortifications at that port, and on April 27 Admiral Sampson's flagship, the *New York,* supported by the monitor *Puritan* and the unarmored cruiser *Cincinnati* bombarded the defences. The Spanish shooting was very bad, only three shots coming near the *New York,* and none hitting the *Cincinnati,* which was much exposed. The American shooting, on the other hand, was good, from the guns of the *Puritan* to the rapid-fires of the *Cincinnati.* The Spanish batteries and earth-works were badly shattered and broken up, and many guns dismounted. As the Captain-General of Cuba announced that only one mule was killed, we may conclude with almost absolute certainty that there must have been a very considerable loss of life among the troops exposed to the American fire. Except as a warning to the Spaniards, and as a test of American marksmanship, the affair of April 27 at Matanzas was of trifling importance, although great attention was given to it at the moment because it was the first action of the war by land or sea. But while the fleet was thus carrying out its orders by its vigorous blockade, by opening a bombardment on the lesser ports, and by harassing the coast batteries and garrisons, events were occurring elsewhere which determined the future course of the war.

On April 23 the President called for 125,000 volunteers, and on April 25 Congress adopted a formal declaration of war, which stated that war had existed since

April 21—an unquestioned truth. On the 26th the President announced that the United States, although not a signatory, would adhere to the agreement of Paris, and permit no privateers. The wisdom of this prompt and righteous declaration was seen at once in the approval which it received abroad, and in the embarrassment which it caused to Spain, where hopes were entertained that, all social and national efficiency being dead, something might still be done by legalized piracy. International opinion was still further conciliated by our giving thirty days to all Spanish ships to leave our ports. Thus, while Congress was voting money and preparing a bill for war revenue, while the call for volunteers was going through the land, while camps were being formed, men mustered in, the regulars brought together from all parts of the country and mobilized at Tampa, we were settling rapidly and judiciously our relations with the other powers of the earth. There was never a moment when any European power could or would have dared to interfere with us, although columns of speculations, predictions, and mysterious warnings filled the newspapers on this subject. And as there was no danger that any one power would interfere, so after Manila there was no peril to be apprehended from any combination of powers. That was the crisis, and when England refused to join the concert of Europe in interfering with us in the Philippines—an act not to be forgotten by Americans—all possible danger of interference from any quarter was at an end. Nevertheless, as we adjusted our relations to the rest of the world wisely and quickly, when we caught Spain by the throat, so the rest of the world made haste to define their relations, both to us and to our antagonist.

England declared her neutrality on April 23, the same day on which the Governor-General of Hongkong requested Commodore Dewey to leave English waters within forty-eight hours—a polite invitation fraught with much meaning to what remained of Charles V's empire in the East. But we were not the only people who had a fighting fleet in neutral waters. For some time past Spain had been collecting a torpedo-boat flotilla and a squadron of armored cruisers. The fleet thus brought together had come to the Canaries, and thence had proceeded to the Cape Verde Islands. In the days after the *Maine* explosion, when relations between the two countries were straining to the breaking point, the movements of these Spanish ships excited intense interest. It was rumored that they were to come to Puerto Rico, and had they done so their arrival would have precipitated war. But they did not start; they remained quietly at the Cape Verde Islands, and when war came they still lingered. It may well be doubted whether they would have moved at all if they had been in a Spanish harbor, but, unluckily for them, the Cape Verde Islands were Portuguese, and although Portugal was entirely friendly to Spain, she was obliged to issue a proclamation of neutrality on April 29. Thereupon the Spanish fleet departed, under orders from Madrid. The light torpedo boats, unprotected cruisers, and transports went north to the Canaries, and thence to Spain. The fighting-squadron was lost sight of steering westward. This squadron consisted of the *Colon*, the *Almirante*

THE SPANISH SQUADRON AT CAPE VERDE ISLANDS

Oquendo, the *Viscaya,* and the *Maria Teresa,* armored cruisers of the first class, all new, all the best work of European dock-yards, with heavy batteries of the finest modern rifles, eight inches of armor, and a contract speed of over twenty knots, and of three large torpedo-boat destroyers, the *Furor, Pluton,* and *Terror,* just out of English yards, the last expression of Scotch and English building, and with a contract speed of thirty knots. The squadron, as it appeared on paper and in the naval registers, was, as a whole, powerful in armament, fast, and very formidable. There it was, then, loose on the ocean, and the question which at once arose and overshadowed all others was where Admiral Cervera and his ships were going, for they represented the Spanish sea power. When they were found and destroyed, the campaign on the Atlantic side would be over, and the expulsion of the Spaniards from the American hemisphere could be effected at the pleasure of the United States. Until they were destroyed no movement could be safely or conclusively undertaken against either Cuba or Puerto Rico. It was the old, ever-recurring problem of the sea power, as crucial and decisive to the United States in the spring of 1898 as it was to Rome when Hannibal faced the legions, or to the English when Napoleon banded all Europe together against Great Britain.

The Spanish fleet was somewhere in the mid-Atlantic; that was all that was known, and speculation was rife as to its destination. The people of the Atlantic seaboard thought that a descent upon the coast towns was at hand—an obviously impossible solution, because in the waters of New England the Spaniards, far removed from any base, would have courted destruction. So this opinion was rejected by the Navy Department. Another opinion was that Cervera was steaming away southward to cut off the *Oregon*. Here, unfortunately, there was much greater probability of truth than in the chimera of the descent on the Atlantic coast towns. But the Strategy Board wisely decided that to divide or scatter the fleets in an effort to protect the *Oregon* would be a mistake of the first order. The great battle-ship must take her chance. Either she would slip by her enemies safely, or, if she met them, she would so cripple them that their effectiveness would be gone. So the *Oregon* was left to her fate.

Thus two possibilities for the Spanish fleet were considered and set aside. A third was that, after making a wide turn, the fleet would return to Spain, and rumors of its reappearance at Cadiz kept coming until the moment when the truth was known. Such a proceeding as this, however, seemed too absurd, even for a Spaniard, to a world which had not yet seen Admiral Camara go back and forth through the Suez Canal; and the authorities in Washington, in consultation with Admiral Sampson, decided that Cervera was intending to do the sensible thing from a naval standpoint and make for a port from which he could operate toward the relief of Havana. It was further conjectured, and on all the known facts and conditions very wisely conjectured, that the Spanish fleet would come to Puerto Rico, the natural and only strong Spanish base for operations directed toward Cuba. On the speed to be fairly estimated for such a fleet the time of their arrival at Puerto Rico could easily be determined. So it came about, on

this theory of the conditions, that soon after noon on
May 3 the battle-ships *Iowa* and *Indiana* left Key West,
whence the flag-ship *New York* followed them at night.
The rendezvous was at Juruco Cove about twelve miles
east of Havana. There they were joined by the two
monitors *Terror* and *Amphitrite*, from the blockading
squadron, the two unarmored cruisers *Detroit* and
Montgomery, the torpedo-boat *Porter*, the tug *Wompatuck*, and a collier. Then they started east to find the
Spanish fleet. A more ill-assorted squadron it would
have been difficult to imagine, and the necessity which
made it so came from the insufficient, unsystematic
naval authorizations of Congress running back over
many years. In the two essential qualities of the
modern fleet, homogeneity of type and evenness of
speed, they were painfully deficient. The squadron
was composed of the most discordant types, and varied
in speed from the twenty knots or more of the *New
York* to the monitors' maximum of less than ten. The
monitors, in fact, were nothing but a perilous incum-
brance. Their low speed and limited coal capacity
made it necessary to tow them, and they thus reduced
the speed of the fleet to about seven knots. In any sort
of seaway it was impossible to fight their guns, and if
an enemy had been encountered in the open ocean, they
would have been a hindrance and a danger, not a help.
Thus burdened with ships fit only for the smooth waters
of a harbor, and with a fleet-speed of seven knots, Admiral Sampson, thanks to the parsimony of Congress,
set forth in pursuit of a powerful squadron of homogeneous armored cruisers, with a uniform contract
speed of twenty knots.

His departure was the end of the crude idea with
which the war opened, that we were to batter down the
Morro Castle and the Cabanas forts, land a few thous-
and troops, and take Havana out of hand. Before the
war a high authority was reported to have said that in
ten days we could have 40,000 men ready for operations
in Cuba. April 23 the President called for 125,000
volunteers, and a month later for 75,000 more. It was
at once discovered that but very few of the regiments
furnished by the States were fully equipped; most
of them were only partially prepared, and many were
not equipped at all. Instead of being able to mobilize
40,000 soldiers in ten days, it was found that it was not
possible to even muster them in that time. While
sundry newspapers were clamoring for an immediate
advance on Havana, it was becoming quite clear to all
men, even in those confused days, that it would take
weeks and months, rather than days, to make these
really fine volunteers into an army; that the machinery
of transportation, supplies, hospital service, and the rest
was utterly inadequate for the strain suddenly put upon
it, even if it had been good, and that it was not good,
but bad and rusty. On May 14, ten days after Sampson's departure for Puerto Rico, there were only a little
over 10,000 men at Tampa, and the wise men who had
said from the beginning that we ought to move on
Puerto Rico, the Spanish base, and not begin in early
summer on Havana, ultimately carried their point because of facts more potent than the best reasoning.

But no military movement being possible until we
had command of the sea, the pursuit of Cervera's fleet,
from both the military and the naval point of view, was

the one thing to which all else had to be subordinated. So while the generals and admirals of civil life were laying out and discussing campaigns in the newspapers, facts were putting the real war into the right channels; and while the prepared navy was off after Spain's sea power, the unprepared army was occupying the time thus fortunately given in getting ready with an energy and speed most remarkable when one understood the wretched system imposed upon it by Congress, and the weight of needless clerks, endless red-tape, and fear of responsibility which had grown up in choking luxuriance during the long, neglectful peace.

But although the direct attack on Havana so confidently looked for at the outset was thus practically abandoned the work of blockading the island and cutting it off from all outside communication went diligently forward. Various expeditions were undertaken to open connection with the Cuban insurgents and supply them with arms and ammunition, as the exaggerated estimate then existing of their numbers and efficiency made the belief general that they could be developed into a powerful offensive force, and be used with effect against the Spaniards. Then and later various expeditions were sent forth in the *Leyden, Gussie,* and *Florida,* but they had no result. The earlier landings, managed and conducted in large measure by Captain Dorst of the regular army, a most gallant and accomplished officer, were effective sometimes in the face of a sharp fire. The first skirmishing took place on one of these expeditions, much courage was shown, some blood was shed, arms were landed, and communication opened with the insurgents, but that was the end of it. There was no trouble about the expeditions, but nothing was developed by them among the insurgents.

More serious work was that entailed by the blockade and by attacks upon the lesser ports to break down the defences and destroy any lurking gunboats. Before the *New York* went eastward she had broken up some parties of Spaniards who, with strange absence of humor, had opened on her with Mauser rifles at Mariel, but she was drawing very near to San Juan when, on May 11, a far more serious affair than any which had yet taken place occurred at Cardenas. Off that port the gunboats *Machias* and *Wilmington*, the torpedo-boat *Winslow*, and the converted revenue-cutter *Hudson* were maintaining the blockade. After a time it was learned that there were three Spanish gunboats in the harbor, and on the 8th of May an attempt was made to decoy them out of the harbor, which so far succeeded that one came within range of the *Machias*, got a 6-pounder shell landed upon her, and quickly retreated. It was obvious, after this, that to fight the Spaniards it was necessary to go after them wherever they might be, a discovery which became later an accepted principle of the war. Acting on this theory, the *Wilmington*, *Winslow*, and *Hudson*, on May 11, made their way into the bay along an unused channel, which was free from mines, until they were within a mile and a half of the wharves where the enemy's gunboats were lying. Then the water became too shoal for the *Wilmington*, and the *Winslow* was ordered ahead to attack. It was a most reckless piece of work to undertake, for the *Winslow* was a torpedo-boat, not a fighting-ship, her sides were not over a quarter of an inch thick, and she was going to meet ships carrying 12-pounders. Her daring commander, Lieutenant Bernadou, and his officers and men, were, however, only too eager to make the attempt. On they went, opening vigorously with their 1-pounders to which the Spaniards replied fiercely. Presently they found themselves among some red buoys, which, as it proved, marked ranges, and the shots from the batteries and the gunboats began to come home. Ten struck the unprotected boat; Lieutenant Bernadou was badly wounded, but managed to keep his feet, the steering-gear was smashed, and one engine. Then came the eleventh shot, which killed Ensign Bagley and four men. The brave little boat was now floating helplessly in full range of the Spanish guns. Her destruction seemed certain, but the *Hudson*, really nothing more than an armored harbor tug, but commanded by a gallant revenue officer, Lieutenant F. H. Newcomb, came bravely to the rescue. The *Hudson* had crept slowly after the *Winslow*, and firing rapidly on the Spaniards, now started, in the midst of a storm of projectiles, to bring off the disabled torpedo-boat. Twice she got a line to the *Winslow*, and twice it parted. Then the *Hudson* got alongside, and towed the wounded boat, with her blood-stained decks and broken sides, out of range and into safety. There were five killed and five wounded out of the *Winslow's* complement of twenty-one officers and men, a terrible percentage, and the heaviest loss incurred by the American navy in any action of the war. It was a rash undertaking, but most gallantly faced and brilliantly attempted, a proof, to those who rightly interpreted it, of a very high and victorious spirit in the navy of the United States, waiting only for a large opportunity to win corresponding triumphs. Nor did the blow dealt the *Winslow* go unavenged. When the *Hudson* and her consort were out of the way, the *Wilmington* drew in, destroyed the Spanish gunboat which had been engaged, and smashed and silenced all the shore batteries, with a heavy loss to the garrisons. There was nothing more to be feared from the gunboats or defences of Cardenas.

The same day that the *Winslow*, the *Hudson* and the *Wilmington* were having their action at Cardenas, far away on the southern coast of Cuba another fight was taking place, in the progress of the work of separating the great island from the rest of the world. On the night of May 10, Captain McCalla of the *Marblehead* called for volunteers to protect the cable-cutters in their work. The roll was soon filled, and the next morning the steam-launches of the *Marblehead* and *Nashville*, towing the two sailing-launches under command of Lieutenants Winslow and Anderson, started into the harbor of Cienfuegos about quarter before seven. They carried a squad of marines picked for proficiency as marksmen, and a machine-gun in the bow of each boat. The *Nashville* and *Marblehead* then opened fire on the Spanish batteries, and under cover of this, and that of the steam-launches, the crews of the other boats went to work. It was a perilous business, but the sailors grappled and cut successfully the two cables they had been ordered to destroy. They also found a third small cable, but the grapnel fouled the bottom and was lost. Meantime the Spanish fire grew

CUTTING THE CABLES UNDER FIRE AT CIENFUEGOS

hotter and hotter, pouring out from the batteries and machine-guns, and the boats began to suffer. The well-directed fire from the rifles of the marines and from the one-pounders kept the Spaniards from reaching the switch-house which controlled the submarine torpedoes, but launches could not contend with batteries at close range, and when the work for which they came, and which had all been performed under a heavy fire, was done, they withdrew to the ships. Nine men, including Lieutenant Winslow, had been wounded, some seriously, and three, as was reported later, mortally. It was a very gallant exploit, coolly and thoroughly carried through, under a galling fire, and it succeeded in its purpose of hampering and blocking in the enemy at the important port of Cienfuegos, which was the road to Havana from the southern coast. It was another twist in the coil which the United States was tightening about Cuba.

CHAPTER V

THE PURSUIT OF CERVERA

MEANTIME the ill-assorted fleet under Admiral Sampson was making the best way it could eastward, and the pursuit of Cervera's fleet had fairly begun. It was known when the Spaniards had sailed, but whither they had gone could only be a matter of guess. They might be going to harry the New England coast, or at least, as has been said, some persons thought this possible. More reasonable was the second theory already alluded to that they intended to intercept the *Oregon*. The great battle-ship had arrived on March 9 at San Francisco, and on the 19th, with Captin Clark in command, she started on her long voyage round Cape Horn, to join the North Atlantic Squadron. On April 7 she left Callao, where she coaled, for Sandy Point, running steadily on through heavy seas, and maintaining high speed. On April 16 she reached the strait, and rode out a severe gale at her anchors, at Port Tamar. The next day the battle-ship was at Sandy Point, where she coaled again, and picked up the gunboat *Marietta*. On the 21st the ships ran through the strait by which Magellan passed to found Spain's empire in the East, and turned northward in Atlantic waters. Here came the shadow of a new danger, for the Spanish torpedo-boat *Temerario* was at Montevideo, menacing an at-

tack in the night. But there was no change in speed or direction. On the ships forged, with guns shotted, the rapid-fires ready, and lights screened at night. Officers and men stood double watches, and those carried insensible from the fire-room begged to return as soon as they came to themselves. Luckily for her, the *Temerario* never became visible, and on April 30 the American ships were at Rio. Here they met a cordial reception, and once more were coaled. Here too came news of the existence of war, and of the sailing of the Spanish fleet with an unknown destination. Four powerful armored cruisers and three torpedo-boats, somewhere, perhaps on the track to the north: heavy odds these for one ship. But Captain Clark leaves Rio on May 4, drops his slower consorts, the *Marietta* and *Nictheroy*, off Cape Frio, and there is no quiver in his despatch of May 9, from Bahia. He says, quite simply, "The *Oregon* could steam fourteen knots for hours, and in a running fight might beat off and cripple the Spanish fleet," and those who read these words think of Sir Richard Grenville in the years gone by, and know that the sea spirit of the north, drawn from a far-distant past, is still burning strong and clear in this American captain and his crew. So he leaves Bahia, and on May 18 he is at Barbadoes, and then comes another space of anxiety, deeper among men on land than among those on the battle-ship, and then the country hears, on May 24, that the *Oregon* is at Jupiter Inlet, Florida, her great voyage done. A pause, and then the world knows that the *Oregon*, after her 14,000 miles through all seas and weather, is on her way to join the fighting-line, not a rivet, nor a bolt, nor a gearing broken or out of place. It appears very sharply in this fashion that, despite wise critics in Europe, American battle-ships can make great voyages and face the seas as well as fight, and that there is a capacity for true and honest workmanship in the United States very comforting to think on. Very clear, too, is the still greater fact that the American seamen, captain and crew, are filled to-day with the old spirit of the sea-conquerors shining undimmed and strong.

So the Spanish fleet did not seek the *Oregon*, and would have been crippled and shattered if it had made the attempt, and the department very wisely left the battle-ship to take care of herself, and would not divide the fleet. And it was also decided, as has already been said, that the enemy would not go to New England, but that, on the assumption (a very violent one, as appeared later) of intelligent action, they would go to the obvious and all-important Spanish base of Puerto Rico. So thither went Admiral Sampson, warned at Cape Haitien from Washington not to risk damage to his ships in a bombardment, and on May 11, when the *Winslow* was fighting desperately at Cardenas, and other American sailors were cutting cables at Cienfuegos, the fighting-fleet was drawing near to San Juan. It was still dark when the lights of the town became visible the next morning, and when the sun rose the city lay before them. The admiral's flag was shifted to the *Iowa*, the tug *Wompatuck* was anchored to mark the ten-fathom line, and then the ships, with the *Detroit* leading, went in and opened fire, while the *Montgomery* ran by and silenced the batteries of Fort Canelo, on the other side of the bay. The Spanish gunnery

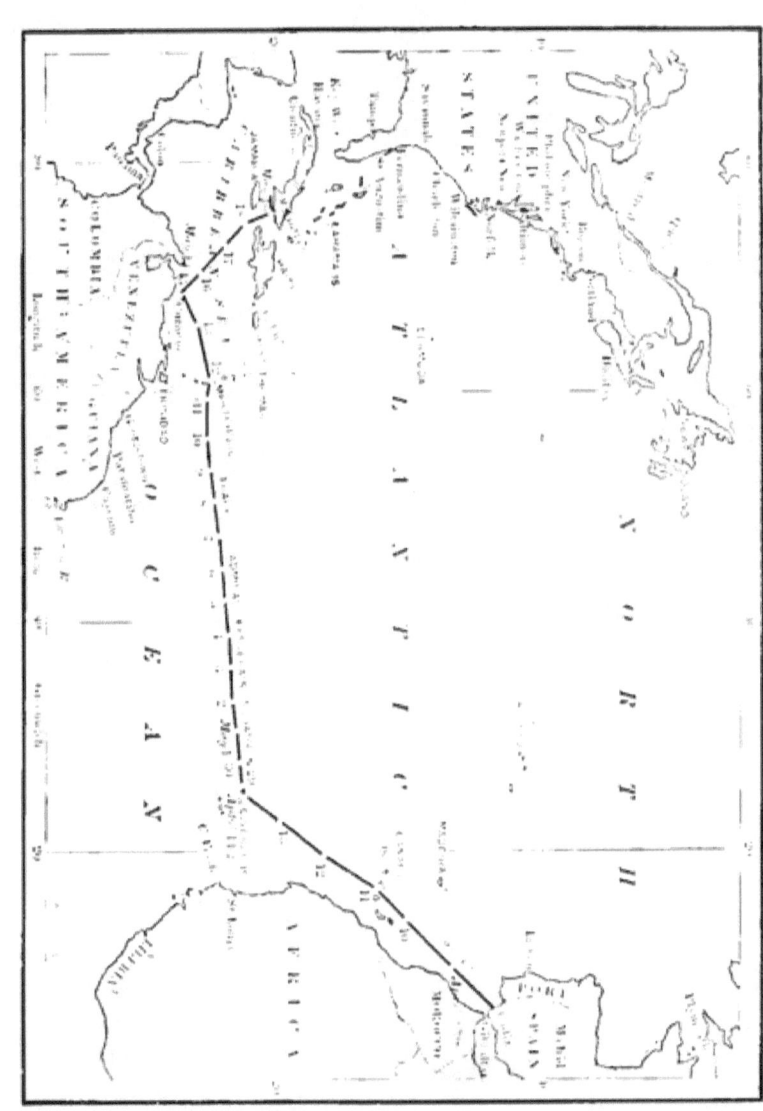

THE DAILY POSITIONS OF THE SPANISH SQUADRON UNDER ADMIRAL CERVERA

Taken from the log-book of the *Cristóbal Colon*

was bad, the American, improving after the first round, very good. The forts were seriously damaged, but neither destroyed nor silenced. Some shells passed over into the town, wrecking and setting fire to certain buildings. In the third round both the *New York* and *Iowa* were hit, but not seriously, and one man was killed and seven wounded. The best reports obtainable put the Spanish loss at forty killed and seventy wounded. After three hours of this work the signal was made to cease firing, and the bombardment of San Juan was over. It had answered entirely its purpose, which was merely that of a reconnoissance in force. That it was a mistake to send the fighting-ships on such an errand is probably true but at least it had been demonstrated that the Spanish fleet was not there, which was of high importance, and that the surrender of the city could be compelled, knowledge, of which no advantage was taken at any time, and which was useless at the moment, as we had no landing force. Such were the results of the affair of San Juan to the Americans; but there was another outcome, which affected only the Spaniards.

The authorities at Washington were striving to guess accurately the probable destination of the Spanish fleet, and they very naturally based their reasoning on what was publicly known of the character and quality of the enemy's ships, and upon the proposition that they had a plan, and would endeavor to do the best and most effective work possible. We know now that the Spaniards had no plan whatever, that their ships were defective in guns and ammunition, and that, instead of having a homogeneous and high speed rate, they were in poor condition, and the *Vizcaya* in such a state that, in Admiral Cervera's words, she was "a boil on the fleet." All calculations, therefore, based upon the contract speed of the Spanish cruisers, and upon the theory that the Spaniards had a plan, were quite idle in regard to an enemy with ships in bad condition and no plan at all. So while Washington was carrying the Spanish fleet rapidly over the ocean at ten to twelve knots an hour toward a well-defined objective-point, in reality they were creeping along at seven knots an hour and making vaguely for some point in the West Indies, to do they did not know what. On May 12, without any apparent reason, they brought up at the friendly French port of Martinique, and there they heard of the bombardment of San Juan, which had its last result in convincing the Spaniards that, whatever happened, they would not go to Puerto Rico and run into the arms of Admiral Sampson. So, leaving behind the *Terror,* which had been damaged by the voyage they went on in purposeless fashion to the Dutch island of Curacoa, like Martinique, within touch of cables, so that the wastes of ocean no longer sheltered them, and their whereabouts was published to the world. This fact and the laws of neutrality made a stay impossible, and on May 15 the poor, aimless, vaguely wandering fleet, after getting a little coal, set forth again and went to Santiago de Cuba, for no better reason, seemingly, than that it was the nearest port under the Spanish flag where they could hope to coal and refit.

This haven, the last they were ever to enter, was a typical Cuban harbor. A narrow entrance, with a channel only a hundred yards wide, cuts sharply between

BOMBARDMENT OF SAN JUAN

high hills, one of which is crowned by the picturesque "Morro Castle." An island faces the entrance channel, which, dividing, passes on either side, and then opens out in a broad and beautiful bay, with the city lying at the foot of the encircling hills. Everything in the harbor is quite invisible from the open sea. No more secure place could be imagined; for no hostile fleet, unsupported by an army could pass that narrow channel sown with mines; while on the other hand, no harbor could be more readily blockaded, and to go out unperceived in the face of an alert and watchful enemy was impossible.

Here, at all events, was a chance to rest. There was no military or naval purpose to be served in Santiago, which had no communication with Havana except by telegraph, but it was better than helpless wandering. Coal, slow in delivery, as well as provisions, was to be had there, and it was a very inviting hiding-place if not trusted in too long. In this wise, at all events, whatever their reasons, the Spaniards hid themselves, and the more active part of the game was meantime carried on by the Americans, whose one object now was to seek and find. This was a very difficult task. We knew when the Spaniards reached Martinique, we knew again when they left Curacoa, and then the veil dropped, and Washington went to guessing and conjecturing, much hampered by the difficulty of getting news and orders to the fleets before the former had been superseded by fresh information and the latter had become obsolete. Nevertheless the department did its best in all the confusion of reports and conjectures. On May 13, the day after the arrival of the Spaniards at Martinique, the Flying Squadron under Commodore Schley, consisting of the *Brooklyn, Massachusetts,* and *Texas,* which had been kept for this contingency in Hampton Roads, sailed for Key West, and every effort was made to convey information to the Puerto Rican expedition.

The same day Admiral Sampson, knowing now that Cervera was not in San Juan, with prompt decision sailed for Havana, the central point to be guarded in case Cervera was aiming to break the blockade there, as he ought to have been. When Sampson reached Cape Haitien he received despatches announcing the appearance of the Spaniards at Martinique, and then at Curacoa, with the subsequent departure from the latter island. Telegrams went at once to warn blockaders at Cienfuegos and to the scout *Harvard.* In the latter, dated May 15, the admiral said that the destination of the Spaniards was unknown, but was probably Santiago or San Juan—an instance of sagacity and insight which is most remarkable, for at that time nobody had thought of Santiago, which on the face of things was a most unlikely refuge. This done, the admiral left his slow-going squadron, and in the *New York* steamed as rapidly as possible to Key West. On the way he got tidings from a despatch-boat, which told him that Schley had sailed, and that Cervera had with him munitions of war (which is now known to have been untrue), and that therefore his object must be to connect in some way with Havana. The statement as to the munitions pointed directly to Cienfuegos as the obvious destination of the Spanish fleet. Therefore, on arriving at Key West he sent the Flying Squadron, con-

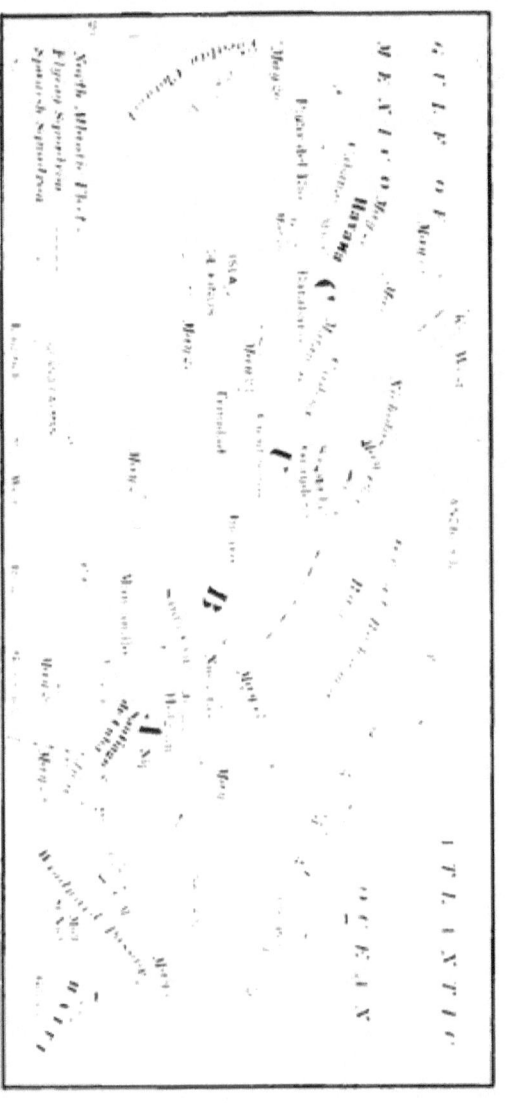

sisting of the *Brooklyn, Massachusetts, Texas,* and *Scorpion,* on May 19, with orders to proceed as rapidly as possible to Cienfuegos. The following day the *Iowa, Castine,* and the collier *Merrimac,* with over 3,000 tons of coal on board, were despatched to re-enforce them. Although she did not leave until eleven o'clock on May 20th, twenty-seven hours after Commodore Schley and looked in at Havana on her way, the *Iowa* when she reached Cienfuegos shortly after noon on May 22, had gained nearly twenty hours on the Flying Squadron. Commodore Schley in starting after the enemy went fifty miles wide of Cape San Antonio and did not reach Cienfuegos until after daybreak on May 22 consuming nearly seventy-two hours with every reason and incentive to hurry in traversing a distance which Captain Evans in the *Iowa* had covered in fifty hours. The *Iowa* carried a note from the admiral to Commodore Schley repeating the information as to Cervera's munitions of war which seemed to make Cienfuegos their absolutely necessary destination and advising the close blockade of that port.*

---

*NOTE.—Particular mention is made of this note because Admiral Schley produced it in his reply to the communication made to the Senate on February 6, 1890, by the Secretary of the Navy. He called especial attention to it with the object of apparently showing: first, that this important despatch had been suppressed by this department, an inference certain newspapers were quick to draw; and second, that this despatch furnished a complete explanation and defence of his doings and his delays at Cienfuegos. The department did not suppress the "Dear Schley" note, for it had no knowledge of its existence on February 6th and did not receive a copy of it until February 9th. The note existed only in the original in Commodore Schley's possession and he alone had the power to withhold or suppress it. It is impossible to suppose that he was so disingenuous as to intend to convey the impression that the Department or Admiral Sampson had suppressed some-

Just after the *Iowa* and her consorts had gone word came from the department that press despatches reported the Spaniards at Santiago. The next day, May 21, the press report corresponding with his own opinion, Admiral Sampson sent the *Marblehead* with orders to Commodore Schley to go to Santiago if he was satisfied the Spaniards were not at Cienfuegos. Later in the day, after he had left Key West for Havana, and evidently growing more certain as to Santiago, he sent the *Hawk* with another message to Commodore Schley, ordering him imperatively and without qualification to go to Santiago, and, as the *Hawk* would reach Cienfuegos on May 23, to leave before daylight on the 24th.

Turning now to the Flying Squadron it appears that Commodore Schley reached Cienfuegos on the 21st, and on the 22d he wrote that he could not say whether the Spanish fleet was there or not, and complained of the difficulty of coaling. On the 23d he wrote, in reply to the unqualified orders conveyed by the *Hawk*, that on account of the smoke visible in the harbor he believed that the Spaniards were there, that he doubted the report about Santiago, that he thought it unwise to chase a probability, and should remain where he was. In other words he said that he proposed to disobey the unqualified "*Hawk*" orders for the reasons he stated.

thing not in their possession, but this impression got abroad, and once for all should be shown to be entirely false. As to the second point, the "Dear Schley" note furnished neither defence nor excuse for the delay at Cienfuegos, for on arriving on May 22nd at one o'clock it was superseded together with the original instruction of May 19 at 7.30 A. M., on May 23d, when the *Hawk* arrived with imperative orders to proceed at once to Santiago, orders which were not obeyed by Commodore Schley until the late afternoon of May 24th.

Later in the day he sent another despatch, saying that a steamship, the *Adula,* just in reported seven ships seventy miles south of Santiago, but that from the firing of guns which he had heard in the harbor, a salute of welcome, as he guessed, although obviously very belated, he still believed the Spaniards to be there. The next day May 24, at 8 A. M., the *Marblehead* arrived and Captain McCalla at once asked permission to communicate with the Cubans in camp at Colorados point and find out from them whether the Spanish fleet was in the harbor or not. This was a sure means of getting absolute information as to the presence of Cervera in Cienfuegos but Commodore Schley had contented himself with guessing from the appearance of smoke or the sound of guns and had refrained from asking the simple direct question from those who knew because he considered that the surf was heavy and did not think that he could land boats to make the necessary inquiries. Captain McCalla was less anxious about the surf and having obtained the required authority ran in, opened communication with the Cubans, learned at once that Cervera was not in Cienfuegos and had never been there and before three o'clock Commodore Schley had the information. He sent on that day a long despatch complaining of the difficulty of coaling where he was, and declaring that he could not coal off Santiago, but saying that he should start eastward on the following day. But after the direct knowledge obtained in quick and energetic fashion by Captain McCalla there was no possible reason or excuse for further delay and at quarter before six on May 24 the squadron started having lost two days, for if the

Hawk orders had been obeyed they would have been at Santiago on May 24th as Sampson expected instead of just leaving Cienfuegos. So, on May 25, while Sampson, disturbed by Schley's reply to the *Hawk* despatches, and by the delay he foresaw, when every hour was precious, was sending still another boat to Cienfuegos with orders for Santiago more imperative than any which had gone before, the Flying Squadron, convinced at last by Captain McCalla's direct information from the insurgents that the enemy were not in Cienfuegos, was steaming to the eastward very slowly in order to allow the little *Eagle* which was of no importance whatever to the fighting line to keep up. On the 26th, at noon, they were forty-seven miles west-southwest of Santiago's Morro; at eight o'clock in the evening, twenty-two miles to the southward of the castle. There the three scouts the *Minneapolis*, *St. Paul* and *Yale* were met and Captain Sigsbee of the *St. Paul* who had been there since the 21st of May reported that he had not seen the Spanish fleet but that he thoroughly believed it to be there and the Cuban pilot Nunez although of opinion that the Spanish vessels could not enter the harbor admitted that they might have got in with tugs.* Acting on this information and without an effort to find out whether Cervera

---

*Note.—Admiral Schley in his letter to the Senate Committee states that Captain Sigsbee assured him that he did not believe that the Spanish fleet was in Santiago. Captain Sigsbee in his letter of February 24th to the Secretary of the Navy says that his belief constantly and openly expressed was the exact contrary of that attributed to him by Admiral Schley and that Nunez admitted that Cervera's fleet might have got in by the aid of tugs, a statement Admiral Schley omits to repeat in giving the opinion of Nunez.

was in Santiago, Commodore Schley then signalled,
"Destination, Key West *via* south side of Cuba and
Yucatan Channel as soon as collier is ready; speed,
nine knots." For one week the door of Santiago had
been open to Cervera, coaling slowly and feebly within,
to issue forth and go where he pleased. At last an
American fleet was in the neighborhood, and still the
door stood open. Obeying the signal of the flag-ship,
the fleet started slowly westward for Key West. On
the morning of May 27th the retreating Flying Squadron which had gone some eighteen miles to the westward and was forty miles from Santiago when it
stopped, met the *Harvard* and Captain Colton gave Admiral Schley the following order from the Navy Department:

WASHINGTON, *May 25, 1898.*

HARVARD, *St. Nicholas Mole, Haiti:*

Proceed at once and inform Schley, and also the senior officer
present off Santiago, as follows: All Department's information
indicates Spanish division is still at Santiago. The Department
looks to you to ascertain facts, and that the enemy, if therein, does
not leave without a decisive action. Cubans familiar with Santiago say that there are landing places 5 or 6 nautical miles west
from the mouth of harbor, and that there insurgents probably
will be found, and not the Spanish. From the surrounding
heights can see every vessel in port. As soon as ascertained, notify the Department whether enemy is there. Could not squadron
and also the *Harvard* coal from *Merrimac* leeward of Cape Cruz,
Gonaives Channel or Mole, Haiti? The Department will send
coal immediately to Mole. Report without delay situation at Santiago de Cuba.   LONG.

To this unqualified order Admiral Schley made the
following reply.

KINGSTON, *May 28, 1898.*

SECRETARY OF THE NAVY, *Washington:* (written May 27, 1898.)
The receipt of telegram of May 26* is acknowledged. Deliv-

ered by *Harvard* off Santiago de Cuba. *Merrimac* engines disabled; is heavy; am obliged to have towed to Key West. Have been unable absolutely to coal the *Texas, Marblehead, Vixen, Brooklyn* from collier, all owing to very rough sea. Bad weather since leaving Key West. The *Brooklyn* alone has more than sufficient coal to proceed to Key West; can not remain off Santiago present state squadron coal account. Impossible to coal leeward Cape Cruz in the summer, all owing to southwesterly winds. *Harvard* reports coal sufficient for Jamaica; leaves to-day for Kingston; reports only small vessels could coal at Gonaives or Mole. *Minneapolis* only coaled for Key West; also *Yale*, which tows *Merrimac*. Much to be regretted, can not obey orders of Department. Have striven earnestly; forced to proceed for coal to Key West by way of Yucatan passage. Can not ascertain anything respecting enemy positive. Obliged to send *Eagle*—admitted no delay—to Port Antonio, Jamaica; had only 25 tons of coal. Will leave *St. Paul* off Santiago de Cuba. Will require 10,000 tons of coal at Key West. Very difficult to tow collier to get cable to hold.

SCHLEY.

This telegram repeated to Admiral Sampson at Key West, May 29.

This was direct and admitted disobedience of orders. Far from striving earnestly, he had made no effort further than to ask the opinion of the scouts to determine whether Cervera was in Santiago or not and now announced that he was forced to proceed to Key West for coal and that he was unable to coal at sea. Neither statement was correct. The coal supply on the ships was as follows.

Extracts from logs of vessels for May 27.

	Tons
Massachusetts:	
Coal remaining on hand at noon 5 to 6 days' supply....	789
Texas:	
Coal remaining on hand at noon 5 to 6 days' supply....	394
Brooklyn:	
Coal remaining on hand at noon 10 to 12 days' supply..	940

CAPTAIN EVANS OF THE *Iowa* SIGHTING THE *CRISTÓBAL COLON* AND THE *MARIA TERESA* IN SANTIAGO HARBOR

The first man to sight the fleet was Lieutenant-Commander Rogers, Executive Officer of the *Iowa*, who described the

Marblehead: Tons
    Coal remaining on hand at noon 3 to 4 days' supply....   116
Iowa:
    Coal remaining on hand at noon 8 to 10 days' supply...   762
Merrimac:
    Coal at noon, on hand..............................   4,300

As to not being able to coal at sea from the *Merri-mac* with her 4,300 tons on board the ships were coaled from her at sea during the two following days.

The *Merrimac* before this had broken down and the Squadron had drifted about while efforts were made to repair her and while the *Yale* was trying to take her in tow but after sending his despatch announcing that he could not obey the orders of the Department, Admiral Schley started again to the westward away from Santiago. The Squadron made about twenty-five miles and then stopped and remained where it was performing the impossible feat of coaling at sea until between one and two o'clock on May 28th. Then being about forty-eight miles west of Santiago the door all this time having remained wide open to Cervera to go whither he pleased Admiral Schley apparently changed his mind once more and made a signal from the flag-ship to move to the eastward. Steaming slowly, the squadron reached Santiago that evening. The next morning, at quarter before eight, the *Iowa* made out the *Colon* and two other cruisers in the harbor. The game of hide-and-seek was at an end, and the Spanish fleet had been found at last. There was and could be no question now as to going away, and the squadron during May 30 stood to and fro off Santiago, well out from the land with the *Marblehead* and *Vixen* patrolling nearer inshore. During that day the *New Orleans* appeared with the collier *Sterling*, and on the next day when night came the squadron went away out of sight from land giving Cervera ample opportunity to run out in the darkness: Admiral Schley's theory being apparently that a close blockade by daylight was sufficient. On May 31, the *Massachusetts* leading, with Admiral Schley on board, and followed by the *New Orleans* and *Iowa*, ran in and opened fire upon the ships and batteries in the harbor. The ranges began at 7,500 yards and were increased to 11,000, the bombardment lasting half an hour, the shots falling short, and no damage whatever being done to the Spaniards. Then the ships drew off to their station, well out from the land, to continue during the daytime this somewhat remote blockade and to retire out of sight from land at night.* Cervera's door was closing upon him. He could still come out at his pleasure more readily at night than by day but at the cost, perhaps, a fight.

The anxiety in Washington and on board the flagship of the North Atlantic fleet during these perilous days, while the Flying Squadron was making its slow way eastward from Cienfuegos and drifting about some forty miles away from Santiago, was intense, and grew more feverish as the presence of the Spanish fleet became more assured and the despatches from Commodore Schley more uncertain. On May 27, after sending, as

---

*NOTE.—The *Marblehead* at night remained within about six miles of the Morro, and the other ships steamed to and fro before the entrance, where they could make out the entrance clearly, but so far off that they could not be seen from land at all. See diary of Lieutenant Muller y Fejeiro, published by Bureau of Naval Intelligence, pages 16 and 17.

has been said, imperative orders for the third time to leave Cienfuegos, Admiral Sampson received Commodore Schley's despatch of the 24th depicting the difficulties of coaling and announcing his departure for Santiago. Thereupon he ordered Captain Folger, in the *New Orleans*, to proceed at once to Santiago, direct Commodore Schley to maintain the blockade there at all hazards, and to use the collier *Sterling* (a stenographer's mistake for the *Merrimac*) for the obstruction of the channel by sinking her in the narrowest part. The next day, May 28, at midnight, came news from Secretary Long of Schley's despatch of the 27th announcing his departure from Santiago for Key West, which had made the day of its arrival the darkest of the whole war to the Navy Department. The Secretary asked if Sampson could go with the *New York*, *Oregon*, and *Indiana* to Santiago, and how long he could blockade. Sampson replied that he could blockade indefinitely, and asked leave to go at once with the *New York* and *Oregon*. Permission came in the evening, and at eleven o'clock Sampson left Key West in the *New York*, was joined the next morning by the *Oregon*, the converted yacht *Mayflower*, and the torpedo-boat *Porter*, and set off at high speed for Santiago. On the way, filled with anxiety because the last news was that the Flying Squadron had left Santiago, the admiral met the *Yale* and the *St. Paul*, and received from Captain Sigsbee a despatch from Commodore Schley of May 29, announcing that the Spanish cruisers had been seen and that he was blockading the port. Greatly relieved, the admiral sped on, and at six in the morning of June 1 he saw the *Colon* inside the

Morro point, and the Flying Squadron lying off the narrow entrance. All was well; the Spaniards had been found, they were still in their hiding-place, and now the door was really to be closed by night as well as day so that Cervera would only be able to choose between capture in the harbor, or breaking open the door and rushing to destruction outside.

The first movement of Admiral Sampson was to obstruct the narrow channel. He did not hope to block it permanently, for he knew that any obstruction could sooner or later be removed by dynamite. But he believed, and with reason, that he could obstruct it temporarily, and his object was to gain time for the arrival of the troops, whose coming was already announced, and whose presence would be absolutely necessary to enable him to get at the Spaniards, either by forcing Cervera to leave the harbor, or by obtaining control of and clearing the mine-fields so that he could himself enter and attack. To attain this object he had decided to sink a collier in the channel, and gave orders to that effect to Captain Folger when he sent him off on May 27 to Santiago. On the 29th he opened the subject to Lieutenant Richmond Pearson Hobson, a young naval constructor of marked ability and energy, and by the time the fleet reached Santiago on June 1 Hobson had prepared his plan, which was so thorough and excellent that the admiral decided to place the perilous and important work wholly in the hands of that young officer. Thus far nothing had been done toward closely locking Cervera up in his retreat, but as soon as Admiral Sampson arrived the *Merrimac* was selected to be sunk in the channel, and the work of stripping her and making ready the anchors which were to hold her, and the torpedoes which were to shatter her bottom, went forward with hot haste under the direction of Lieutenant Hobson. The call for volunteers was made by signal, and hundreds of the sailors came forward. Men begged to be taken, implored Hobson to choose them, and turned away utterly miserable because they could not go on a desperate undertaking which every one believed meant certain death while those who were chosen thanked their officers weeks afterwards for kindly allowing them to go when so many were seeking this terrible chance. Here again was a very fine and noble spirit, telling what the American navy was, and why it was soon to be victorious—something here quite worthy of the consideration of Spain, which had so insisted upon senseless war.

Hobson finally selected from the crowd of applicants Phillips, Kelly, Mullen, and Deignan, of the *Merrimac*, because they were familiar with the ship: then he took Charette, a gunner's mate, and Montague, chief master-at-arms, from the *New York*, and thus completed his little crew. Captain Miller of the *Merrimac* was bitterly disappointed when the admiral told him he could not go, but that did not prevent him from giving every advice and help to the men who were going on his ship. The preparations, although pushed with such intense energy, were so many that it was difficult to get them finished, and the night was far gone when all was done. At last the ship started, and then there was more delay in trying to tow the launch, which was to run in as near as possible and wait to rescue any survivors after the ship had sunk. When they finally set forth there was already a streak of light in the east, and as the *Merrimac* was steaming to the harbor entrance, the torpedo-boat *Porter* dashed up with an order of recall from the admiral. Back went the *Merrimac,* and a day of waiting and suspense followed, not easy to bear when men's nerves were strung to such work as lay before Hobson and his crew. Mullen, utterly exhausted by his labors in preparing the ship, gave out, and his place was taken by Murphy, a coxswain on the *Iowa.* Robert Crank, the assistant engineer of the ship, with bitter disappointment, was ordered away at the last moment and not allowed to go. Finally the long day passed, night came, and at half past three in the morning the *Merrimac* started again, this time with an additional man, Clausen, who was coxswain of the barge, and had come on board with Ensign Powell. He asked permission to go, and was accepted by Hobson, thus getting his chance at the great prize of death in battle. This time there was no recall; on she ran, every man at his post, the young lieutenant standing upright and alone on the bridge, Deignan at the wheel, steering coolly and taking every order with absolute correctness, and not a sailor moving except at the word of command. Nearer and nearer the doomed ship went, with gradually slackening speed. Then the Spaniards saw her, and there came a storm of shot and shell, fierce, resistless, like a torrent. Still on the ship steered, still slackening in speed—goes too far, as the event proved, her steering-gear having been shot away, and the lashings of Montague's anchor, which dropped too soon—and then, torn by her own torpedoes and by those of the enemy, she sinks far up

THE LAST OF THE *MERRIMAC*

in the channel. The parting of the anchors, the loss of the steering-gear, and consequent running in too far, the sweep of the current, combine, and she goes to the bottom, lying lengthwise, and not across. The crew, every task performed, lie at the appointed place upon the deck in the storm of projectiles, the torpedoes exploding beneath, and go down with the reeling ship into the whirl of dark waters. They have done their duty. The *Merrimac*, as she lies now, makes the entrance perhaps a little more difficult, but does not block it. So far the attempt fails, but the brave deed does not fail, for such gallantry is never a failure. It rouses and uplifts the American people, for these men are theirs; it appeals to the lovers of daring the world over; it is a shining and splendid feat of arms; it tells to all what the American navy is; it ranks Hobson with Cushing when he pushed his torpedo against the *Albemarle*, with Decatur when he fired the *Philadelphia*. And the men who did the deed cling, chilled and spent in the water, to the raft which is fast to the sunken ship, and in the darkness are not hit or found, but in the morning are taken off by Admiral Cervera, who greets them as "valiente." On the American side, brave young Powell, creeping about with his launch, in the midst of a heavy fire from the batteries, on the chance of rescuing Hobson and his men, comes out at last, much fired at, but with none of the *Merrimac* crew on board, and when he closes his report, saying simply, "and no one came back, sir," the fleet fear the worst, and believe that the gallant deed has been paid for with eight lives. But later in the day comes out a Spanish boat, with a flag from Admiral Cervera, to announce that Hobson and his sailors are prisoners, alive and well, and little hurt. It is sad that for the sake of Spain they could not have remained with Admiral Cervera—a brave man facing inevitable ruin with courage—but they were turned over to the military authorities on land, who placed them and kept them for some days in the Morro Castle, in range of the American bombardment—an act rather sullying to a people who are fond of talking about honor, but appear to think that in that connection words are enough.

So closed the first move of Admiral Sampson to blockade the enemy. The second, which began at the same time, lasted for many weary days, and was neither suddenly brilliant nor vividly picturesque, but like much of what is best in the world, without show, with no chance of ever getting the due meed of praise, except from history and posterity did efficiently and well the work that was there to do. This second move was the establishment of the blockade of the harbor by the ships. Foreign experts doubted whether it were possible to blockade four cruisers and two fine torpedo-boat destroyers in any harbor. The latter, it was thought, would surely slip out in the darkness, and then would come in a moment's space the destruction of a battleship or two, and so an end of the blockade. But there was no darkness in the entrance of Santiago Harbor after the 8th of June. Two battle-ships, relieving and supporting each other, went in every night within four miles, and the rays of the powerful search-lights made the narrow channel as bright as day. So great was the glare that when the fatal moment came Admiral Cervera did not dare to issue forth into that zone of white light, where he, blinded by the glare, would have been a helpless target for an enemy veiled in the darkness. At night also picket-launches ran in less than a mile from the shore, and there, within rifle range, tossing often on rough seas, watched through the long hours, ready to give warning of the slightest movement from inside the harbor. The close blockade by day begun on June 1 was kept up and constantly increased in stringency. The ships, at first stationed at six miles from the harbor mouth, were drawn in to four miles a little later, and the enemy thus hemmed in, so that at no hour in the twenty-four could he come forth without meeting the American fleet in carefully chosen positions, ready for battle, and with orders which left no room for doubt as to just what they should do. In this blockade, where nothing was overlooked and nothing forgotten, Admiral Sampson, by strenuous honest work, by keen foresight, and by unwearying and unceasing vigilance, made not only possible, but humanly speaking, certain, the victory which was to come, a great feat in naval warfare, and a very fine and lasting service to the American campaign.

The blockade was varied by a bombardment on June 6, by an attack on the battery east of the Morro by the *New Orleans* on June 14, and by another general bombardment on June 16. In all these attacks the American gunnery was excellent, and the batteries were for the time silenced. To these bombardments were added the assaults of the *Vesuvius*, which arrived on June 13, and began at once to run in at night and hurl her dynamite shells at the forts and harbor. The ship had a terrible weapon, but as she was unable to get direction

or aim, the falling of her shells was largely a matter of
accident. If by chance they struck near a battery, a
ship, or a building, wreck and ruin followed, but wherever they dropped the explosion was so terrific, coming
as they did silently out of the darkness, that they carried consternation and alarm, and had a moral effect
wholly out of proportion to their actual results, tending
in this way, no doubt, to prevent any attempts on the
part of the Spaniards either to seek escape at night or to
send out torpedo-boats.

Only one point remained to be covered in order to
assure the successful maintenance of the blockade, and
that was to possess a safe harbor for shelter, coaling,
and repairs. This indispensable adjunct Admiral Sampson secured by sending the *Marblehead* and *Yankee* to
Guantanamo, where they drove the Spanish gunboats
to the inner harbor, which was protected by mines in the
channel, and made themselves masters of the outer harbor, which was excellently suited to the needs of the
fleet. To make possession useful as well as complete,
it became necessary to hold a position on shore and
drive back the enemy, so that they could not annoy the
ships and boats in the bay. For this work the first battalion of marines, which had left Key West on June 7,
was employed, and on June 10 their transport, the *Pan-
ther*, arrived in Guantanamo Bay. The marines, between five and six hundred strong, landed immediately,
and established themselves on a low hill where a Spanish block-house had been destroyed by the guns of the
Yankee. The next evening they were attacked by the
Spaniards concealed in the chaparral, and two men on
outposts were killed. The attack was renewed in the

SOLDIERS OF THE CUBAN ARMY

From a photograph taken at the time of the landing of the American army

night by the unseen enemy and Surgeon Gibbs was killed and two privates wounded. The next day the camp was shifted to a better position, and some sixty Cubans came in and joined the Americans. The firing of the Spanish continued throughout the night, and Sergeant Good was killed, but on the 13th, with the aid of the Cubans, who knew the country, they were easily repelled. On the 14th the Americans took the offensive. Two companies of marines, supported by the Cubans, left the camp at nine o'clock to destroy the well at Cuzco, which was the only water-supply for the Spaniards within twelve miles. They failed to cut off the enemy, as they had hoped, but they drove the Spaniards steadily before them, reaching the intervening hill first, and carrying the crest under a sharp fire. As the marines descended into the valley the Spaniards broke cover and retreated rapidly, and at three o'clock the fight was over, the well filled up, and the heliograph signal station captured and destroyed. One lieutenant and seventeen men were taken prisoners, and they reported a Spanish loss of two officers and fifty-eight men killed, and a large number of wounded. On the American side one marine was wounded, and about a dozen were overcome by heat. This was the end of the Spanish attacks. They had had enough, and withdrew, leaving the American post undisturbed to the end of the campaign. The marines had done their work most admirably. For three days and nights they had met and repelled the attacks of a concealed enemy, never flinching under the strain which had been upon them without a moment's relief. Then they had taken the offensive, and had marched and fought for six hours under the

tropical sun and through a dense forest and undergrowth with the steadiness and marksmanship of experienced bushfighters. It was a very brave, honest,
and effective piece of work, showing admirable discipline and a surprising readiness to meet new and strange
conditions.

On June 15 the work of the marines was followed up
by the *Marblehead, Texas,* and *Suwanee* going into
Caimanera, silencing the batteries, and driving the
Spaniards completely away. The ships penetrated so
far into the channel of the inner harbor that they ran
on to torpedoes, the *Marblehead* picking up one on her
propeller, fortunately so thick with barnacles that it
did not explode by contact, as it was intended to do.
Thus the affair at Guantanamo Bay was finished, and a
secure refuge, base, coaling and repair station were
secured for the fleet, which assured its ability to continue the blockade—a very important operation, performed with the thoroughness, foresight, and minute
care which characterized all Admiral Sampson's work.
But the best arranged and most systematic blockade,
the most vigorous and sustained bombardments, the
workmanlike establishment of a fine naval base—none
of these things could bring the American ships alongside the Spanish cruisers. It was not the comparatively feeble batteries of the Morro, the Socapa, or Es-
trella Point which stood in the way. That which held
back the American fleet was the mine-field at the entrance of the harbor, sown thick with torpedoes and
submarine mines, exploding either by contact or by
electric wires leading to batteries on shore. The navy
which offered hundreds of volunteers to accompany

Hobson had plenty of officers and men who would have cheerfully dared all the dangers of that narrow channel, defying alike shore batteries and sunken mines. But such an attempt would have been not only perilous, and worthless, but a blunder of the first magnitude. Small ships, which perhaps might have slipped in, would have been utterly useless against the heavy Spanish cruisers, and a battle-ship sunk by torpedoes in the narrow channel would have been a useless and crippling sacrifice, and would have blocked the entrance so that the Spaniards could never have been forced out and the American fleet could never have gone in. Once the mine field was cleared, the ships could enter, but the mines could not be reached or removed until the batteries at the entrance were taken and the garrisons driven away. For this land-work the fleet had no adequate force. To reach and destroy the sea power of Spain in the West Indies, upon which the whole campaign against both Cuba and Puerto Rico turned, an army was needed to support the fleet, to take the entrance forts and thus permit the ships to enter, or else to capture the town itself and force the Spaniards out into the open. Thus it was that while Admiral Sampson was perfecting his blockade at every point, he was urgently asking that land forces be sent to his support, and all the officers and men of the fleet were waiting impatiently for the coming of the army which should deliver the Spanish cruisers into their hands.

CHAPTER VI

SANTIAGO—THE LAND FIGHT

THE American navy was ready, as ships of war must always be, and when the President signed the Cuban resolutions, the fleet started for Cuba without a moment's delay. With the army, the case was widely different. Congress had taken care of the army in a spasmodic and insufficient manner, consistently doing nothing for it except to multiply civilian clerks and officials of all kinds, who justified their existence by a diligent weaving of red-tape and by magnifying details of work, until all the realities of the service were thoroughly obscured. Thus we had a cumbrous, top-heavy system of administration, rusted and slow-moving, and accustomed to care for an army of 25,000 men. Then war was declared. An army of 200,000 volunteers and 60,000 regulars was suddenly demanded, and the poor old system of military administration, with its coils of red-tape and its vast clerical force devoted to details, began to groan and creak, to break down here and to stop there, and to produce a vast crop of delays, blunders, and what was far worse, of needless suffering, disease, and death, to the brave men in the field. Thereupon came great outcry from newspapers, rising even to hysterical shrieking in some cases, great and natural wrath among the American people, and much anger and fault-finding from Senators and Representatives. Then came, too, the very human and general desire to find one or more scapegoats and administer to them condign punishment, which would have been eminently soothing and satisfactory to many persons—just in some cases, perhaps, unjust in most, but in any event of little practical value. There was undoubtedly a certain not very large percentage of shortcomings due to individual incapacity, which should have been sharply rooted up without regard to personal sensibilities. But the fundamental fact was that the chief and predominant cause of all the failures, blunders, and needless suffering was a thoroughly bad system of military administration. An inferior man can do well with a good system better than a superior man with a bad system, for a good administrative organization will go on for generations sometimes, carrying poor administrators with it. But a really bad system is wellnigh hopeless, and the men of genius, the Pitts, the Carnots, and the Stantons, who, bringing order out of chaos and strength out of weakness, organize victory, are very rare, and are produced only by the long-continued stress of a great struggle, and after bitter experience has taught its harshest lessons. At the outset of our war we had a bad system, and men laid the blame here and there for faults of system and organization which were really due to the narrowness and indifference of Congress, of the newspaper press, and of the people, running back over many years. To-day the system stands guilty of the blunders, delays, and needless sufferings and deaths of the war, and war being over, reforms are resisted by patriots who have so little faith in the republic that they think a properly organized army of 100,000 men puts it in danger, and by bureau chiefs and their friends in Congress who want no change, for reasons obvious if not public-spirited.

Thus much by the way of preface, essential to the comprehension of even the barest outline of our military operations in the war of 1898, and to make clear not merely why there were shortcomings, which any account must notice, but also the fact that the wonder of it all lies not in the blunders and failures of organization, but in the indomitable energy and force of the American people which made the rusty, clumsy machine work in some fashion, and in the ability and bravery of American officers and soldiers which brought unbroken victory out of such conditions.

On April 23, 125,000 volunteers were called for, and a month later, on May 25, 75,000 more. It was soon found that it was one thing to call out volunteers, and quite another to make them into an army, which, strangely enough, appeared to surprise the country. Even the mobilization of the regulars was not rapid, and the middle of May had passed before they were assembled at Tampa. By the beginning of June, however, the regulars were gathered; but of all the volunteers, slowly mustering in different camps and in various stages of unreadiness, only three regiments were sufficiently prepared to join the forces at Tampa. These three were the Seventy-first New York, the Second Massachusetts, and the First United States Volunteer Cavalry. It was to this army of regulars and volunteers that the government turned when it became evident that troops were needed at Santiago, and the command of the expedition was given to General Shafter, a brave Michigan soldier of the war of the rebellion and an officer of the regular army.

On the night of June 7 orders came from Washington that the army should leave the next morning, and then was displayed a scene of vast confusion. The railroad tracks were blocked for miles with cars filled with supplies tightly shut by red-tape, at which men unused to responsibility and to the need of quick action gazed helplessly. The cars not only kept the supplies from the army, but they stopped movement on the line, and hours were consumed where minutes should have sufficed in transporting troops from Tampa to the Port. Once arrived, more confusion and a widening of the area of chaos. No proper arrangement of transports— no allotment at all in some cases, and in others the same ship given to two or three regiments. Thereupon much scrambling, disorder, and complication, surmounted at last in some rough-and-ready fashion, and the troops were finally embarked. Then came orders to delay departure. There was a false report brought of a Spanish cruiser and torpedo-boats seen by the *Eagle* and *Nashville*. Admiral Sampson put no faith in the report, guessed accurately that the *Eagle* had been misled in the darkness by certain ships of our own; but unfortunately he was at the other end of the line, and in the United States the false but definite report of hostile ships was accepted, and the army waited, sweltering on board the crowded transports, many of them lying near the wharves in the canal or channel, which was festering with town sewage. A very heavy price this to pay for a mistaken vision of the night, and for hasty acceptance of its truth. But the long hot days, laden with suffering and discomfort to the troops, finally wore by, and at last the transports, on June 14, made their way down the bay, pushed on the next day, were joined near Key West by some dozen ships of war as convoy, and then on the 16th were fairly on their way to Santiago. Far pleasanter this than broiling in Tampa Harbor, and the spirits of the troops improved. Yet the movement, so infinitely better than the hot, still waiting, was deliberate enough. Some of the transports were very old and very slow, and as they set the speed, the fleet crept along about eight knots an hour over a sapphire sea, with beautiful star-lit nights, and glimpses by day of the picturesque shores and distant mountains of Cuba. On Sunday, June 19, they were off Cape Maisi, and at daybreak the next morning they came in sight of the waiting war-ships and of Santiago Harbor. Then came consultations between General Shafter and Admiral Sampson and the Cuban generals Garcia and Castillo. The plan of capturing the Morro and the other entrance batteries, as the admiral desired, so that the mine-field could be cleared, the fleet go in, destroy the Spanish cruisers, and compel the surrender of Santiago, was abandoned. General Shafter decided to move directly upon the city, and orders were given to make the landing at Daiquiri. The army had neither lighters nor launches. They had been omitted, forgotten, or lost, like an umbrella, no one knew exactly where; so the work of disembarking the troops fell upon the navy. Under cover of a heavy fire from the ships, the landing began, and was effected without any resistance from the enemy. On an open coast, without any harbor or

shelter, with nothing but an iron pier so high as to be useless, smoothly, rapidly, efficiently, through a heavy surf, on the beach and at an unfloored wooden wharf, the boats and launches of the navy landed 15,000 officers and soldiers, with a loss of only two men. It was a very excellent piece of work, thoroughly and punctually performed, exciting admiration among foreign onlookers, who had just beheld with amazement the very different performances connected with the embarkation at Tampa.

The next morning General Wheeler, commanding the division of dismounted cavalry, under direct orders from General Shafter, rode forward, followed by two squadrons of the First volunteer cavalry, and one each of the First and Tenth regular cavalry. When General Wheeler reached Juraguacito, or Siboney, he found that the Spaniards had abandoned the block-house at that point, retreated some three miles toward Sevilla, and had there taken up a strong position, their rear having been engaged by some 200 Cubans with little effect. By eight o'clock that night the cavalry division reached Siboney, and General Wheeler, after consultation with General Castillo, determined to advance and dislodge the enemy lying between the Americans and Santiago. The next morning before daylight the movement began. The troops marched along two roads, which were really nothing more than mountain trails. The First and Tenth regular cavalry, under the immediate command of General Wheeler, and General Young who had with him some Hotchkiss guns, marched by the main or easterly road to Sevilla. Along the westerly road went the First volunteer cavalry.

nearly five hundred strong. This regiment, enlisted, officered, disciplined, and equipped in fifty days, may well be considered for a moment as it moves forward to action only two days after its landing. It is a very typical American regiment. Most of the men come from Arizona, New Mexico, and Oklahoma, where the troops were chiefly raised. There are many cowboys, many men of the plains, hunters, pioneers and ranchmen, to whom the perils and exposure of frontier life are a twice-told tale. Among them can be found more than two score civilized but full-blooded Indians—Americans by an older lineage than any of those who are fighting just now for the final domination of the New World. Then there are boys from the farms and towns of the far-western territories. Then, again, strangest mingling of all, there are a hundred or more troopers from the East—graduates of Yale and Harvard, members of the New York and Boston clubs, men of wealth and leisure and large opportunities. They are men who have loved the chase of big game, foxhunting and football, and all the sports which require courage and strength and are spiced with danger. Some have been idlers, many more are workers, all have the spirit of adventure strong within them, and they are there in the Cuban chaparral because they seek perils, because they are patriotic, because, as some think, every gentleman owes a debt to his country, and this is the time to pay it. And all these men, drawn from so many sources, all so American, all so nearly soldiers in their life and habits, have been roughly, quickly, and effectively moulded and formed into a fighting regiment by the skillful discipline of Leonard Wood, their colonel,

GENERAL GARCIA AND BRIGADIER-GENERAL LUDLOW
Taken during their conference at the time of the landing of the American army

a surgeon of the line, who wears a medal of honor won in campaigns against the Apaches; and by the inspiration of Theodore Roosevelt, their lieutenant-colonel, who has laid down a high place in the administration at Washington and come hither to Cuba because thus only can he live up to his ideal of conduct by offering his life to his country when war has come.

These Rough Riders, as they have been popularly called, marched along the westerly trail, so shut in by the dense undergrowth that it was almost impossible to throw out flankers or deploy the line, and quite impossible to see. And then suddenly there were hostile volleys pouring through the brush, and a sound like the ringing of wires overhead. No enemy was to be seen. The smokeless powder gave no sign. The dense chaparral screened everything. Under the intense heat men had already given way. Now they began to drop, some wounded, some dead. The Rough Riders fire and advance steadily, led onward by Colonel Wood and Lieutenant-Colonel Roosevelt. A very trying place it was for perfectly new troops, with the burning tropical heat, the unseen enemy, the air filled with the thin cry of the Mauser bullet. But there was no flinching, and the march forward went on.

Along the eastern road the regulars advanced with equal steadiness and perfect coolness. They do not draw the public attention as do the volunteers, for they act just as every one expected, and they are not new, but highly trained troops. But their work is done with great perfection, to be noted in history later, and at the time by all who admire men who perform their allotted task bravely and efficiently in the simple line of daily duty.

Thus the two columns moved forward constantly, along the trails and through the undergrowth, converging to the point at which they aimed, and Colonel Wood's right flank finds the anticipated support from the advancing regulars. The fire began to sweep the ridges and the strong rock forts on the ridge. Spaniards were seen at last apparently without much desire to remain in view; the two columns pressed forward, the ridge was carried, the cross-road reached, and the fight of Las Guasimas had been won.

There was no ambush or surprise about it, as was said by some people in the first confusion, and by others later without any excuse for the misstatement. The whole movement was arranged and carried out just as it was planned by the commanding general of the division. It had been a hot skirmish, and victory had come to the steady American advance, unchecked by the burning heat, the dense, stifling undergrowth, and the volleys of an unseen enemy. That night the Spanish soldiers said in Santiago: "Instead of retreating when we fired, the Americans came on. The more we fired the more they advanced. They tried to catch us with their hands." The Spanish official report stated that they had repulsed the Americans and won, but as the Americans had 10,000 men they had retreated, which was, perhaps, to the Spanish mind, dwelling these many centuries among mendacities, and thereby much confused, a satisfying explanation. The plain truth was that the entire American force amounted to 964 officers and men. The Rough Riders suffered most severely, having 8 killed and 34 wounded. The regulars lost 8 killed and 18 wounded. The Spanish accounts give

JOSEPH WHISTLER.

their own force in various figures from 2,500 down to 1,400, the last statement being made long after the battle, when the number of Americans who had defeated them could no longer be concealed. A comparison of their varying statements and all the best evidence would seem to indicate that the Spanish troops engaged were not less than 2,000. Forty-two Spaniards were found dead on the field; 77 were reported in the Santiago newspapers the next day to have been killed, and after the surrender General Toral admitted to General Wheeler a loss of killed and wounded of 265 at Las Guasimas and in the brushes with the Cubans of the two preceding days.

This action, in which, in less than an hour, American regulars and volunteers had driven a superior Spanish force from a strongly intrenched position on high ground, put the army in high spirits. It also encouraged the mistaken idea which Admiral Sampson had expressed at first, and which General Shafter apparently held to firmly, that the soldiers of the United States had nothing to do but to press forward, drive the Spaniards from them, and take the town in forty-eight hours. If the Americans had gone on at once, there is every reason to believe that they might have gone through successfully to the city itself. But to take the town in forty-eight hours in the first advance was one thing, and to attempt to take it on the forty-eight-hours plan after a week's delay was another and widely different business. In a short time it was to be proved that a strong line of defences, constructed for the most part while the advance begun at Las Guasimas was halted, lay between the Americans and Santiago, and

that the Spaniards, after their fashion, would fight hard
and stubbornly under cover of entrenchments and
block-houses. Nevertheless, it was with such views
prevailing that the army finally moved forward. Lawton's and Chaffee's brigades came up to the front the
day of the fight at Las Guasimas, and the other troops
advanced during the following days to the high ground
around Sevilla, which the victory of the cavalry division had brought within American control. During
three days there seems to have been great confusion in
the movement of troops, and still more in the transportation of supplies. The narrow trails, bad at the
best, were soon torn up by wagons, and were choked
by the advancing regiments, which moved slowly and
with difficulty. The army stretched back for three
miles from El Pozo, where an outpost was stationed, and whence the Spaniards could be seen hard at
work, the line of entrenchments and rifle-pits length-
ening continually along the hills of San Juan, and the
defences of El Caney constantly growing stronger.
Yet during these days of waiting no battery was
brought to El Pozo to open on the Spanish works, no
effort was made to interfere with the enemy in
strengthening his position, which meant the sacrifice
of just so many more lives by every hour that it went
on unimpeded. There was no attempt during these
comparatively unoccupied days to make new roads
through the forest and undergrowth, so that the troops
could emerge all along the line of woods instead of in
dense narrow masses from the two existing trails.
There were officers who saw, knew, and suggested all
these things, but they were not done. So, too, the val-

WILLIAM R. SHAFTER

ley or basin which lay between the heights we held and the heights of San Juan remained silent, unpenetrated, unexplored. There does not appear to have been any reconnoitring done at all, except by General Chaffee, who, with the skill and coolness of an experienced Indian fighter, explored the ground in front of his command thoroughly, even to the Spanish lines at El Caney, a village lying toward the northeast of Santiago, and very strongly defended by block-houses and a fort.

It was at this point, finally, that it was determined to make an attack, and this was, so far as can be judged, the only operation that was planned beforehand. All the rest of the fighting which ensued came about largely by chance. The movement against El Caney was intrusted to Generals Lawton, Chaffee, and Ludlow, brave, skilful, and gallant soldiers, in command of the Second Division, with the addition of an independent brigade under General Bates, in all a trifle over six thousand men. The plan was that they should capture El Caney, which it was calculated would consume about half an hour to an hour, and then, swinging to the left, cut off and take in the flank the Spaniards on San Juan hill, against which the main army was then to move in direct assault. So, on the afternoon of June 30, the order came at three o'clock that the whole army was to move at four, and then began a slow advance as the troops crushed and crowded into the narrow trail. Part of Lawton's division got off first, then the rest, and they all marched on silently during the night, making their way over the ground General Chaffee had reconnoitred through woods and underbrush. By dawn they were in position and it was arranged that Chaffee's brigade

was to attack from the north and east, and Ludlow's
from the south and west, and so carry the position.
But to take a strongly fortified town with infantry
quickly and without needless loss it is absolutely essential to clear the way by a powerful and destructive artillery fire. For this all-important object the division
had only Capron's battery of four guns, so absurdly inadequate to its task that the fact needs only to be stated.
This meagre battery opened on the Fort at El Caney
with a deliberate fire at half past six, producing little
more effect than to very slowly crumble the walls.
Moreover, the battery was not only grossly inadequate,
but it used black powder, and immediately established
a flaring target for an enemy concealed and perfectly
familiar with the ranges. Why were there no more
guns? Why were they left at Tampa or in the transports? The fact requires no committee of investiga-
tion to prove it, and somebody was responsible for the
scores of men shot at El Caney because there were only
four guns there to open the way. Why was the powder
black, so that a target of smoke hung over the American position after every discharge? Any smokeless
powder was better than none. Even poor, broken-
down Spain had smokeless powder for her artillery.
Why did not we have it? While the War Department
had been passing years in trying to find a patent powder
just to its liking, our artillery was provided with black
powder and went to war with it, and men died need-
lessly because of it. No need of a committee to establish
this fact, either. Who was responsible? One thing
is certain—a system of administration which is capable
of such protracted inefficiency is little short of criminal,

and the Congress and the people who permit such a system to exist, now that it has been found out, will share in the heavy responsibility of a neglect for which men's lives have dearly paid if they do not promptly remedy it.

But these reflections did not help matters at El Caney that July morning, and the feeble battery, the slow fire and the target-smoke soon disposed of the pleasant headquarters plan of taking the village in the course of an hour. There was nine hours' savage work ahead before the desired consummation could be reached. The Spaniards, although without artillery or siege-guns, numbered about eight hundred men; were entirely protected and under cover in a stone fort, rifle-pits, and strong block-houses; knew perfectly and accurately all the ranges; could not retreat without rushing on destruction after our troops surrounded them —a sharp incentive to desperate resistance. So, while the slow artillery fire went on, the infantry began to suffer seriously from the deadly Spanish fire. They worked their way forward, creeping from point to point, but it was very slow, and equally costly. At half past one the situation looked badly. The Americans were holding their own, but losing far more heavily than the Spaniards. An order from General Shafter at this moment to neglect El Caney and move to the assistance of the troops at San Juan must have seemed like a grim satire, and was disregarded. But the evil hour had really passed. The artillery fire was quickened, and the fort began at last to go rapidly to pieces under the steady pounding. Colonel Miles's brigade joined General Ludlow in pressing the attack on the south; and then at last General Chaffee, whose men had been enduring the brunt of the fight, gave the order to storm, and the Twelfth regiment sprang forward at the word, eager for the charge. Up the ravine they went to the east side, then swung to the right, broke through the wire fences, rushed upward to the top of the hill, and the fort was theirs. The enemy who had fought so stubbornly at rifle range could not stand the American rush; they had no desire to be taken "by the bare hands." The price paid had been heavy, but the dearly bought fort, in the words of an eye-witness, was "floored with dead Spaniards," a grewsome sight. Yet, even as the wild cheers went up, it was seen that they were still exposed, and a heavy fire came from the block-houses. Lining up in the fort, the Americans poured volley after volley into these other strongholds; and the other brigades pressing home their charge, the Spanish gave way, even retreat seeming less hopeless now than resistance, and fled from the village, dropping fast as they went under the shots of Ludlow's men. By four o'clock the firing had died away, and El Caney, at a cost which proper artillery would have greatly reduced, had been won by the unyielding, patient gallantry of the American regular infantry.

The Spaniards had less than a thousand men at El Caney, but they were under cover, strongly fortified, and knew the ranges. Shut in, desperate, and almost surrounded as they were, they appeared at their best, and fought with a stubborn courage and an indifference to danger which recall the defence of Saragossa and Gerona. Worthless as the Spanish soldiers have too often shown themselves to be, behind defences and

THEODORE ROOSEVELT

penned in by enemies, they have displayed a fortitude
worthy of the days, three centuries ago, when the infantry of Spain was thought the finest in Europe. Of
this tradition El Caney offered a fresh and brilliant
illustration. The Spaniards lost nearly five hundred
men in killed, wounded, and prisoners, much more
than half their number, and among the killed was the
commander, General Vara del Rey, his brother, and
two of his sons. On the American side the killed numbered 4 officers and 84 men; the wounded, 24 officers
and 332 men—the loss falling chiefly on Ludlow's and
Chaffee's brigades, comprising the 4,000 men who were
actively engaged throughout the day. The force was
composed entirely of regulars, with the exception of
the Second Massachusetts Regiment, in Ludlow's brigade. These volunteers, never in action before, behaved extremely well, coming up steadily under fire,
and taking their place in the firing-line. But the moment they opened with their archaic Springfields and
black powder, which they owed to the narrow parsimony of Congress, and to the lack of energy and efficiency in the system of the War Department, they became not only an easy mark for the Spanish Mausers,
but made the position of more peril to all the other
troops. In consequence of this they had to be withdrawn from the firing-line, but not until they had suffered severely and displayed an excellent courage. The
lack of artillery and the black powder made the assault
on El Caney a work to which infantry should not have
been forced. Yet they were forced to it, and supported
by only four guns, but splendidly led by Lawton, Chaffee, and Ludlow, they carried the position at heavy

cost by sheer courage, discipline, and good fighting, manifesting these great qualities in a high degree, and one worthy of very lasting honor and remembrance.

Lawton and Chaffee and Ludlow had gone to El Caney with a well-defined purpose but it is difficult, even after the most careful study and repeated reading of the official reports, to detect any plan whatever in the movements of the rest of the army. The troops had been moved up the narrow trail the night before, and at seven in the morning Captain Grimes's battery opened from El Pozo hill. Black powder again, and a magnificent target, so that the Cubans in the farmhouse, Rough Riders in the yard, and the First and Tenth Cavalry, all thoughtfully massed by some one in the immediate neighborhood of the battery, where they could be most easily hit, began to suffer severely. Then the two brigades of the cavalry division under General Sumner, the First, commanded by Colonel (now General) Wood, leading, moved down the road to Santiago. When the Rough Riders reached the ford of the San Juan, they crossed and deployed in good order. Then a captive observation-balloon was brought along and anchored at the ford where the troops were crossing and were massed in the road. As one reads the official statement of this fact, comment and criticism alike fail. That such a thing should have been done seems incredible. The balloon simply served to give the Spaniards a perfect mark and draw all the rifle and artillery fire to the precise point where our men were densely crowded in a narrow road. Fortunately the balloon was quickly destroyed by the enemy's fire, but it had given the place and the range, and there

the troops remained for nearly an hour, exposed to heavy fire from the forts and block-house, and from guerillas in trees, who here and elsewhere devoted themselves especially to picking off surgeons, wounded men, and Red Cross nurses. ' There the men staid, dropping under the shots of the Spaniards, able to do nothing, waiting orders. No orders from headquarters came; the situation was intolerable; retreat meant not only defeat, but useless and continual exposure to a slaughtering fire. No other resource remained, except to take rifle in hand and, with infantry alone, carry strong intrenchments and block-houses, defended by well-covered regulars supported by artillery. Still no orders, and at last the division, brigade, and regimental commanders acted and ordered for themselves. Colonel Roosevelt led his Rough Riders forward from the woods, and asking the men of the Ninth to let him pass through, the regiment of regulars rose and followed him, and then the whole cavalry division went out and on up the first hill, where there was a red-roofed farm-house, whence they drove the enemy. A pause here, a taking breath, exposed all the time to a heavy fire from the strong main intrenchments now in plain view. Again Colonel Roosevelt calls on his men, starts, comes back because they had not heard, and off they go again over the long open space, more than half a mile, which separates them from the Spanish post. The line of blue figures looks very thin and very sparse to those who are watching it. It seems to move very slowly. But it is moving all the time. Men stagger and drop, but the line goes on and up. It nears the top, the Spaniards break and run, and the cavalry di-

vision—six regiments—all mingled now, finds itself
with the heights carried, and the intrenchments on the
right in its firm but tired grasp. With it has gone the
Gatling battery under Captain Parker, who in really
splendid fashion has kept his guns right at the front,
a powerful ally and support in these trying moments.
Colonel Roosevelt, who rode at first, has left his horse
at a wire fence, and now finds himself the senior officer present and in command of all that is left of the
six gallant regiments, having led dauntlessly and un-
hurt one of the most brilliant charges in our history.

Meantime over on the left the regular infantry are
repeating against the fort of San Juan—the strongest
of all the Spanish positions, and on a larger scale—the
splendid work of the dismounted cavalry. This division, consisting of eight regiments of regulars and one
of volunteers, was admirably commanded and led by
General Kent. They moved up the road on the afternoon of June 30, and started again early on the next
morning as soon as Captain Grimes's battery opened
at El Pozo, with the First Brigade, under General Hawkins, in the lead. Their orders were to keep their
right on the main road to Santiago. They too were held
back by the crowd in the narrow trail, and still further
delayed by waiting for the passage of the cavalry division, who were given the right of way. As they began
at last to advance slowly they too came under the Spanish fire, they too received the punishment brought upon
the army by the luckless balloon, and thus crowded together, at a halt almost, suffered severely. The enemy's
fire steadily increased, the shrapnel poured in where
the balloon had marked the position, and the sharp-

shooters in the trees busied themselves, as they were doing already with the cavalry division. General Kent attempted to send the Seventy-first New York through a by-path, so as to bring them out in their proper position with the First Brigade, but when they came under the heavy fire of the enemy the first battalion broke, and were only held from a panic by the exertions of General Kent's staff-officers. The other two battalions remained steady, for the regiment was of first-rate material, and the trouble arose from their being badly officered and besides being endowed with a colonel who apparently did not come on to the field of action. In the end they rallied, and many went forward in the final charge with the regulars, notably the company under the gallant lead of Captain Rafferty. But at the moment the confusion in the New York regiment still further checked the already impeded advance. The First Brigade had gone on without the volunteers, and the Third regiment was hurried forward by General Kent into the blocked road, and finally pushed through the New York regiment. As they came out and crossed the lower ford Colonel Wikoff was killed, and two lieutenant-colonels who succeeded him in command of the brigade were quickly shot down, all in the course of ten minutes. Yet nothing could shake the nerve or break the discipline of this splendid brigade. Following orders, making all the formations, operating in companies, battalions, and regiments, on they went through the heavy under-growth, waist-deep through the streams, and across barbed-wire defences. Nothing could break them as they went steadily and fiercely onward. The Second Brigade,

finely led by Colonel Pearson, was pushed through in
the same way beneath a galling fire, out of the narrow
trail and across the ford. Two regiments of Pearson's men went to the support of the Third Brigade,
one to that of the First. Meantime the Third
Brigade, connecting with the First on the right and
sweeping round through a heavy fire, turned the enemy's right, and shared with the First in the assault.
On they went up a steep hill 125 feet above the level,
tangled with barbed wires, and crowned with deep
trenches and the strong brick fort of San Juan. No
artillery to help them. Regular infantry, rifle in hand,
were going to take this high and heavily fortified position. Steadily and quickly they went at it, General
Hawkins, a noble figure, white-haired, and with all
the fire of youth in his gallant heart, leading the
charge at the head of his two regiments. To those who
watched, it seemed to take a long time. But it was
twenty minutes past twelve when the Third Brigade
followed the First out of the death-trap in the woods,
and at half past one the steady, strong-moving mass of
infantry had cleared an outlying knoll, crossed the valley, scaled the rough steep hill, and with Hawkins at
their head, and the men of the Third Brigade sweeping
up on the left, stood triumphant on the crest, where they
fell to intrenching themselves, and sent the Thirteenth
Infantry off to support the cavalry division, while the
Twenty-first regiment pushed on 800 yards farther
and took an advanced position. Altogether a very
splendid feat of arms, very perfectly performed.

One other movement was made on July 1st at the
extreme left. General Duffield was ordered to move

along the railroad by the coast and make a demon-
stration at Aguadores, in order to keep the Spaniards
engaged at that point and prevent their attacking our
left. General Shafter especially ordered General Duffield not to sacrifice his men, but to "worry the
enemy." When he reached the river at the point of
crossing, he found that the bridge had been in part
destroyed. The river also was deep, and, according
to General Duffield's estimate, 600 to 700 feet wide.
He therefore made no attempt to cross, but kept
the enemy under fire until three o'clock, engaging
them again the next day, and carrying out in this
way his orders to the entire satisfaction of General
Shafter, who recommended him for gallantry and good
conduct at Aguadores. The total loss in their skirmishes, when the Thirty-third Michigan behaved very
well, was two killed and fifteen wounded.

The battle of San Juan, as it is called, consisted
really of two detached attacks on the hill of that name
and the separate action of El Caney. There were 6,464
officers and men at El Caney, and 7,919 engaged at
San Juan, apart from the small brigade (323 all told)
of light artillery. There were among them three regiments of volunteers, but the Second Massachusetts, after
suffering severely, had to be withdrawn from the firing-
line on account of its black powder, and the Seventy-
first New York was only partially engaged. Deducting
these two regiments, there were 12,507 officers and
men engaged, including, of volunteers, only the Rough
Riders, who, like the regulars, were armed with modern magazine rifles, and who showed themselves on
that day the equal of any regulars in desperate fight-

ing; but they numbered only 583 of the more than 12,-000 men brought into action. The battle of San Juan, therefore, was pre-eminently the battle of the American regulars, of the flower of the American standing army. With scarcely any artillery support, armed only with rifles, they were set to take heights and a village strongly held by regular soldiers and defended by forts, intrenchments, batteries, and a tangle of barbed-wire fences. This is something which the best military critics would declare well-nigh impossible and not to be attempted. The American army did it. That is enough to say. They lost heavily, largely through the awkward manner in which they were crowded and delayed at the start. There were 21 officers and 220 men killed, and 93 officers and 1,280 men wounded, the percentage of the officers being remarkably high, except at Aguadores, where none were injured. On the Spanish side it is almost impossible to get any figures of the slightest value, even their official reports being filled with obvious falsehoods and contradictions. General Wheeler gives the number at El Caney as 460; the official Spanish report puts it at 520, of whom only 80 returned unwounded. Captain Arthur Lee, of the British army, who has written by far the best account of El Caney, says there were somewhat less than 1,000 Spaniards in the works, and that at least half were killed and wounded. As his estimate of the losses agrees with the Spanish report, I have accepted it. The Spanish statement of their numbers at El Caney is so absurd, on their own report of losses, that Captain Lee's dispassionate estimate of the total force must also be accepted. The case at San

Juan is much more difficult. According to Lieutenant Muller y Tejeiro, quoting what professes to be official reports, there were only 3,000 men defending Santiago, including the sailors, and only 250 men at San Juan heights. This is so grotesquely false that it is easy to throw it aside, but it is not easy to reach the truth. Muller gives 520 men at El Caney and 250 at San Juan, and in one place gives the total killed and wounded as 593, and in another as 469, both manifestly absurd losses for 770 men. The Spaniards said at different times that they had as few as 1,400 and as many as 2,500 at Las Guasimas, which hardly coincides with the statement that there were only 3,000 men in the city. Deducting Escario's force, which came in on July 2, there were 13,000 rifles, Mausers and Remingtons, surrendered in Santiago city when it capitulated, which indicates a total force of that number, unless we assume that each of Lieutenant Muller's 3,000 soldiers carried four rifles. As a matter of fact, the Spaniards had ultimately 12,000 to 13,000 men in Santiago; they had over 9,000 along the line of defences on the east side confronting the Americans*; and the works at San Juan were strongly held by at least 4,000 men, as stated by Mr. Ramsden, the British consul, a thoroughly trustworthy witness. Their actual losses it is not easy to detect through the clouds of falsehood in the official reports; but as we know that they were heavier than the American at El Caney, and also at Las Guasimas, we may safely assume that the case was nearly the same at San Juan, although they had all the advan-

---

* General Wood puts the number of men on the whole eastern line of defences at 9,600.

tage of cover and position. It is certain that when the city surrendered they had more men in hospital than the Americans. The Spaniards stood their ground bravely, fired heavily in volleys, and bore their punishment unflinchingly, but nowhere did they face the American rush and onset when they came close upon them. It was a hard-fought battle, and both sides suffered severely, but the steady and irresistible American advance won.

After the victorious charge there was still no rest for the men who had climbed the steep sides of San Juan. Worn and weary as they were, they went to work to make intrenchments, and with scant food—Colonel Roosevelt's men feeding on what the Spaniards had left behind—they all toiled on through the night. At daylight the Spaniards attacked, opening a fire which continued all day. Yet, despite the fire and the drenching rain, the men worked on, and the new intrenchments, now frowning down toward the city, grew and lengthened. At nine o'clock in the evening another attack by long range firing was made by the Spaniards, and repulsed. The losses on the American side during this fighting on the 2d were not severe, as they were protected by breastworks, and the Spaniards were utterly unable to take the hill they could not hold, from the men who had driven them from it when they had every advantage of position. Nevertheless, the situation was undoubtedly grave. With 3,000 men only on the extreme ridge at first, we were confronted by 9,000 Spaniards. Our men were exhausted by battle, marching, and digging. They were badly fed, transportation was slow, and supplies scarce, and they

GENERALS IN THE SANTIAGO CAMPAIGN

were at first unsheltered. Under these conditions some officers thought about and urged withdrawal, while General Wheeler, backed strongly by many of the younger officers and later by Lawton and Sumner, opposed any such movement. The spirit which carried the heights of San Juan held them, but to General Shafter, away from the front and the firing-line, the voices of doubt and alarm came with effective force. During the day he fluctuated from doubt to confidence. He wanted Sampson to try at once and at all hazards to break in, and he proposed to General Wheeler to move against the entrance forts of the harbor, thus giving a tardy adhesion to the wise plan of Sampson and Miles, which he had abandoned. Early on the morning of July 3 there came a despatch from him, written under the first depressing influences, to the War Department, saying that he had Santiago well invested, but that our line was thin, the city strongly defended, and not to be taken without heavy loss; that he needed re-enforcements, and was considering withdrawal to a position which an examination of the map showed to mean a retreat to the coast. This news—the first received in twenty-four hours—came upon those in authority at Washington with a depressing shock. General Shafter was urged to hold the San Juan heights, and in a confused hurry every effort was made to get together more transports—none having been brought back from Santiago—and to drive forward the departure of troops. It was the one really dark day of the war, and the long hot hours of that memorable Sunday were heavy with doubt, apprehension, and anxiety.

CHAPTER VII

SANTIAGO—THE SEA FIGHT

By one of the dramatic contrasts which fate delights to create in human history, at the very time when the Shafter despatch was filling Washington with gloom, the sea-power of Spain was being shot to death by American guns, and her ancient empire in the West Indies had passed away forever. It matters little now why Cervera pushed open the door of Santiago Harbor and rushed out to ruin and defeat. The admiral himself would have the world understand that he was forced to do so by ill-advised orders from Havana and Madrid. Very likely this is true, but if it is, Havana and Madrid must be admitted to have had good grounds for their decision. It did not occur to the Spaniards, either in Santiago or elsewhere, that the entire American army had been flung upon El Caney and San Juan, and that there were at the moment no reserves. Their own reports, moreover, from the coast were wild and exaggerated, so that, deceived by these as well as by the daring movements and confident attitude of the American army, they concluded that the city was menaced by not less than 50.000 men. Under these conditions Santiago would soon be surrounded, cut off, starved, and taken. It is true that Admiral Cervera had announced that if the Americans entered Santiago he would shell and destroy the city, and he would probably have done so, with complete Spanish indifference to the wanton brutality of such an act. But it is difficult to see how this performance would have helped the army or saved the fleet. With the American army on the heights of San Juan, and extending its lines, the ultimate destruction or capture of the entire squadron was a mere question of time. The process might be made more or less bloody, but the final outcome could not be avoided, and was certain to be complete. On the other hand, a wild rush out of the harbor might result possibly in the escape of one or more ships, and such an escape, properly treated in official despatches, could very well be made to pass in Spain for a victory. In remaining, there could be nothing but utter ruin, however long postponed. In going out, there was at least a chance, however slight, of saving something. So Cervera was ordered to leave the harbor of Santiago. He would have liked to go by night, but thanks to the precautions of Admiral Sampson the narrow entrance glared out of the darkness brilliant with the white blaze of the search-lights, and beyond lay the enemy, veiled in darkness, waiting and watching. The night was clearly impossible. It must be daylight, if at all. So on Sunday morning at half past nine the Spanish fleet with bottled steam came out of the harbor with a rush, the flag-ship *Maria Teresa* leading; then the other three cruisers about 800 yards apart; then, at 1,200 yards distance, the two crack Clyde-built torpedo-boat destroyers *Furor* and *Pluton*. As Admiral Sampson was to meet General Shafter that morning at Siboney, the *New York* had started to the eastward, and was four miles away from her station when, at the sound of the guns, she swung round and rushed after the running battle-ships, which she could never quite overtake, although she came up so fast that she was able to get two shots at the torpedo boat destroyers before they went down which was only twenty minutes after they had emerged from the harbor entrance. It was a cruel piece of ill fortune that the admiral, who had made every arrangement for the fight, should, by mere chance of war, have been deprived of his personal share in it. Equally cruel was the fortune which had taken Captain Higginson and the *Massachusetts* on that day to Guantanamo to coal. These temporary absences left (beginning at the westward) the *Brooklyn, Texas, Iowa, Oregon, Indiana,* and the two converted yachts *Gloucester* and *Vixen* lying near inshore, to meet the escaping enemy. Quick eyes on the *Iowa* detected first the trailing line of smoke in the narrow channel and signal was made at 9.34 "Enemy Escaping" which was acknowledged on the *Brooklyn* at 9.35. Then all the fleet saw them and there was no need of any other signals. Admiral Sampson's order had long since been given: "If the enemy tries to escape, the ships must close and engage as soon as possible and endeavor to sink his vessels or force them to run ashore." Every ship was always stripped for action, each captain on the station knew by heart this order which was posted in every conning tower, his crew needed no other, and the perfect execution of it was the naval battle at Santiago.

The Spanish ships came out at eight to ten knots' speed, cleared the Diamond Shoal, and then turned

PASQUALE DE CERVERA

sharply to the westward. As they issued forth they opened a fierce, rapid, but ill-directed fire with all guns, which shrouded them in smoke. The missiles fell thickly and seemed to come in a dense flight over all the ships. Around the *Indiana* the projectiles tore the water into foam, and the *Brooklyn*, which the Spaniards are said to have had some vague plan of disabling, because they believed her to be the one fast ship, was struck several times, but not seriously injured.* The Spanish attack, with its sudden burst of fire, was chiefly in the first rush, for it was soon drowned in the fierce reply. The American crews were being mustered for Sunday inspection when the enemy was seen. They were always prepared for action, and as the signal went up the men were already at quarters. There was no need for Admiral Sampson's distant signal to close in and attack, for that was what they did.

This signal had no importance so far as the action was concerned for it was merely a repetition of the

---

*Note.—Through the kindness of the Hon. Charles H. Allen, Assistant Secretary of the Navy, I have been able to procure the exact amount expended to repair the damage caused by the Spanish shots in the battle of July 3d. The statement is as follows:

Cost of Repairing Damage Caused by Spanish Guns in Battle of July 3d:

Oregon	None
Texas	$ 752.32
Brooklyn	1,303.15
Indiana	4,078.58
Iowa	4,993.65

This table is instructive and seems to dispose of the proposition that the Brooklyn suffered more than the other ships, bore the brunt and was the especial object of Spanish attack.

standing order posted up in the conning towers. But it
has importance in another respect because it was a signal made by the commanding admiral. Technically Admiral Sampson was in command of the fleet throughout the action for he was never out of signal distance.
The signal which he made when he started for Siboney
"Disregard movements of flag-ship" never implies relinquishment of command and did not then. So long as
he was within signal distance he was in command and
he remained within that distance constantly shortening
it, from beginning to end of the action. His first signal
when seeing the enemy coming out, he turned his ship
was neither needed nor heeded but his orders to the
Iowa later to stop by the *Vizcaya* and similar orders
to other ships were seen and obeyed as the *New York*
rushed along after the *Oregon* and *Brooklyn*. He was
within easy signal distance when the *Colon* surrendered and her surrender was at once reported to him.

As it is undoubtedly true that Admiral Sampson was
technically in command throughout it is equally true
that Admiral (then Commodore) Schley the next in
rank was never technically in command for a single
moment. As to actual command the case is equally
clear. At 9.35 the *Brooklyn* acknowledged the *Iowa's*
signal "Enemy escaping." The signal-book of the
Brooklyn shows that she then made signal "Clear for
action" which was superfluous when addressed to ships
which had been cleared for action for thirty days. She
then made signal to close with the enemy a mere repetition of Sampson's standing order which all the ships
were carrying out to the fullest extent. The *Brooklyn's* signal-book also shows that these signals were

William T. Sampson

Winfield S. Schley

Henry C. Taylor

Charles E. Clark

Robley D. Evans

John W. Philip

NAVAL OFFICERS IN SANTIAGO CAMPAIGN

not acknowledged and as a matter of fact they were never heeded or noticed and probably were never seen by the other ships. In a word Admiral Schley neve. controlled or directed in the slightest degree the movements of any ship but the *Brooklyn* and exercised no general command whatever. There was no fleet action. Each ship followed the standing order and fought under it for its own hand. The result was harmonious but it was a captain's fight without a single fleet movement directed at the time by anybody.

Each ship following the standing order to close put its helm to starboard and bore down on the enemy. The *Brooklyn* alone disobeyed not only the standing order but the order which she herself had just set directing the other ships to close. The *Brooklyn* put her helm to port came round in the reverse of the other ships, with her stern to the enemy and after this wide sweep away from them bore on to the westward parallel to and outside the Spanish ships. Admiral Schley had signalled to the other ships to close but he made no signal when he reversed his own order by putting his helm to port. In this unexpected movement he not only took himself out of the way of the enemy but he checked the advance of the *Texas*. Had he put his helm to starboard and borne down like the other ships or even if he had not held the *Texas* back the Spanish ships would probably never have been able to clear the shoal and turn to the westward. They would in all probability have been headed and never got out of the pocket in which they were and which was opened for them by the movement of the *Brooklyn* and the consequent checking of the *Texas*.

Admiral Schley's first explanation of his movement was that he was afraid of being rammed it being understood that the Spaniards were especially anxious to destroy the *Brooklyn* because she was so fast. His second explanation of his turning away from the enemy in a direction contrary to that taken by the other ships was that he wished to avoid blanketing their fire. For the ship in the lead, and with the highest speed to blanket ships in the rear seems difficult on its face but for the leading ship to blanket the fire of four battleships strung out over a mile that fire being directed against four ships strung out over an equal or greater distance appears practically impossible.

This necessary definition as to the command with proof that the captains fought the action for themselves under the standing order of Admiral Sampson* together with the closely related description of the exceptional and isolated movements of the *Brooklyn* have led us away from the general narrative of the battle itself.

The only disadvantage to the Americans at the outset was that they were under low steam, and it took time to gather way, so that the Spaniards, with a full head of steam, gained in the first rush. But this did not check the closing in, nor the heavy broadsides which

---

*Note.—See report of Captain Clark of the *Oregon* addressed to Admiral Sampson in which he says: "Acting under *your* orders" i. e.

Under Sampson's standing orders which Admiral Schley repeated by signal from the *Brooklyn* and then disobeyed. That is, he did not follow his own order and gave no notice or signal to the other ships that he was going to do just the opposite to what he had ordered them to do; namely, "close with the enemy."

were poured upon the Spanish ships as they came by
and turned to the westward. Then it was that the
Maria Teresa and the *Oquendo* received their death-
wounds. Then it was that a 13-inch shell from the
Indiana struck the *Teresa* exploding under the quarter-
deck; and that the broadsides of the *Iowa*, flung on
each cruiser as it headed her in turn, and of the *Oregon*
and *Texas*, tore the sides of the *Oquendo*, the *Vizcaya*,
and the flag-ship. The Spanish fire sank under that
of the American gunners, shooting coolly as if at target
practice, and sweeping the Spanish decks in a manner
which drove the men from the guns. On went the
Spanish ships in their desperate flight, the American
ships firing rapidly and steadily upon them, always
closing in, and beginning now to gather speed. The
race was a short one to two of the Spanish ships, fatally
wounded in the first savage encounter. In little more
than half an hour the flag-ship *Maria Teresa* was
headed to the shore, and at quarter past ten she was a
sunken, burning wreck upon the beach at Nima Nima,
six miles from Santiago. Fifteen minutes later, and
half a mile further on, the *Oquendo* was beached near
Juan Gonzales, a mass of flames, shot to pieces, and a
hopeless wreck. For these two, flight and fight were
alike over.

At the start, the *Brooklyn* as has been said putting
her helm to port, had gone round, bearing away from
the land, and then steamed to the westward, so that,
as she was the fastest in our squadron, she might be
preserved to head off the swiftest Spanish ship. In
the lead with the *Brooklyn* was the *Texas*, holding
the next position in the line and checked temporarily

by the *Brooklyn's* movement. But the *Oregon* was about to add to the laurels she had already won in her great voyage from ocean to ocean. With a burst of speed which astonished all who saw her, and which seemed almost incredible in a battle-ship, she forged ahead to the second place in the chase, for such it had now become. The *Teresa* and the *Oquendo* had gone to wreck, torn by the fire of all the ships. The *Vizcaya* had also been mortally hurt in the first outset, but she struggled on, pursued by the leading ships, and under their fire, especially that of the *Oregon*, until, at quarter past eleven, she too was turned to the shore and beached at Asseraderos, fifteen miles from Santiago, a shattered, blazing hulk. Meantime the two torpedo-boats, coming out last from the harbor, about ten o'clock, had made a rush to get by the American ships. But their high speed availed them nothing. The secondary batteries of the battle-ships including that of the *New York* as she came driving past were turned upon them with disastrous effect, and they also met an enemy especially reserved for them. The *Gloucester,* a converted yacht, with no armor, but with a battery of small rapid-fire guns, was lying inshore when the Spaniards made their break for liberty. Undauntedly firing her light shells at the great cruisers as they passed, the *Gloucester* waited, gathering steam the while for the destroyers. The moment these boats appeared, Lieutenant-Commander Wainwright, unheeding the fire of the Socapa battery, drove the *Gloucester* straight upon them at top speed, giving them no time to use their torpedoes, even if they had so desired. The fierce, rapid, well-directed fire of the *Gloucester* swept the decks of the torpedo-

The *Platon*

The *Færøy*

boats, and tore their upper works and sides. Shattered by the shells from the battle-ships, and overwhelmed by the close and savage attack of the *Gloucester*, which fought in absolute disregard of the fire from either ships or shore, the race of the torpedo-boat destroyers was soon run. Within twenty minutes of their rush from the harbor's mouth the *Furor* was beached and sunk, and the *Pluton* had gone down in deep water. At the risk of their lives the officers and men of the *Gloucester* boarded their sinking enemies, whose decks looked like shambles, and saved all those who could be saved. There were but few to rescue. Nineteen were taken from the *Furor*, 26 from the *Pluton;* all the rest of the 64 men on each boat were killed or drowned. It is worth while to make a little comparison here. The *Furor* and *Pluton* were 370 tons each, with a complement together of 134 men. They had together four 11-pounders, four 6-pounders, and four Maxim guns, in addition to their torpedoes. The *Gloucester* was of 800 tons, with 93 men, four 6-pounders, four 3-pounders, and two Colt automatic guns. The Spanish boats were fatally wounded by the secondary batteries of the battle-ships, but they were hunted down and destroyed by the *Gloucester*, which, regardless of the fire of the Socapa battery, closed with them and overwhelmed them. There is a very interesting exhibition here of the superior quality of the American sailor. The fierce rapid, gallant attack of the *Gloucester* carried all before it, and showed that spirit of daring sea-fighting without which the best ships and the finest guns are of little avail, and which has made the English-speaking man the victor on the ocean from the days of the Armada.

When the *Vizcaya* went ashore at quarter past eleven, only one Spanish ship remained, the *Cristóbal Colon*. She was the newest, the fastest, and the best of the squadron. With their bottled steam, all the Spanish cruisers gained at first, while the American ships were gathering and increasing their pressure, but the *Colon* gained most of all. She did, apparently, comparatively little firing, kept inside of her consorts, hugging the shore, and then raced ahead, gaining on all the American ships except the *Brooklyn*, which kept on well outside to head her off. When the *Vizcaya* went ashore, the *Colon* had a lead of about six miles over the *Brooklyn* and the *Oregon*, which had forged to the front, with the *Texas* and *Vixen* following at their best speed. As the *New York* came tearing along the coast, striving with might and main to get into the fight, now so nearly done, Admiral Sampson saw, after he passed the wreck of the *Vizcaya*, that the American ships were overhauling the Spaniard. The *Colon* had a contract speed five knots faster than the contract speed of the *Oregon*. But the Spaniard's best was seven knots below her contract speed, while the *Oregon*, fresh from her 14,000 miles of travel, was going a little faster than her contract speed, a very splendid thing, worthy of much thought and consideration as to the value of perfect and honest workmanship done quite obscurely in the builder's yard, and of the skill, energy, and exact training which could then get more than any one had a right to expect from both ship and engines. On they went, the Americans coming ever nearer, until at last, at ten minutes before one, the *Brooklyn* and *Oregon* opened fire. A thirteen-inch

shell from the great battle-ship, crushing her way at top
speed through the water, fell in the sea beyond the
Colon while the eight-inch shells of the *Brooklyn* began
to drop about her. But the big shell from the *Oregon*
turret was enough; and without waiting for another of
those grim messengers from the battle-ship, without
firing another shot, the Spaniard hauled down her flag
and ran at full speed ashore upon the beach at Rio Tar-
quino, forty-five miles from Santiago. Captain Cook
of the *Brooklyn* boarded her, received the surrender,
and reported it to Admiral Sampson, who had come up
just in time to share in the last act of the drama. The
Colon was only slightly hurt by the shells, but it was
soon found that the Spaniards, to whom the point of
honor is very dear, had opened and broken her sea-
valves after surrendering her, and that she was filling
fast. The *New York* pushed her in nearer the shore,
and she sank, comparatively uninjured, in shoal water.

So the fight ended. Every Spanish ship which had
dashed out of the harbor in the morning was a half-
sunken wreck on the Cuban coast at half past one. The
officers and men of the *Iowa*, assisted by the *Ericsson*
and *Hist*, took off the Spanish crews from the red-hot
decks and amid the exploding batteries and ammunition
of the *Vizcaya*. The same work was done by the
Gloucester and *Harvard* for the *Oquendo* and *Maria
Teresa*. From the water and the surf, from the
beaches, and from the burning wrecks, at greater peril
than they had endured all day in battle, American officers and crews rescued their beaten foes. It was a
very noble conclusion to a very perfect victory. The
Spanish lost, according to their own accounts and the

best estimates, 350 killed or drowned, 160 wounded, and 99 officers and 1,675 men prisoners, including, of course, those on the *Furor* and *Pluton*, as already given. The American loss was one man killed and one wounded, both on the *Brooklyn*. Such completeness of result and such perfection of execution are as striking here as at Manila, and Europe, which had been disposed at first to belittle Manila, saw at Santiago that these things were not accidental, and considered the performances of the American navy in a surprised and flattering, but by no means happy, silence. At Santiago the Spaniards had the best types of modern cruisers, three built by British workmen in Spanish yards, and one, the *Colon*, in Italy, while the torpedo-boat destroyers were fresh from the Clyde, and the very last expression of English skill. The ships of the United States were heavier in armament and armor, but on the average much slower. The Americans could throw a heavier weight of metal, but the Spaniards had more quick-fire guns, and ought to have been able to fire at the rate of seventy-seven more shots in five minutes than their opponents.* According to the contract speed, the Spanish cruisers had a great advantage over all their American opponents, with the exception of the *Brooklyn*, and of the *New York*, which was absent at the beginning. If they had lived up to their qualities as set down in every naval register, they ought to have made a most brilliant fight, and some of them ought to have escaped. They also had the advantage of coming out under a full head

---

* See the admirable article in *Harper's Magazine* for January (p. 291) upon the "Naval Lessons of the War," by H. W. Wilson, author of "Ironclads in Action."

of steam, which their opponents lacked, and yet in less than two hours all but one were shattered wrecks along the shore, and in less than two hours more that one survivor had been run down and had met the same fate. It is no explanation to say, what we know now to be true, that the *Colon* did not have her ten-inch guns, that the *Vizcaya* was foul-bottomed, that much of the ammunition was bad, and the other ships more or less out of order. One of the conditions of naval success, just as important as any other, is that the ships should be kept in every respect in the highest possible efficiency, and that the best work of which the machine and the organization are capable should be got out of them. The Americans fulfiled these conditions, the Spaniards did not; the *Oregon* surpassed all that the most exacting had a right to demand; the *Colon* and *Vizcaya* did far less; hence one reason for American victory. It is also said with truth that the Spanish gunnery was bad, but this is merely stating again that they fell short in a point essential to success. They fired with great rapidity as they issued from the harbor, and although most of the shots went wide, many were anything but wild, for the American ships were all hit repeatedly. When the American fire fell upon them, the Spanish fire, as at Manila, slackened, became ineffective, and died away. Again it was shown that the volume and accuracy of the American fire were so great that the fire of the opponents was smothered, and that the crews were swept away from the guns. The overwhelming American victory was due not to the shortcomings of the Spaniards, but to the efficiency of the navy of the United States and to the quality of the crews. The officers and seamen, the gunners and engineers, surpassed the Spaniards in their organization and in their handling of the machinery they used. They were thoroughly prepared; no surprise was possible to them; they knew just what they meant to do when the hour of battle came, and they did it coolly, effectively, and with perfect discipline. They were proficient and accurate marksmen, and got the utmost from their guns as from their ships. Last, and most important of all, they had that greatest quality of a strong, living, virile race, the power of daring, incessant dashing attack, with no thought of the punishment they might themselves be obliged to take. The whole war showed, and the defeat of Cervera most conspicuously, that the Spaniards had utterly lost the power of attack, a sure sign of a broken race; and for which no amount of fortitude in facing death can compensate. No generous man can fail to admire or to praise the despairing courage which held El Caney and carried Cervera's fleet out of the narrow channel of Santiago; but it is not the kind of courage which leads to victory, like that which sent American soldiers up the hills of San Juan and into the blood-stained village streets of El Caney, or which made the American ships swoop down, carrying utter destruction, upon the flying Spanish cruisers.

Thus the long chase of the Spanish fleet ended in its wreck and ruin beneath American guns. As one tells the story, the utter inadequacy of the narrative to the great fact seems painfully apparent. One wanders among the absorbing details which cross and recross the reader's path, full of interest and infinite in their complexity. The more details one gathers, puzzling what

Cristobal Colon

Oregon Brooklyn

G. H. Traves

to keep and what to reject, the denser seems the complexity, and the dimmer and more confused the picture. The historian writing calmly in the distant future will weave them into a full and dispassionate narrative; the antiquarian will write monographs on all incidents, small or large, with unwearying patience; the naval critic and expert will even now draw many technical and scientific lessons from everything that happened, and will debate and dispute about it, to the great advantage of himself and his profession. And yet these are not the things which appeal now, or will appeal in the days to come, to the hearts of men. The details, the number of shots, the ranges, the part taken by each ship, the positions of the fleet—all alike have begun to fade from recollection even now, and will grow still dimmer as the years recede. But out of the mist of events and the gathering darkness of passing time the great fact and the great deed stand forth for the American people and their children's children, as white and shining as the Santiago channel glaring under the search-lights through the Cuban night.

They remember, and will always remember, that hot summer morning, and the anxiety, only half whispered, which overspread the land. They see, and will always see, the American ships rolling lazily on the long seas, and the sailors just going to Sunday inspection. Then comes the long thin trail of smoke drawing nearer the harbor's mouth. The ships see it, and we can hear the cheers ring out, for the enemy is coming, and the American sailor rejoices mightily to know that the battle is set. There is no need of signals, no need of orders. The patient, long-watching admiral has given direction for every chance that may befall. Every ship is in place; and they close in upon the advancing enemy, fiercely pouring shells from broadside and turret. There is the *Gloucester* firing her little shots at the great cruisers, and then driving down to grapple with the torpedo-boats. There are the Spanish ships, already mortally hurt, running along the shore, shattered and breaking under the fire of the *Indiana*, the *Iowa*, and the *Texas;* there is the *Brooklyn* racing by outside to head the fugitives, and the *Oregon* dealing death-strokes as she rushes forward, forging to the front, and leaving her mark everywhere she goes. It is a captain's fight, and they all fight as if they were one man with one ship. On they go, driving through the water, firing steadily and ever getting closer, and presently the Spanish cruisers, helpless, burning, twisted wrecks of iron, are piled along the shore, and we see the younger officers and men of the victorious ships periling their lives to save their beaten enemies. We see Wainwright on the *Gloucester,* as eager in rescue as he was swift in fight to avenge the *Maine.* We hear Philip cry out: "Don't cheer. The poor devils are dying." We watch Evans as he hands back the sword to the wounded Eulate, and then writes in his report: "I cannot express my admiration for my magnificent crew. So long as the enemy showed his flag, they fought like American seamen; but when the flag came down, they were as gentle and tender as American women." They all stand out to us, these gallant figures, from the silent admiral to the cheering seaman, with an intense human interest, fearless in fight, brave and merciful in the hour of victory.

And far away along the hot ridges of the San Juan heights lie the American soldiers, who have been fighting, and winning, and digging intrenchments for forty-eight hours, sleeping little and eating less. There they are under the tropic sun that Sunday morning, and presently the heavy sound of guns comes rolling up the bay, and is flung back with many echoes from the surrounding hills. It goes on and on, so fast, so deep and loud, that it is like continuous thunder filling all the air. A battle is on; they know that. Wild rumors begin to fly about, drifting up from the coast. They hear that the American fleet is coming into the harbor; then for an hour that it has been defeated and that the Spaniards have escaped; and then the truth begins to come, and before nightfall they know that the Spanish fleet is no more, and the American soldier cheers the American sailor, and is filled anew with the glow of victory, and the assurance that he and his comrades have not fought and suffered and died in vain.

The thought of the moment is of the present victory, but there are men there who recognize the deeper and more distant meanings of that Sunday's work, now sinking into the past. They are stirred by the knowledge that the sea power of Spain has perished, and that the Spanish West Indies, which Columbus gave to Leon and Castile, shall know Spain no more. They lift the veil of the historic past, and see that on that July morning a great empire met its end, and passed finally out of the New World, because it was unfit to rule and govern men. And they and all men see now, and ever more clearly will see, that in the fight off Santiago another great fact had reasserted itself for the consideration of the world. For that fight had displayed once more the victorious sea spirit of a conquering race. It is the spirit of the Jomsberg Viking who, alone and wounded, ringed round with foes, springs into the sea from his sinking boat with defiance on his lips. It comes down through Grenville and Drake and Howard and Blake, on to Perry and Macdonough and Hull and Decatur. Here on this summer Sunday it has been shown again to be as vital and as clear as ever, even as it was with Nelson dying at Trafalgar, and with Faragut and his men in the fights of bay and river more than thirty years before.

CHAPTER VIII

THE SURRENDER OF SANTIAGO

DESPITE the depressing despatch to Washington saying that he was considering withdrawal, General Shafter, at 10 o'clock on Sunday morning, sent to General Toral a demand for immediate surrender, threatening to shell the city, although he had no siege-guns and nothing but light artillery to carry out his threat in case his demand was not complied with. General Toral answered at once, declining to surrender, and saying that he would notify the foreign consuls and the inhabitants of the proposed bombardment. Thereupon the foreign consuls appeared at General Wheeler's headquarters, and asked that the bombardment be postponed until the 5th; that the non-combatants, women and children, and the foreign residents, be allowed to leave the town and pass into the American lines, to be there fed and cared for. General Shafter granted the respite until the 5th, provided that there was no firing from the Spanish lines. By the evening of the 3d it was known that Cervera's fleet had been completely destroyed, and the purpose of the expedition had been fully attained. But in effecting that purpose the army had been so far advanced toward Santiago that, although the purely military value of the place was next to nothing after what had happened, not to take it would have been a blow to the prestige of the United States which could not be accepted. If the army had never advanced toward Santiago, but had confined its operations to the capture of the Morro and other harbor defences, thus allowing the navy to clear the mine-fields, the fleet could have entered, destroyed Cervera's ships in the harbor, and forced the surrender of the city. In this event the bulk of the troops could have been placed immediately on the transports and despatched to Puerto Rico, the natural Spanish base in the Antilles, and the point which General Miles rightly believed from the beginning should be the main objective of the American campaign, subject only to the destruction of the cruisers which represented the Spanish sea power in the West Indies. But since the plan of attacking the shore batteries and clearing the channel had been abandoned, and the army marched straight against Santiago, it was no longer possible to withdraw the troops in order to send them to Puerto Rico, or for any other purpose. The capture of Santiago had become by the operations of our army a moral and consequently a military necessity.

The brilliant victory of the American fleet raised every one's spirits, and gave assurance of the final triumph on land. General Shafter, who had first sent out the telegram intimating withdrawal, telegraphed General Miles later that he was master of the situation and could hold the enemy for any length of time, and in the evening, after the news from the fleet had been fully confirmed, cheerfully sent word that his line completely surrounded the town from the bay on the north of the city to a point on San Juan river on the south, and that he thought General Garcia would be able to check the advance of Pando's column. Nevertheless the situation of the American army was in some respects serious. The defenses of Santiago in the immediate neighborhood of the city, General Shafter said, were "almost impregnable." They were certainly very strong, and it would have cost many lives to carry them with troops insufficiently provided with artillery. This was a very grave fact, because time had become extremely important to the American forces, and it was pressingly necessary to bring the siege to an end. Haste was imperative, not on account of anything to be feared from the enemy, but through the surrounding conditions. The entire force of the United States, with the exception of Duffield's brigade, had gone through the battle of the 2d of July, and had suffered severely in killed and wounded. For the next thirty-six hours they had been exposed to the enemy's fire, repeatedly obliged to repel an advance, always on the alert, and, in addition, constantly digging and laboring on the intrenchments. The tenacious, unwavering courage with which they clung to the advanced line, laboring and fighting, was as fine in its way as the daring, irresistible rush with which they had swept up the slopes of San Juan. But courage and energy could not prevent the exhaustion incident to so much fighting and digging. There was no reserve. All the troops practically were on the line, with no chance for any substantial relief. The transportation was bad, so that the men were underfed and insufficiently tented. With their exhausting labors, and not fortified by food, with a hospital service which had in large measure broken down, the men were exposed to scorching tropic heats and torrential rains, all in a climate famous for malarial fevers. It was only a question of a very short time when these fevers would become general, striking first the sick and wounded, who were insufficiently cared for and who could not be restored to health on a diet of pork and beans, and then the well and unwounded men in the trenches. Worst of all, behind the climatic diseases lurked the dread epidemic of yellow fever, hidden in the cabins of Siboney, which ought to have been burned at once as the marines burned the fishing villlage at Guantanamo, and in the hordes of refugees who were presently to come out of the besieged city.

On the other side, the Spaniards were in reality much worse off, although it may have appeared at Havana and in Madrid as if they had only to hold firm and trust to the climate and the ravages of fever to inflict severe losses upon the Americans, delay them, and possibly force them to withdraw. The Spanish commmanders were in the midst of a hostile population. The Cuban insurgents had for some time practically shut them up in the city on the land side, breaking their communications and cutting off their supplies. They believed that the American forces numbered fifty thousand men, and although they were mistaken in this, they knew that their opponents could easily receive unlimited re-enforcements, new regiments, as a matter of fact, soon arriving and extending the lines rapidly around the doomed city. They knew, also, that Cervera's fleet had been destroyed, and that no relief coming oversea could possibly be hoped for. To draw in the outlying troops from other parts of the province was a work of time and difficulty, and meanwhile, with a beaten and discouraged army which had suffered severely in battle, with disease rife, and their water supply impaired, they were face to face with a vigorous enemy constantly increasing in numbers. Under these conditions the surrender of the city was only a question of time, but how long that time would be was of infinite importance to the American army when delay meant disease and death.

The first truce of two days following Toral's curt and useless refusal to consider surrender did not help the American situation, for it brought on July 5 a general exodus of non-combatants from the city. These unhappy refugees, mostly women and children, came pouring into the American lines at El Caney to the number of twenty-two thousand. They were in sad plight—ragged, sick, starved. They made a fresh strain upon the American resources, for they had to be fed; they brought yellow fever with them as they scattered through the camps, and they relieved very much the situation of the Spanish forces in the city. After their arrival there was skirmishing along the lines, sometimes of quite a lively character, varied by flags of truce and consequent intervals of repose. Our losses were slight, as the men were now well protected by intrenchments and breastworks. This condition of affairs lasted until the 9th, when another demand for surrender was made. The Spaniards, in reply, offered to evacuate if allowed to withdraw untouched to Holguin, which was declined. They then peremptorily refused to surrender, being encouraged in their attitude probably by the fact that General Escario, with the Pando column, consisting of 3,300 men, had come in some days before.* General Garcia had endeavored to stop this re-enforcement, and had fought an action in which the Spanish loss is said to have been 27 killed and 67 wounded; but General Escario forced his way through, apparently without serious difficulty, and reached the city in safety. Whether the arrival of these fresh troops was the cause or not, the surrender was declined, and thereupon the American lines opened with small guns and artillery, and continued the fire until nightfall of Sunday, the 10th, being supported on that afternoon by the eight-inch guns of the *Brooklyn, Indiana,* and *Texas,* which came in near shore and fired, most of their shells falling short. The Spaniards replied steadily, but, according to their own accounts, slowly, owing to their desire to economize their ammunition. The American losses were trivial; the Spanish, by their own reports, 7 killed and 47 wounded; but the result of the bombardment was neither substantial nor effective. The next day the *New York, Brooklyn,* and *Indiana* came in to within 400 yards of the shore at Aguadores, anchored, and opened fire with their eight-inch guns over the coast hills, at the city they could not see, with a range of 8,500 yards. This time the practice was excellent. The army officers watching the fall of the shells, although they could not tell exactly what happened, saw enough to make it clear that the shots were effective, and that fires broke out in several places. It was found afterwards to have been far more destructive than the watchers on the hills supposed. Captain West reported forty-six shots, but was unable to tell

*The night of July 2.

the result of most of them. After the surrender naval officers found fourteen houses wrecked by shells, and nineteen shells in the Calle de la Marina near the waterfront; while Lieutenant Muller states that fifty-nine houses were wrecked or injured, and that no lives were lost, solely because the inhabitants had deserted the city. As General Linares said in the pathetic despatch which he sent to Madrid describing his hopeless and miserable situation. "The fleet has a perfect knowledge of the place, and bombards by elevation with a mathematical accuracy." General Shafter considered that the bombardment had been sufficiently accurate and effective to warrant him in advancing the lines and demanding again an unconditional surrender. At the same time he desired a continuous bombardment from heavier guns, and Admiral Sampson brought down the *Oregon* and *Massachusetts* and prepared to open with the 13-inch guns the next day; while General Miles, who had just arrived, was ready to land fresh troops. But neither the 13-inch guns nor the re-enforcements were needed. The Spaniards knew that the naval bombardment was effective, whatever doubts the officers of our own army may have had in regard to it. The navy, despite the long range and the intervening hills, had managed to supply the place of the lacking siege-guns, and the Spaniards had had enough. A truce was agreed to on July 12; and on July 13 General Miles, who had come up from the coast after ordering the burning of Siboney, a precaution which ought to have been taken two weeks before, joined General Shafter and General Wheeler, and going through the lines with them, had a long interview with General Toral, commanding the Spanish forces. It was evident then, and is still clearer now, that the fight was really over, and that nothing remained but an arrangement of the terms of surrender. General Toral asked for a day to consult Madrid as to the deportation of the Spanish troops, which was granted. The next day there was another meeting of the generals, and it was supposed that all was arranged; but it appeared that there had been misunderstandings; other meetings followed, and it was not until after midnight that the preliminary agreement was finally signed. This was sent to Madrid, and being accepted there, was put into due form as articles of capitulation, and signed on July 16. The terms of capitulation provided that all the Eastern District and the troops therein should be surrendered; that the United States should transport the Spanish troops to Spain at its own expense; that the Spanish officers should retain their side arms, but that all other arms and ammunition of war were to be surrendered, the American commissioners recommending to their government, as a sop to Spanish pride, that the soldiers should be allowed to keep the arms they had so bravely defended, to which recommendation no heed was or could be paid.

So the city and Eastern District of Santiago passed into American hands, the outward and visible sign of the victorious fighting of the army, as the twisted wrecks to the westward were of that of the navy. The ceremonies of surrender took place on July 17. Early in the morning General Shafter, with General Wheeler by his side, started from the American lines, followed by the division and brigade commanders and their staffs. They were plainly dressed, without stars or orders—hard fighters all—and presented a contrast to General Toral and his staff, who were glittering with decorations. It was half past nine when the two commanders met and shook hands, and the American congratulated the Spaniard upon his gallant defence. Then a battalion of Spanish infantry marched past, piled their arms, and marched back again, in sign of the surrender, and setting the example soon to be followed by the rest of the army. This done, the generals and their staffs rode forward into the city. Along the road lay the carcasses of horses, and the shallow graves of soldiers torn open by vultures—grim and silent witnesses of the work which had brought the Spaniards to defeat. Presently the Spanish lines were reached, and the cavalcade passed through the intrenchments, wire fences, and barricades of paving-stones, which it would have cost many brave lives to force. So on through streets lined with Spanish soldiers, silent, but apparently relieved to have it over, and bearing the inevitable with cheerful philosophy. When the plaza was reached the generals entered the palace, while the Ninth Infantry and two troops of cavalry cleared the square. In the palace General Shafter received the head of the Church, gorgeous in purple robes and many decorations. Possibly, as the archbishop, after his brief interview, took his way across the square through the bowing crowds, he may have thought upon the after-dinner speech in which he had so lately declared that with ten thousand men he would hoist the Spanish flag over the Capitol at Washington, and thus pondering, have found fresh force in the words of Ecclesiastes. The time slipped

by as the crowds waited—the natives rejoicing, th
Spanish soldiers cheerful, the Spanish officers an
priests sad and dejected—until, as all watched th
cathedral clock, the hand came round to five minute
before twelve. Then a sharp command rang out, the in
fantry and cavalry came to attention and stood motion
less. The five minutes dragged on with leaden feet, an
then at last the bells began to sound from the cathedra
and the American flag went up on the staff over th
palace. The band played "The Star-Spangled Banner,'
the officers bared their heads, the troops presented
arms, the artillery thundered from the trenches, and al
down the long and distant line ran the American cheer:
—strong, vigorous, inspiring, the shout of a conquer
ing people.

It was all over. Santiago had passed away from
Spain, and with it all Cuba, for what had been done
there could not be hindered elsewhere, as was now very
plain to all men. It was one of the dramatic points in
the war. It was the moment when the American flag,
mounting proudly in the air, told the world that Spain's
empire in America had finally and forever departed.
Out of that harbor, famous before, more famous now,
Grijalva and Cordova had sailed on the perilous voyages which had discovered Central America. Thence
in the early dawn of a November morning in 1518
Cortez had slipped away with his fleet to escape an unfriendly Governor, and raising afterwards at Havana
his standard of black and gold, with a red cross flaring
in the centre, had passed on to conquer Mexico and pour
untold wealth into the coffers of the Spanish King.
The last Spanish fleet had just left that harbor a des-

OPENING THE AMERICAN CHURCH ON THE SIMLA ROAD AT SANDBAGH

perate fugitive, and had perished in its mad flight a few miles beyond the harbor mouth. Now the speech of the men who, three hundred years before, had hunted the Armada and saved English freedom was heard in the market place of Santiago, repeating the old message of liberty, grown wider and stronger than ever before in the hands of the great republic. The flag of the United States fluttered in the breezes which for three centuries had carried the arms and colors of Spain, now fallen and gone. Only outward symbols these, but representing many facts and many events worthy of much attention and consideration from those who think tyranny, falsehood, and bigotry are suitable instruments for the government of mankind.

It is well also not to forget that while these great and conclusive events were happening at Santiago, while Sampson was shutting in Cervera with his strong and patient blockade, the better to crush him when he rushed out to fight, while the American army was advancing from the coast, winning the hot fight at San Juan and taking the city in token of victory, other Americans in ships of war were diligently and efficiently carrying steadily forward the work which was cutting off Cuba from the rest of the world, and making inevitable the surrender of the island, even as the eastern province had surrendered. North and south, all along that far-stretching and broken coast-line, American gunboats and cruisers kept up a ceaseless patrol. Ships at the western end were scarce enough, but nevertheless the blockade was held tight and firm around Havana and the ports covered by the first proclamation. To tell in fitting detail all the work that was done would fill many pages, and would be no more than the officers and sailors deserve who performed hard and often obscure duty with an efficiency equal to that shown by their more fortunate comrades in a larger and more brilliant theatre. But it is impossible here to render this justice to all. The work was patient and unceasing, and the incidents of fighting were of almost daily occurrence. Now a great blockade-runner was hunted down and destroyed, as the *Eagle* dealt with the *Santo Domingo* at Rio Piedras, and the *Hawk*, aided by the *Castine*, with another six-thousand-ton ship at Mariel, the men on the ships or in boats facing a heavy fire in their relentless pursuit. Blockade-running became a dangerous, almost impossible, business under the conditions imposed by the American navy. Again it was the landing of an expedition to bring aid and supplies to Gomez, as was done by the *Peoria* and *Helena* convoying the *Florida*, with a fight in consequence against the batteries and block-houses at Las Tunas. Again it was the *Dixie* smashing the block-houses at the San Juan and Guayximico rivers, and the gunboats at Casilda. These are but samples of the manner in which the Spanish defences were harried and broken up all along the coast, and the efforts to get supplies to the main army at Havana frustrated and brought to naught.

More serious was the affair of June 26 at Manzanillo. On the morning of that day the *Hist*, under command of Lieutenant Young, the senior officer present, together with the *Hornet* and the *Wompatuck*, attacked a gun-boat near the block-house in Niguero Bay, and, after a sharp action, destroyed her. They pushed on to the harbor of Manzanillo in the afternoon, and came upon nine vessels, including four gunboats and a torpedo-boat, drawn up in crescent formation, and supported by four pontoons and strong shore batteries. Nothing daunted, these two converted yachts and one tug, with their light batteries, pressed forward and attacked vigorously, under a heavy fire. The odds were strongly against them; the *Hist* was hit eleven times; the *Hornet*, also struck many times, was disabled finally by a shot through her main steam-pipe, and was towed off by the *Wompatuck*, which received her share of shots, fighting her guns steadily and effectively. The Spanish torpedo-boat was disabled, one gunboat sunk, as well as a sloop loaded with soldiers, and a pontoon was destroyed. It was a very plucky fight against a far superior force. The next day the *Scorpion*, under command of Lieutenant Marix, and accompanied by the tug *Osceola*, went in and vigorously renewed the attack, but was inadequate to dispose of such odds against them. These affairs made it obvious that a stronger force was necessary in order to really destroy the Spanish ships assembled in the harbor. On July 18 the five small vessels which had already been engaged, re-enforced by the gunboats *Helena* and *Wilmington*, Commander Todd of the latter being the senior officer present, went in early in the morning and opened fire at ten minutes before eight. At the end of two hours and a half they had destroyed three large transports, the *Ponton*, a guard-ship, and three gunboats. As they worked in closer, batteries opened from the shore, and soldiers with rifles, to which they replied effectively; but when the shipping was disposed of, the American flotilla withdrew, the work to which it had been assigned having been performed with entire thoroughness, excellent shooting, cool courage, and in the same spirit of completeness as had been shown to the world at Manila.

Three days afterwards the *Annapolis*, commanded by Commander Hunker, supported by the *Topeka*, with the *Wasp* and *Leyden* leading, went in through the mine-sown channel of Nipe bay, on the northern coast. There they found the gunboat *Don Jorge Juan*, of 935 tons and armed with 6-inch rifles, lying at anchor in the restful belief that no enemy would dare to venture past the mines. Unluckily the enemy inconsiderately did that very thing, faced the fire of the *Don Jorge Juan*, closed in, and in half an hour the Spaniard, shot to pieces, had surrendered and sunk. Again, three days later, the *Nashville*, under command of Commander Maynard, took possession of Gibara, supporting the Cubans who were already in the town. Thus the seaports of Cuba were falling rapidly and steadily into American hands, and thus the net was being drawn ever closer and tighter upon the main army at Havana. In pursuance of this policy it was determined to complete the work at Manzanillo, where the shipping had been so thoroughly destroyed, by taking the town itself, which, strongly held by a large force of troops and well defended by batteries, was a source of trouble to the American campaign on land, as well as a constant temptation to blockade-running. With this object in view, the *Newark*, under Captain Goodrich, on her way to the Isle of Pines to conduct certain operations ordered by Admiral Sampson, gathered together the *Resolute*, *Suwanee*, *Hist*, *Osceola*, and the *Alvarado*—a

NAVAL OFFICERS IN PUERTO RICAN CAMPAIGN

recently captured Spanish gun-boat—and entered Manzanillo Harbor on August 12. A demand for surrender under pain of bombardment was refused, and the ships opened upon the batteries at twenty minutes before four. In half an hour white flags were seen on a Spanish gunboat; the American fire stopped; the *Alvarado*, running in under a flag of truce, was fired upon, and the action was immediately renewed. Cuban forces then appeared in the rear of the town, and opening fire, were supported by the ships. At half past five the ships anchored; a slow fire from the *Newark* was kept up through the night, and preparations were made to renew the bombardment and force the surrender of the town the next morning. When daylight came, white flags were seen in Manzanillo, and the Captain of the Port brought off to Captain Goodrich a brief despatch, saying, "Protocol of peace signed by the President; armistice proclaimed." No more bombardment, therefore, and Manzanillo was to be yielded without a struggle. The road of peace was opened again, hostilities were suspended, and the last shot of war from American guns in Cuban waters had been fired.

CHAPTER IX

THE CAMPAIGN IN PUERTO RICO

THE island of Puerto Rico, the easternmost and the most beautiful of the Greater Antilles, with its large population and commanding strategic position, was constantly in the minds of both army and navy as soon as war began. It was there that Admiral Sampson had gone to find Cervera at what seemed the most probable place, but the Spanish fleet was not in the harbor of San Juan. The noise of the bombardment died away, and the people of the island continued to believe that all was well, that Spain was triumphant and had won a great victory at Manila. American cruisers fluttered about the coast, and it was true that there seemed always to be a ship off San Juan. But this did not shake the general confidence, and there was much elation when the crack torpedo-boat destroyer *Terror*, detached at Martinique because out of order, came into the harbor. On June 22 it seemed that it would be a good thing for the *Terror* to go out, with the cruiser *Isabel II*, and attack the *St. Paul*, commanded by Captain Sigsbee of the *Maine*, just then watching the port. The *St. Paul* was only a huge Atlantic liner hastily armed and converted into an auxiliary cruiser, and probably the Spaniards thought her an easy prey, if only she would not run away. It is said that they invited their friends

down to the shore to see the performance. The cruiser came out first, apparently did not like the outlook, and clung to the shelter of the batteries, firing ineffectively, while the *St. Paul*, apparently undisturbed, took a few shots to try the ranges. Then came the *Terror*, and as she steamed to the eastward the *St. Paul* steamed along outside and parallel. Then the torpedo-boat made a dash, and the *St. Paul*, instead of running away, waited to be torpedoed, and when the *Terror* got within 5,400 yards, opened on her, sweeping her decks with fragments of shell and rapid-fire projectiles. It was clearly easier to blow Captain Sigsbee up in a peaceful harbor at night than in broad day, and the *Terror* turned round. Then a beautiful shot at nearly three miles distance from the *St. Paul's* 5-inch gun hit her on the starboard side, smashed her engine, and killed the chief and assistant engineers, so that the dreaded boat was just able to struggle back and be dragged sinking to the beach by a couple of tugs. This disposed of that member of Cervera's fleet for the time being, and the pretty bit of shooting which was responsible for it was the only incident until the *Yosemite* appeared and drove the *Antonio Lopez* ashore, and caused the *Alphonso III., Isabella II.*, and a torpedo-boat to seek shelter in the harbor.

General Miles, from an early period of the war, was convinced that it would be an error to undertake a summer campaign on a large scale in Cuba and directed against the principal Spanish army at Havana. He thought, and very justly, that the correct objective, from a military point of view, was Puerto Rico, which was the Spanish base for all operations in the West Indies, and where the climate was much better for

Northern troops than was the case in Cuba. This plan was laid before the War Department, which was still considering the advisability of a general movement against Havana. The coming of Cervera's fleet and its final imprisonment in the harbor of Santiago changed the situation and made that city the objective of the highest moment. General Miles, appreciating the importance of this expedition, telegraphed on June 5, from Tampa, that he desired to go at its head: but the command was given to General Shafter, and on June 6 General Miles, instead of being sent to Santiago, was asked, in a despatch from the Secretary of War, how soon he could have a sufficient force ready to go to Puerto Rico. General Miles replied that it could be ready in ten days, and there the matter seems to have dropped. On June 8 the Santiago expedition was ready, and on June 14 it sailed with 15,000 men and 800 officers, instead of the 25,000 it was expected to send. This was owing to a break-down in the ocean transportation, due to lack of knowledge of the steamships, which proved insufficient, and compelled the leaving behind at Tampa of 10,000 men who ought to have gone, and whose presence at Santiago would have greatly quickened the results and thereby saved much of the mortality caused by fever. The day after the Shafter expedition finally departed, General Miles was summoned to Washington, and there, on June 26, an order was finally given to organize an expedition to operate against the enemy in Cuba and Puerto Rico, and General Miles was directed personally to take the command. For some little time before, efforts had been making to collect transports for Puerto Rico, and this work went slowly for-

AN ANCIENT GATEWAY, SAN JUAN, PUERTO RICO

ward, for everything connected with the business of transportation was tardy and imperfect. Then came a spur to the lagging transport service, which had already appealed to the navy for aid, and secured the help of vessels of war in carrying troops. It was a very sharp spur too, and struck home hard, being nothing less, in fact, that General Shafter's despatch of July 2, saying that he was considering withdrawal, depicting the strength of the inner defences of the city, and the impossibility of carrying them with the force he had with him. General Miles replied, congratulating him upon the splendid fighting of his army, and said that he expected to be with him in a week. But General Miles overrated the transport service. Even under the tremendous pressure then existing he did not get away until July 8, and as it was he went on the *Yale*, a vessel of the navy, with 1,500 troops on board, accompanied by the *Columbia*, and followed by the *Duchesse* with more soldiers. When he reached Santiago, on July 11, however, no time was lost, for General Miles had a good plan already made, and knew just what he meant to do —a very great advantage in affairs requiring action, where even a poor plan is better than none at all, and is always an immense advance over chaos. So General Miles, knowing what he wanted, arranged at once with Admiral Sampson—delighted to meet with a plan and cordially acquiescing—that everything should be prepared to land the new force on the west side of the bay, and either attack the harbor forts and open the way to the fleet, or else, if it seemed better, march on to the city and take the Spanish position in reverse. This done, General Miles landed, burned the cabins at Sibo-

ney, and the next morning rode to the front and joined
General Shafter. After taking part in the negotiations which resulted in the capitulation of the city, and
issuing orders looking to the proper camping of the
troops and their protection, so far as possible, from disease, and especially from yellow fever, which had now
become menacing, General Miles betook himself to the
Yale, and telegraphed to Washington, asking permission to proceed as soon as possible to Puerto Rico. After
some delay the necessary authority was given. All the
troops at Santiago were more or less infected, so that
it was not safe to take any of them, as had been orig-
inally planned in connection with the fresh regiments
which had been kept on shipboard. This reduced the
effective force which General Miles had with him to
3,300 men, and he was obliged to rely on these alone
until the re-enforcements, which were expected, arrived
from the United States, to face the Spanish forces in
Puerto Rico, amounting, it was reported, to over
17,000 men. Tugs, launches, and lighters were ordered
and anxiously awaited, but none came, and the expedition finally started on July 21, trusting to the navy and
to what they could find at their destination to land the
troops. The fleet consisted of seven transports carrying troops, and the *Massachusetts, Dixie, Gloucester,
Yale* and *Columbia* as convoy, the last two also having
troops on board. The plan was to land at Fajardo, on
the eastern side of the island a little south of the cape,
and not far from the city of San Juan. This continued
to be the objective until the expedition started; but
General Miles, being satisfied that Fajardo had been
widely advertised as the landing-place, and that, owing

to the delays and the publicity, the Spaniards had had ample opportunity to concentrate at that point, very wisely decided that he would not go where the enemy expected him, but to Guanica, where nobody looked for him, on the southwestern coast. He also had trustworthy information, which events subsequently verified, that at Guanica he could get sugar-lighters, and still more at Ponce, the principal city of the island in the immediate neighborhood, whence a fine military road ran to San Juan, and that the people of that region were disaffected to Spain and friendly to the Americans. Captain Higginson objected, naturally, to this change, because at Guanica he could not get in with his heavy ships to support the troops, whereas he could cover their landing at Fajardo. So it was first decided to go to Fajardo, observe the conditions, and if they were unfavorable, return. Later this plan too was changed, and the *Dixie* being sent to pick up the *New Orleans* at San Juan, and the transports which were supposed to be on their way to the original point of attack, the fleet went on direct to Guanica. They reached their destination a little after five o'clock on the morning of July 25, and the *Massachusetts* and *Gloucester*, standing in, came to anchor at quarter before nine. The battle-ship could go no farther, and although it was clear that there were no entrance batteries, no one knew what batteries might be concealed inside, or what mines might be placed in the channel. Lieutenant-Commander Wainwright at once asked permission to go forward, and on the request being granted, the *Gloucester* ran briskly in, firing as she entered. A landing party, consisting of Lieutenant Wood and twenty-eight men,

under command of Lieutenant Huse, was put ashore,
and, on their hauling down the Spanish flag the enemy
opened upon them on both sides and from the village.
Deploying, they drove the enemy back through the village, and at the end of the street built a stone wall and
strung barbed wire to meet the re-enforcements reported to be coming from Yauco. This attack and the
fire from the *Gloucester* scattered the small body of
Spanish regulars who had resisted the landing. Meantime Captain Higginson, listening anxiously and atten-
tively after the *Gloucester* had disappeared from sight,
became satisfied that there were no inside batteries, and
ordered the transports to go in. This was quickly done;
it was found that the men of the *Gloucester* had seized
a lighter, and soldiers from Colonel Black's regiment of
engineers were at once landed at Captain Wainwright's
request to support the *Gloucester* landing party. In
a few minutes, as soon as the naval launches could
tow them in, the town of Guanica was in the
hands of the American army, and the first landing in
Puerto Rico had been successfully accomplished. The
path was opened very swiftly and effectively by the men
of the *Gloucester*, as prompt and efficient in the seizure
of the town as they had been in the destruction of the
Furor and *Pluton*.

The next day at dawn General Garretson, with six
companies of the Sixth Massachusetts and one company
of the Sixth Illinois, moved out and attacked a strong
force of Spaniards at Yauco, driving them before them
and taking the town, which gave us possession of the
railroad and of the highway to Ponce, for the advance
of General Henry's brigade. That evening the *Dixie*

THE LANDING AT GUANICA

returned, and the next day General Wilson, on the *Obdam*, and General Ernst, on the *Grande Duchesse*, arrived with more troops, and the *Annapolis* and *Wasp* also joined the squadron. Captain Higginson was now strong enough to detach a force against Ponce, which it was most desirable to secure with the least possible delay, not only because it was the largest city of the island and the terminus of the military road, but because it had a good harbor and excellent facilities for disembarking, in which Guanica was very deficient. Captain Davis of the *Dixie* was therefore ordered to proceed at once with the *Annapolis*, *Wasp*, and *Gloucester* to Ponce, reconnoitre, seize lighters, and occupy any position necessary for landing the army. The *Dixie*, accompanied by the *Annapolis* and *Wasp*, started at quarter before two, and the *Gloucester* at half past four. At three o'clock the first three ships were in the channel, and by half past five they had all anchored without resistance in the harbor. Captain Davis ordered the *Wasp* to lie in such a way that her broadside would command the main street of La Playa, and Lieutenant Merriam was sent ashore with a flag of truce to demand the immediate surrender of Ponce, under threat of bombardment, which was no idle menace, as the heavy six-inch battery of the *Dixie* entirely commanded the town, the main part of which was a mile and a half distant from the port. When Lieutenant Merriam returned, he reported that the Spanish forces had withdrawn from the port, and that he had been unable to open communications with their commander. He was closely followed on board by the British and German consuls, and several gentlemen representing the com-

mercial interests, who said they had authority from the
Spanish commander to negotiate for surrender. The
fact was that although Colonel San Martin and his 700
Spanish regulars were quite ready to fight, their resistance would have resulted only in the destruction of
the city by bombardment—something much disliked by
the property owners—and the consequent general rising of the hostile people, productive probably of much
bloodshed and disaster to the soldiers themselves.
Hence the readiness to allow the commercial interests
to surrender the town. A delay was asked for, long
enough to permit communication with the Spanish
headquarters at San Juan, which was refused by Captain Davis. Return to the town for further consultation followed, and then they came back and surrendered
the town, subject only to the condition that the Spanish
troops should be permitted to withdraw unmolested,
and that the municipal government should be allowed
to remain in authority until the arrival of the army.
This done, the Americans occupied the night by looking over all the vessels in the harbor and taking such as
were good prize, Lieutenant-Commander Wainwright
of the *Gloucester*, energetic and efficient, gathering in
some seventy lighters, and getting them ready for the
army. At half past five Lieutenant Merriam went in,
followed closely by Lieutenant Haines of the *Dixie*,
with the marines, and received the surrender of the
port. The flag was raised by a cadet of the *Dixie* over
the office of the Captain of the Port, the marines were
posted, and by this formal act Ponce passed into American hands. About seven o'clock the *Massachusetts*,
convoying General Miles with General Wilson and the

THE BANNER OF PONCE

transports, now increased by two more which had just come up with the *Cincinnati,* had joined them. By half past seven General Wilson had landed, and in less than an hour Lieutenant Haines was able to withdraw his sentries and turn over the port to the army. Meantime some officers of the *Dixie* had driven up to the centre of the town, where they were received with enthusiasm by the people, which they soon reported at La Playa. Returning at once, they went to the City Hall, accompanied by Lieutenant Haines, who released the political prisoners found there, and Cadet Lodge of the *Dixie* hauled down the Spanish and raised the American flag, the great crowd in the square cheering wildly, and then received from the Mayor the municipal banner and the formal surrender of the city. Presently Major Flagler appeared with troops and took formal possession. Thus the whole business was quickly done without hesitation or delay, and the American army held the city of Puerto Rico as a base from which they could advance at will to the capital, and by which they controlled the whole southern coast of the island.

Once on shore, thanks to the capture of the lighters and the efficient aid of the navy, General Wilson moved rapidly. That same afternoon he had established his headquarters at Ponce. Then he proceeded to organize the government of the city which had passed into his hands, and at the same time his own command, which was composed of General Ernst's brigade, consisting of the Sixteenth Pennsylvania and the Second and Third Wisconsin—all volunteers—a battalion of regular light artillery, a troop of volunteer cavalry, and a company of the Signal Corps. On August 3 he was able to relieve the brigade of their black-powder Springfields, and supply them with smokeless-powder Krag-Jorgensons—a highly beneficial change, which ought to have been made years before, but for which there should be due gratitude, after the Santiago experience, that it was made at all, even toward the end of a war. So the work, civil and military, was driven rapidly and efficiently forward, and in the midst of it all the country was reconnoitred, and as fast as possible the outposts were advanced along the great road to San Juan.

In this way, and from spies and deserters, it was learned that a force of the enemy, numbering 2,000, had taken position at Aibonito, about thirty-five miles from Ponce, a place of great natural strength, and indeed almost impregnable. Between Aibonito and our advanced parties lay the town of Coamo, also a very strong position naturally, held by 250 men. Coamo was capable of a very stubborn defence, and was still further protected by a block-house on the Banos road, which could open fire upon troops moving along the main military road. General Wilson decided, therefore, to turn the position. The Sixteenth Pennsylvania, under the command of Colonel Hulings, and guided by Colonel Biddle and Captain Gardner of General Wilson's staff, was ordered on the evening of August 8 to move to the rear of the town. In the darkness, over difficult mountain trails and across deep ravines, they made their way, with difficulty and much hard marching. At seven in the morning of the 9th, General Ernst, with the other two regiments of his brigade, and supported by the artillery and cavalry, advanced directly upon the town. Captain Anderson's battery opened at once

upon the block-house, which replied with an ineffective fire, and was in flames in fifteen minutes. The two Wisconsin regiments at the same time moved forward along the Banos and the military roads. As they advanced they heard the sound of sharp firing, and knew that the Pennsylvania troops were engaged. The march was quickened, and the whole force pressed rapidly forward, reaching and entering the town to find the enemy gone and the intrenchments deserted. General Wilson's skilful disposition of the Sixteenth Pennsylvania had given him Coamo with hardly a struggle, and the fight had been made and won in the rear of the town before the main advance reached it.

The flanking regiment, pushing along over the mountains in the darkness, had come out too far to the north, and had been obliged to move to the south by a difficult path, which made them an hour late in arriving at the point agreed upon. But when they reached their destination they found the Spaniards in a strong position, covered by the trees and ditches, and holding the road. The first battalion was rapidly formed along two ridges parallel to the road, whence they at once opened fire, and a sharp skirmish ensued. Meantime the second battalion moved to the left, toward a position whence they could enfilade the road, and the Spaniards surrendered. The action lasted an hour. The Americans lost 6 men wounded. On the Spanish side the commander, who exposed himself with reckless courage, another officer, and 4 privates were killed, and between 30 and 40 were wounded. Five Spanish officers and 162 men were made prisoners.

Within five minutes after the fight Captain Clayton

with his troop of cavalry rode through the town in rapid pursuit of the beaten enemy. The troopers pushed on fast, preventing, except in one instance, the destruction of the bridges, and carrying the American advance forward until they came within range of the strong positions of El Penon and Assomante, where batteries were placed which swept the road. To take these defences by direct assault, it was obvious, would involve a heavy loss of life to the limited forces General Wilson had at his disposal, and he accordingly resolved to again turn the enemy by a flanking movement on the right. Before doing so, however, General Wilson determined to make a reconnoissance with artillery, and our batteries opened on the Spanish positions at one o'clock on the 12th of August. We apparently silenced their batteries, but as we slackened they opened again with a vigorous fire, and once more, as at Santiago, black powder furnished the enemy a fine target, while the smokeless powder made it difficult to get their range or exact place. We lost 2 men killed, and 2 officers and 3 men wounded, and demonstrated the strength of the Spanish position. General Wilson, before beginning to turn the Spaniards, sent in a demand for surrender, which was naturally and quite curtly refused. Then, just as General Ernst was starting on the flank movement which would have forced Aibonito to surrender like Coamo, word came that the peace protocol with Spain had been signed and hostilities suspended. So the movement along the military road into the heart of the island and across to San Juan, which had been pushed so skilfully and successfully, came to a stop, and did not begin again until Spain had surrendered on a

GENERALS IN PUERTO RICAN CAMPAIGN

larger scale and it was able to go forward to the capital without resistance.

Other movements were in progress while General Wilson was operating along the main military road. General Brooke, with the brigade commanded by General Hains, reached Guanica on July 31, and going thence to Ponce, was ordered to Arroyo, about thirty-six miles east of Ponce, the port of the large town of Guayama, and near the point where the coast begins to turn and trend toward the north. Arroyo had surrendered to the little *Gloucester* and the *Wasp* on August 1, but on the arrival of the army the old story of the inefficient transport service—no lighters, no boats, no means of getting the soldiers on shore, always desirable things to have in military expeditions of this character—was repeated, and then, as usual, came the appearance of the navy, and the navy got the troops on shore, to the great relief of the general in command. Once landed, there was little delay. On August 4 General Hains was ordered to move on Guayama, and on the following morning he advanced with the Fourth Ohio, holding the Third Illinois in reserve. Meeting the enemy about a mile east of Guayama, our men drove the Spaniards before them and through the streets, had a sharp skirmish with them on the other side, in which four men were wounded, and in the evening, still advancing, took and held two strong positions on the outskirts of the town. The position was held until the 8th, when a reconnoissance was made by Colonel Coit, with about 110 men, along the road running north from Guayama. Pushing forward, the party had advanced about five miles when they ran into the Spaniards, came under a heavy fire, and had five men wounded Falling back steadily, they were met and supported by the rest of the regiment, and easily checked and drove the Spaniards back. The reconnoissance had developed the fact that the enemy were in force and held strong positions on the north. General Brooke therefore determined to turn the position. He waited until the 13th in order to get two troops of cavalry and four light batteries, and then sending General Hains with one regiment to make a détour and reach the enemy's rear, he advanced with the rest of his force along the road directly against the Spanish position. He moved slowly, in order to give time to the flanking regiment to reach its destination, and when sufficient time had elapsed he brought his guns within range and unmasked them. Just as the men were about to open fire, a message came in from Ponce announcing the signing of the protocol and that all was over. General Brooke retired to camp at Guayama, and there waited until, as one of the commissioners, he rode over the hills to receive the surrender of the island, watch the departure of the soldiers of Spain, and become himself the first American Governor of Puerto Rico.

On the same day that General Brooke received his orders for Arroyo, General Schwan arrived, and on August 6 received orders from General Miles to organize an expedition at Yauco and proceed against Mayaguez, a large town, the centre of a sugar district in the extreme west of the island, and thence, swinging to the right, to advance by Lares to Arecibo, the principal city on the north coast. On August 9 the expedition was ready. It consisted of the Eleventh infantry and two

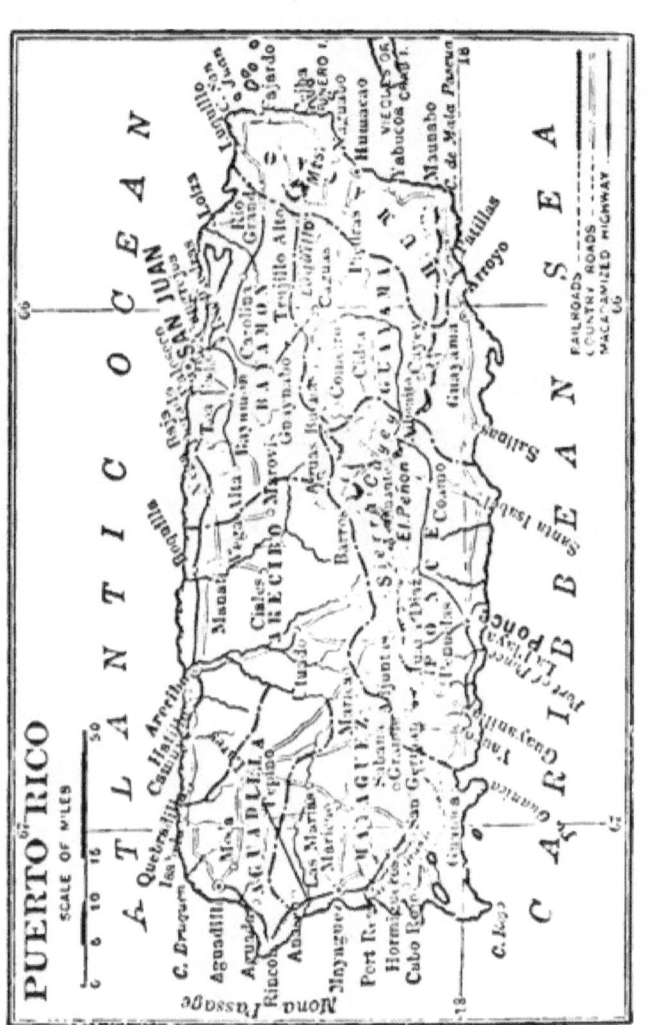

light batteries, all regulars. They marched twelve miles in intense heat and over a bad road to Sabana Grande, where they were joined by Captain Macomb with a troop of the Fifth cavalry, also regulars. Giving his men a good night's rest, General Schwan started at eight o'clock. Having provided himself with guides and spies, and from the beginning having made every arrangement to secure all possible information, General Schwan soon had news that the enemy, whose force was reported to be superior in numbers to his own, had marched out from Mayaguez to contest the American advance. The cavalry and the advance-guard were ordered, therefore, to exercise great care; they were drawn nearer to the brigade, and then the whole force pressed rapidly and steadily forward along the San German road. As they drew nearer to Mayaguez they came into a country intersected by two rivers and their tributaries. The road runs along the valley of the Rio Grande, through flat lands widening out here and there to a thousand yards, fenced with wire and crossed by creeks and streams, some running swiftly and with a considerable depth of water—altogether a rather difficult country for troops to operate in, and susceptible of a strong defence. As the Americans approached the little village of Hormigueros, Spanish scouts opened fire ineffectively from behind the hedges near some sugar-mills. On went the cavalry, and the Spanish skirmishers fled, pursued by the troopers, who rode along under shelter of a railroad embankment, keeping up a steady fire and getting control of a covered wooden bridge. Just beyond this point it had been intended to camp, but General Schwan determined, although his

men had marched thirteen miles in the heat, to finish
with the enemy, now that he had them in his near
neighborhood, and in order to gain possession of an important iron bridge on the main road. The soldiers re-
sponded cheerfully and readily. The whole force
pressed on, and when within four hundred yards of the
bridge the enemy opened with a light fire, and then
heavily with volleys, at the main body of troops. The
artillery was brought up. There was difficulty in decid-
ing the position of the enemy, thanks to their smokeless
powder, but soon the direction was obtained from the
course of the Spanish bullets. Then the artillery
opened, and the whole command moved forward. Unable to cross a creek, the advance made its way over a
bridge. The Gatlings went forward with the infantry,
concentrating their fire and supported by the cavalry.
Still forward, and they were over the iron bridge, and
masters of the approach to Mayaguez. The rest of the
artillery came up again, the infantry pressed forward,
the enemy gave way in all directions, and the Americans occupied the Spanish position and camped there
for the night. Again had it been shown that the Spaniards could not stand the steady onset of the American
troops. They had equal numbers, knowledge of the
country, and the advantage of position. They fired
heavily as at Guasimas as soon as the Americans came
within range, and then as the Americans came on, opening with all arms and going at them without flinching,
the Spaniards, nearly all regulars in this case, gave way
and fled. The action was over at six o'clock. The
American loss was 1 killed and 15 wounded; the Spanish, 15 killed and about 35 wounded. The skirmish

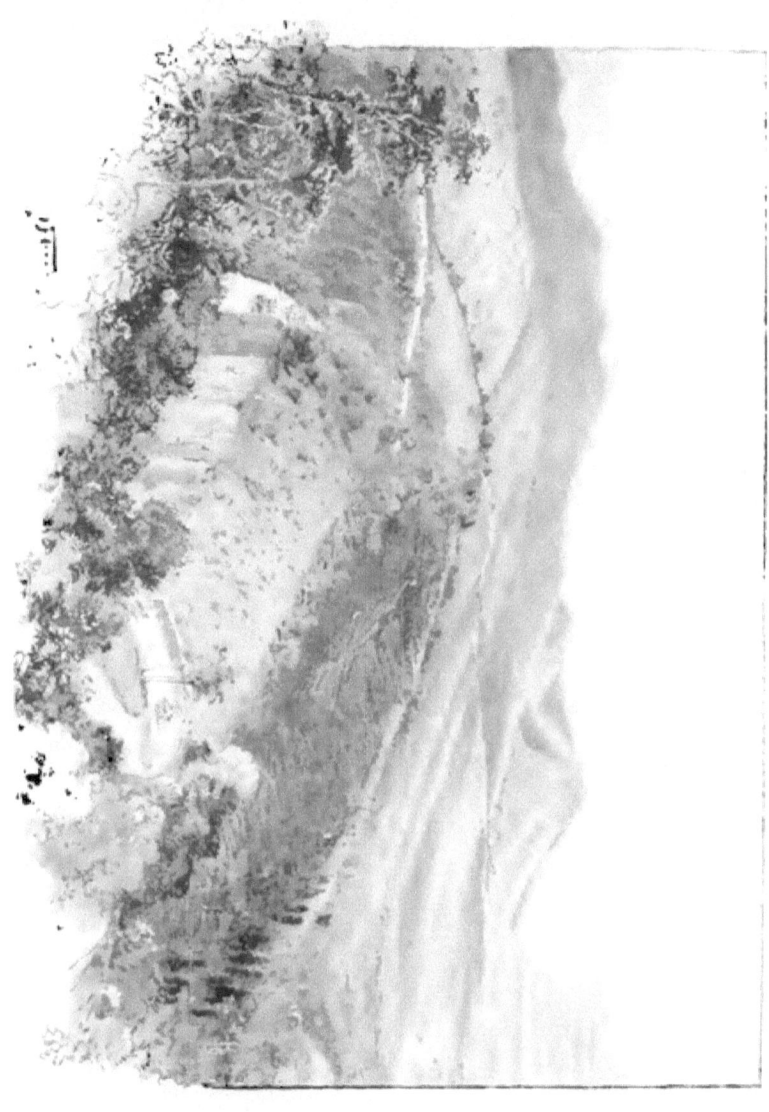

was well and skilfully fought, and illustrated as perfectly as a much larger affair the inability of the Spaniards to either attack, take the initiative, or make a firm stand in the open.

The next morning, August 11, by half past eight, the American scouts were in Mayaguez, an hour later the cavalry, and then came General Schwan and his staff and the infantry, with bands playing and colors flying. The Spaniards had gone, the town gently yielded itself, the Mayor declared himself subject to the orders of the American general, and the people crowded the streets and cheered the American troops. The brigade then went into camp near the town, and the cavalry were ordered to keep in touch with the retreating enemy. Following the easterly road to Lares, the cavalry drove some Spaniards before them, but it was soon discovered that the main body had taken the western road, and the next morning Colonel Burke started in pursuit with about seven hundred men all told. The morning was intensely hot, and the afternoon brought a drenching rain, but the troops kept steadily on, and encamped for the night at the forks of the Las Marias and Maricao roads. Here news came that the Spaniards, with a force variously estimated at 1,200 to 2,500 men, intended to make a stand at Las Marias. As Colonel Burke's one desire was to reach them, he was off at daylight. The utmost speed was made, but the road in places was so bad and so heavy that the artillery could only be got along by the infantry hauling the guns. This caused delay, and there was much anxiety and bitter disappointment when it was reported that the enemy had abandoned Las Marias and were fleeing

toward Lares. Then word came that seven hundred
were still on the hither side of the Rio Grande, which
at that season was running deep and full. The Americans hurried through the town, and presently the cavalry came up with the fugitives, and then the engagement began. A large number of Spaniards had, as reported, failed to cross the river, and they replied with
volleys to our fire. By some means the artillery was
dragged up, the guns opened, and our infantry followed. The Spaniards gave way in all directions, now
thoroughly demoralized. Many were drowned in trying to ford the stream, and the American skirmishers,
advancing rapidly, picked up more than 50 prisoners,
as well as 200 rifles and large quantities of ammunition, which strewed the road. The American loss was
only 6 wounded; 5 Spaniards were buried by our men
in addition to those lost in the river, and many more
were wounded. General Schwan now had the enemy
broken and in full flight. Lares was within his grasp,
and a clear line to the principal northern town of Arecibo. And then came the fatal message announcing the
signature of the protocol, and "no troops ever suspended
hostilities with a worse grace." But a suspension it
had to be, and this expedition, which had marched and
fought with so much spirit and such restless energy,
stopped like the rest.

Not far from them another command was brought
in like manner to a stand-still. General Stone, with a
small party, had pushed along a trail considered impas-
sable, by way of Adjuntas and Utuado, and had made
a practical road through the centre of the western region, along which General Henry marched with his

command. In a day or two more they would have been able to head off the Spanish detachments retreating before General Schwan, and would have effected a junction with the latter, thus gaining complete control of all the west, and at the same time of the northern towns, and of the railroad on the coast. But they too were stopped, and thus the Puerto-Rican campaign came to an end.

The operations of the American army in Puerto Rico have been described in some detail, not on account of the engagements which occurred, for they were hardly more in any instance than sharp skirmishes, but because the result of the campaign was of great importance, and the manner in which the operations were conducted, and the behavior of the troops, merit consideration. There has been an impression that the Puerto-Rican campaign was little more than a parade, and it has even been spoken of contemptuously as a "picnic," owing probably to the too prevalent notion that military operations must be estimated solely by the losses, or, as a British admiral of the last century is said to have put it, in somewhat brutal phrase, "by the butcher's bills." The number of killed and wounded is undoubtedly a test of the severity of fighting, of the force of an attack, and of the strength of the resistance. But a campaign as a whole must be judged, if it is to be judged fairly, by larger and different standards. Malplaquet and Oudenarde were important and bloody battles, but their direct effect upon the final results of the war was but small. Washington forced Howe out of Boston without an action, and with the loss of hardly a man, yet the military and political results were enormous; the feat was so admirable that the last historian* of the Revolution says it gave Washington at once a place in history, and compares it with Napoleon's performance at Toulon in making his future fame.

In nineteen days the different divisions under the command of General Miles had overrun nearly the entire western half of Puerto Rico, and had made it evident that in another fortnight they would have swept over the whole island and cooped up the Spaniards in San Juan, if they had not actually gained possession of the capital itself. The success of the American troops was so rapid and complete, and their future was so clearly assured, that a claim to the island had been established of such an undeniable character that, when it came to signing the protocol, there was no possibility of withholding from the United States the cession of Puerto Rico. Thus the object of the campaign was completely achieved, which, after all, will always weigh heavily in making up the final judgment of history. Coming next to the actual operations of the campaign, it is found that there was the same lack of means for disembarking troops, the same defective transportation service, as in Cuba. These difficulties were overcome by the assistance of the navy, and with their boats or the lighters they had captured. The men were rapidly and skilfully handled at separated points, showing that the two services worked well together; and although many of the soldiers arrived in poor condition from the camps in the United States, with a consequent prone-

*Sir George Trevelyan.

ness to suffer from the climatic diseases, they were so well managed that every division was enabled to push steadily and rapidly forward, making hard marches, very often through difficult country, and carrying out successfully everything which was demanded from them. Last and most important of all, there was an intelligent plan throughout, which, in its execution, was swiftly and comprehensively taking possession of the entire island. Each movement of troops was so arranged as ultimately to support and fit in with every other. The engagements which took place were all marked by the same qualities. General Wilson, General Schwan, and General Brooke all fought their troops with skill. They reconnoitred their country, they knew what they meant to do, they had plans which proved their own soundness when carried into execution. The strong positions were turned by judicious flanking movements, and when the positions were not strong the direct onset drove the Spaniards back in confusion, as at Hormigueros. In every action or skirmish the troops behaved admirably, and their advance was constant and unchecked, so that the general plan developed steadily from the beginning, and showed its merits in its results. It is quite true that the population was friendly, and received the American troops with acclamation, a condition which smooths away many troubles in any campaign. But this was equally true of Cuba, and does not impair the excellence of the operations in the eastern island, or diminish the importance of the general result. To this campaign we owe the island of Puerto Rico, and the manner in which

it was carried forward through many difficulties re-
flects the highest credit on the generals who commanded, and upon the discipline, quality, and courage
of the soldiers, both regulars and volunteers.

ON THE ADJUNTAS TRAIL

CHAPTER X

THE BLOCKADE OF MANILA AND THE CAPTURE OF GUAM

ADMIRAL DEWEY employed the first two days after his victory in making all fast, seizing the arsenal at Cavité and the islands at the harbor mouth, and announcing a blockade of the port of Manila, lying somewhat helpless just now before his guns. Then, having prudently cut the cables, he sent to Washington, by way of boat to Hong-kong, a laconic despatch, telling of his victory in a few simple sentences, and in figures as dry as the multiplication table. It had one great merit—exact truth—a quality much lost and clouded in the Spanish reports which had gone to Madrid, and from which alone the world knew anything of the doings in the distant East on May 1. Yet the victory had been so absolute, the destruction of Montojo's squadron so utter and complete, that even the Spanish could not hide the facts with language, an exercise in which they have great proficiency. The truth tore its way through the thin phrases; it broke the pompous sentences, and made itself sufficiently visible to Europe. To the great powers there it came with a shock. They were not pained by the unhappy lot of Spain, for that they regarded with all the philosophy which had just manifested itself so attractively in regard to poor Greece. The downfall of a broken, bankrupt nation, they bore well enough; and although they were surprised and annoyed by the swiftness, accuracy, and fighting efficiency of the Americans, they were prepared to belittle the whole affair, and to pretend that it was no such great matter, after all. But what shocked and alarmed them very seriously indeed was that a new power, known to be of great wealth and strength, had suddenly swept down on Manila, toppled over in ruin the harmless remains of Spanish power, and in one morning had risen up master of a great port and city, and a disagreeable factor of unlimited possibilities in the East, where they were having a "question" and starting in to divide the vast Empire of China. This was obviously objectionable, and ought to be stopped. It became clear at once to several imperial and many diplomatic minds that something should be done. There was much running about, much sending of cipher despatches, many grave unofficial conversations and representations, and a general urgency to set the concert of Europe, which had performed so beautifully in the Cretan business, to playing again. And then it was found that the most important performer, the great sea power of the world, would not take part. It appeared that these people who had flung Spain's fleet to destruction spoke the English tongue; that as long as they sent their grain across the ocean to Great Britain, England had a base on the Atlantic, and could defy the world; that England rather wanted them as neighbors in the East, and had no mind to be aught but friendly to them. So England would not play her part, and without her fleets, still more with those fleets hostile, there could be no concert of Europe; and that harmonious body sank into silence

GEORGE DEWEY

after this attempt at turning up, and was never heard of in the Philippines. Many results came from this English action. The people of the United States knew instinctively what had happened, although all details were kept quite obscure; they valued the friendly deed, which was not to be forgotten; and they saw in a flash the community of interests which bound them to their kinsmen over-seas. So the two great English-speaking nations drew together—a very momentous fact, well understood and much disliked on the Continent of Europe, and something destined to have serious effect on the world's history in the future. The more immediate and direct outcome of England's refusal to interfere—as well as her evident intention to let no one else interfere in what was going on in the Philippines—was that Admiral Dewey was left with a free hand to work out the situation which he had himself created.

He had sprung in a few hours into the ranks of the world's great admirals. It was now to be seen whether the victorious seaman was also a commander in the widest naval sense, and at the same time a statesman and diplomatist. The conditions were full of peril. He was seven thousand miles from home, the enemy held the city in his front, he had no troops to aid him, and he knew that unfriendly eyes were watching him narrowly, while he could not know at first that the concert of Europe had broken down, and that England was the friend of the United States.

The war-ships of other powers began to collect at Manila—French, English, Japanese, and German, the latter finally reaching five in number, and including two armored vessels. What was their meaning and intent?

—a question very important to Admiral Dewey, and demanding much thought. As they watched him, it quickly became apparent that in England and Japan he had friends and sympathizers. In France an ill-wisher was soon discovered, but nothing more. The ill wishes of the French indeed never took the form of overt action, but we can learn their feelings from the diary of a naval lieutenant at Manila, thoughtfully published in the *Revue de Paris*. The diarist was much disturbed that Europe did not intervene. He writes mournfully that the European powers were doing no more than watching fate, which was true enough. His mind was filled with dark suspicions of England and of the Anglo-Saxon, and he thought that America ought promptly to be shut out from the East. He belittles Dewey's victory, but blames the Spaniards for allowing him to win it, which is, of course, one way of looking at that event. Such a fact ought not to have been, and yet it was. The explanation of it is that we had English gunners, deserters, picked up in Hong-kong —a dear old falsehood which has done much hard service, never harder than in this case, for Dewey's crews, except for a few Chinamen, were practically all American. But the thought soothes the French diarist, who has never heard of Truxtun and *L'Insurgente*, or of some American shooting at French frigates just a hundred years ago. Then comes the conventional cry that the Americans care only for dollars, are treacherous, mean, braggarts (this last a heinous offence in French contemplation), and, saddest of all, have no nobility of soul. And the philosopher, as he reads, wonders about the nobility of soul shown in the Dreyfus case

and some of its attendant incidents, and thinks how
differently the phrase is interpreted in different countries. But the lieutenant's diary is none the less instructive, and, joined to many much louder manifes-
tations by Paris newspapers and Frenchmen generally,
causes Americans to draw some conclusions as to
French friendship not soon to be forgotten. Still whatever they felt or thought, the Frenchmen did nothing
serious while they watched fate, and hostile feelings
certainly troubled Admiral Dewey little enough. But
there was one power present who pushed her hostility
from thoughts and words to action. This power was
Germany. She had no especial claim to be there, no
large or peculiar interests, but she sent more ships than
any other power, kept on meddling, and went to the
verge of war. The Germans broke through Dewey's
regulations, which he had the right to make, and he
called them sharply to order. They would violate the
rules by moving about at night, and then the American
search-lights fell with a glare upon them, and followed
them about in a manner which checked and annoyed
them. One German ship put out her lights and tried
to slip in at night, but a shell across her bows brought
her to. Another made herself offensive by following
and running close up to our transports when they first
arrived. A German ship went up to Subig bay and
prevented the insurgents from taking the Isla Grande.
So the *Raleigh* and *Concord* went up too, stripped for
action, and as they went in the *Irene* went out, and
the Americans took Isla Grande. Very trying all this
to a man charged with great responsibilities and seven
thousand miles from home. There must be no haste,

no rashness, nothing that could give his opponents a hold, and yet there must be no yielding, and no threat except with action behind it, and on a provocation which the whole world would justify. Every annoyance, every improper movement, was quickly checked. The diplomacy was perfect. Then came the sufficient provocation, and the teeth were shown. To the vigilant admiral the opportunity came at last when one of the German vessels was proved to have landed provisions in Manila. Let us read what follows, as it is told by Mr. Stickney, an eye-witness.

"Orderly, tell Mr. Brumby I would like to see him," said Admiral Dewey, one forenoon.

"Oh, Brumby," he continued, when the flag-lieutenant made his appearance on the quarter-deck, "I wish you to take the barge and go over to the German flag-ship. Give Admiral von Diederich my compliments, and say that I wish to call his attention to the fact that vessels of his squadron have shown an extraordinary disregard of the usual courtesies of naval intercourse, and that finally one of them has committed a gross breach of neutrality in landing provisions in Manila, a port which I am blockading."

The Commodore's voice had been as low and as sweetly modulated as if he had been sending von Diederich an invitation to dinner. When he stopped speaking, Brumby, who did not need any better indication of the Commodore's mood than the unusually formal and gentle manner of his chief, turned to go, making the usual official salute, and replying with the customary, "Ay, ay, sir."

"And, Brumby," continued the Commodore, his voice rising and ringing with the intensity of feeling that he felt he had repressed about long enough, "tell Admiral von Diederich that if he wants a fight, he can have it right now!"

Thereupon the German admiral became sorry for what had happened, and, it appeared, did not know what his captains had been doing—a sad reflection upon German discipline. But it seemed that, although

ELWELL S. OTIS

Major-General in command of the American forces in the Philippines

he had two armored ships, and Dewey none, he did not desire a fight, and the meddling abated sensibly. Then much later, in a manner to be described hereafter, when the *Monterey* came in, with her heavy armor and big guns, it was found that important interests required the presence of the German war-ships elsewhere. Why the Germans behaved as they did, manifesting every possible dislike and hostility without doing anything effective, and breeding a strong and just enmity toward them in the United States, is difficult to understand. To the higher and more refined statesmanship of Europe it may have seemed wise. To the ruder and simpler American mind it seems stupid and profitless, and, in any event, Americans will not forget it. But every one can admire the manner in which Admiral Dewey mixed tact with firmness, and in the midst of jealous and meddling neutrals steered his course without an error, and never relaxed for a moment his iron grip on the great bay he had conquered and the city which lay beneath his guns.

To keep the sympathy and support of the friendly powers and hold at bay the hostile nations were difficult and perplexing tasks, trying to nerves, temper, and wits. But this was not all. The war in Cuba had in due course lighted up the flames of insurrection in the Philippines, where Spanish tyranny and extortion, supplemented by the oppression, cruelty, corruption, and outrages of the powerful monastic orders, had been heaping up the material of revolt. To this mass of explosives the troubles of Spain in Cuba had applied the torch. The black robed bodies of the hated monks floating down the Pasig river were grim signals of the coming storm. Rebellion broke out in the back country and in the provinces of Luzon, and a guerrilla warfare began to desolate the country. The Spaniards met the outbreak vigorously and repressed it savagely, shooting down their prisoners by scores to make a holiday spectacle for the crowds on the Luneta. The fighting dragged along, exhausting to the Spaniards and without substantial gain to the rebels, until July, 1897, when the insurgent chiefs surrendered, on condition that certain reforms should be made and that a sum of money should be paid over to the families of those who had been killed in the war or ruined by it. Spain, as usual, broke her word, as she had done with the Cubans in 1878. The reforms were not made, and only a part of the money was ever paid. Emilio Aguinaldo and the other leaders withdrew to Hong-kong in September 1897, bringing with them $400,000, which they had received from the Spanish government. The insurrection was over, although there was fitful fighting here and there; but the chiefs had retired to a safe haven and were helpless at Hong-kong. Such was the situation which Admiral Dewey found when war was declared. The insurgent chiefs, however, stimulated by the approach of trouble between the United States and Spain, put themselves in communication with Mr. Wildman, our consul at Hong-kong, and opened negotiations with him. They declared that they desired annexation to the United States, above all independence of Spain and relief from Spanish rule, and wished to aid the Americans in all possible ways. Admiral Dewey took the obvious course of encouraging them, which from a military point of view was entirely sound.

He caused Aguinaldo to be brought over, and protected his landing on May 19. So little response came at first to Aguinaldo's appeal to his countrymen that he wished to turn round and return to Hong-kong, and was kept only by much pressure. Gradually at first, and then rapidly, the natives began to come in; Admiral Dewey furnished arms from the arsenal at Cavité, and the insurgents had presently a respectable force. They soon found that, with the Spanish sea power destroyed and an American fleet in possession of Manila bay, the situation was widely different from that in which they had struggled alone, desperately and helplessly against the forces of Spain. They began to win victories, to cut off detached bodies of Spanish troops and take outlying towns. With victory their numbers rapidly increased, and they were soon able, under cover of the American war-ships, to surround Manila. So far all went well, and the insurgent forces and their operations put Manila even more securely at Admiral Dewey's mercy. Then the difficulties began. The insurgents forgot that they owed their position entirely to the American fleet, and that but for the American war-ships the chiefs would have been vegetating in exile at Hong-kong, and their followers hewing wood and drawing water for the Spaniards, as of yore. Aguinaldo, who had never adjusted his relations to the universe, began to regard himself as a government and a nation, and started to plan for a dictatorship. Admiral Dewey, who had most carefully avoided recognizing the insurgents or treating them as allies, was obliged to hold them constantly under control. He forced them to conduct their war in a civilized manner; he insisted upon and secured the humane treatment of their Spanish prisoners, and he kept a watchful eye upon their intrigues with foreign powers, which they almost at once began.

Taken altogether, it was a most difficult position, and required all the best talents of the statesman and diplomatist. But the admiral proved himself to be both in high degree, and kept the whole situation always in hand, never losing the mastery for a moment. So the slow days wore by. Very slow and very anxious they must have been to a victorious sailor suddenly charged with vast responsibilities, with hostile European powers on one side, and dangerous and untrustworthy supporters on the other. Very often must he have thought of the seven thousand miles which separated him from home as he paced the deck, counting the days which lay between him and the coming of re-enforcements. For the re-enforcements were very slow in starting, owing to the great delay in getting transports and in mobilizing the troops at San Francisco. So deliberate did the movements seem, so many were the announcements of departure, only to be followed by postponement, that the country began to grow restive, and there were mutterings about the apparent abandonment of Dewey and the fate of Gordon at Khartoum.

But the delays which undoubtedly existed were due to the surprise of Dewey's victory, to the magnitude of its results, and to the unreadiness of the military organization to meet such an emergency. Admiral Dewey had asked on May 13 for 5,000 men, and needed, of course, fresh ammunition and naval re-enforcements

as well. Three weeks elapsed after the eventful 1st of May before the cruiser *Charleston* left San Francisco, and then she went without the troops. The three transports the *City of Pekin*, *Australia*, and *City of Sydney* finally got off on May 25, carrying the First California and Second Oregon regiments of volunteers, five companies of the Fourteenth Infantry United States regulars, a detachment of California artillery—in all, 115 officers and 2,386 enlisted men—under General Anderson, the division commander. They joined the *Charleston* at Honolulu, where she was waiting for them, and started thence on June 4. As soon as they were clear of the land Captain Glass of the *Charleston* opened the sealed orders brought to him by the *Pekin*, and found that he was directed to stop at the Ladrones on his way to Manila and capture the island of Guam. The course was then shaped toward the first land seen by Magellan, after his long wandering over the wastes of the Pacific, and on June 20, at daylight, the American ships were off the island. They looked in at the port of Agana, the capital, found no vessels there, nor any sign of a Spanish force, and so proceeded to the other port of San Luis d'Apra, where rumors at Honolulu had placed a Spanish gunboat and soldiers. When they reached the harbor, shut in by Apepas Island and the peninsula of Orote, the *Charleston* suddenly disappeared from the sight of the watching eyes on the troopships. She had plunged boldly in, following the deep, narrow, and tortuous channel hedged by coral reefs. Against the gray and green of the cliffs, with sudden rain squalls coming and going, the lead-colored cruiser could not be made out from the transports. At last

something white was discovered moving against the
cliffs. Then the white spots were discovered to be the
boats on the superstructure of the *Charleston,* and it
was apparent that the cruiser was going steadily in.
Presently she made out the masts of a vessel beyond
Apepas, and the spirits of the crew rose at the hope of
an action. Then they rounded the end of the island,
and disappointment fell upon them when they discovered that the longed-for enemy was only a peaceful Japanese brigantine. No fight there. On the
cruiser crept through the dangerous waters, past old
Fort St. Iago. No sound, no movement, no enemy
there. All as quiet, one would think, as in Magellan's
day. On again, and now the *Charleston* was opposite
Fort Santa Cruz, and opened sharply with her three-
pounders. The guns cracked, the shells whistled over
the fort, a dozen shots were fired, there was no reply,
and in five minutes the only action seen by Guam was
over. The *Charleston* slipped along a little further,
ever more slowly, and at last stopped. Soon boats put
off from the shore, and the captain of the port and
some other Spanish officers came on board the *Charleston.* They began to apologize in the best Spanish manner for their inability to return the American "salute."
"What salute?" said Captain Glass. It appeared that
they referred to the shelling of Fort Santa Cruz.
"Make no mistake," said Captain Glass. "I fired no
salute. Our countries are at war, and those were
hostile shots." Poor Spanish officers, stranded far
away in the dim Pacific! They had heard no news of
war, and now they were prisoners. Then Captain
Glass demanded the Governor, who was at Agana, and

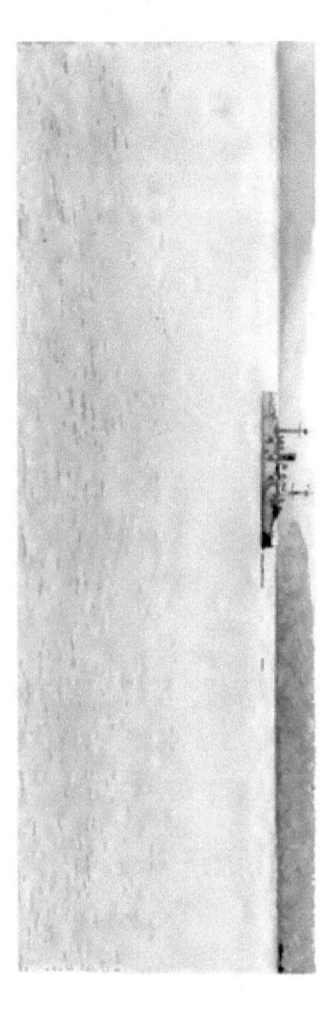

paroled his suddenly acquired prisoners to go ashore and get him. This brought a pause in the operations, and the three transports were convoyed in and anchored near the cruiser. As evening drew on a message arrived from the Governor, stating that the military regulations of Spain forbade his going aboard an enemy's ship, and that he would be happy to see the American commander at his office. This characteristic exhibition of pompous Spanish etiquette and of piteous inability to recognize facts made the American captain hesitate between anger and amusement. But good-nature and the sense of humor prevailed, and word was sent to the Governor that the captain or some officer representing him would call on the following day. The next morning Lieutenant Braunersreuther went ashore with only four sailors, but with two Oregon companies and fifty marines in the background making ready to follow. Before the soldiers and marines could be landed, however—a somewhat slow piece of work—Lieutenant Braunersreuther appeared, his task completed, and the Spanish Governor and his staff prisoners in the whale-boat. The poor Spaniards had faced the inevitable, and bowed to the inexorable argument of an overwhelming force. The Governor had written an order to the commandant of the troops to bring them down and surrender them, had then penned a melancholy letter to his wife, and in deep dejection had followed his captors to the *Charleston*. After they had been assigned to quarters Captain Glass went ashore and inspected Fort Santa Cruz, and there on the southeast corner of the terre-plein the flag was hoisted. As it climbed slowly to the top of the staff

the national salute rang out, gun after gun, from the
cruiser, and the air was filled, as the crash of the reports died away in echoes, with the music of the regimental bands on the troop-ships. Then all was done,
and the flag which had risen first on the distant Atlantic coast floated out before the afternoon breeze of these
remote islands which were henceforth to know new
masters. The ceremony done, the practical work
which the flag symbolized was soon finished. At four
o'clock the two companies, one of Spanish regulars,
and one of native Chamorros, came down to the boat-
house where Lieutenant Braunersreuther, backed by
his bluejackets and forty marines, received the surrender. The Spanish troops were all disarmed, the
regulars were taken on board the ships as prisoners,
and the Chamorros, perfectly overjoyed at the over-
throw of Spain, as is the case with all who have called
Spain master, were left behind. The little play, in
which comedy and tragedy had mingled closely, was
over. The moss-grown, picturesque old forts, the
slender Spanish garrison, the whole civil government
of Spain, had passed into the power of the United
States. There were scenes which seemed to recall the
fantastic conceptions of comic opera, and bring only
laughter to the onlookers. Yet behind the absurdity
was the pathos of the helpless yielding Spaniards, and
the stern historic fact that the first possession in the
Pacific which Magellan had given to the Spain that
dominated and frightened Europe had passed away forever from the Spain which had ceased to rule, and become a part of the Western republic, whose very exist-

THOMAS M. ANDERSON

ence depended on the denial of all that Charles V and
Phillip II, represented among men.

On June 22 the *Charleston* steamed away with her
prisoners, followed by the transports. In the early
afternoon of Tuesday, June 28, they were off Cape
Engano, and in a short time were joined by the *Baltimore*, sent out to meet them. Two days more and they
were running into Manila bay. As they passed Corregidor, three German vessels were lying near by, and
the *Kaiserin Augusta*, a large armored cruiser, got up
steam and followed close to the *Australia*, hung to her
until the flag-ship was reached, and then broke out the
American flag and saluted. The whole movement was
offensive, and to be offensive without doing anything to
support it is not only ill-bred, but stupid. So the performance of the *Kaiserin Augusta* went down in the
American books charged to the German account, and
the ships went on. Before them lay the French ships,
sulky and suspicious, the Japanese, the trim black English ships, with the "old red ensign" looking very
friendly and very welcome to the American troop-
ships. And then came the ships flying the flag they
loved, and which they had come so far to serve. There
was the victor fleet near together off Cavité, and the
salutes rang out from the *Olympia* and the *Charleston*.
Support had come at last, and Dewey had a new cruiser
and troops of the United States at his back. It must
have been a great relief to feel that the long separation
from home was over, and that the *Pekin* and her consorts were but the first in a long line of re-enforcements
now fairly started from the United States. The moral
effect of the arrival of General Anderson and his troops

was great, although in actual numbers the force was a
small one, but it was put to immediate use. The soldiers were quickly landed and established at Cavité,
which had been in American possession since the battle of May 1. Then the admiral faced the situation
again. There was still the hostility of the European
powers to be met. German enmity was still shown in
a way which bordered on intolerable insolence. The
American troops had been barely a week in their new
quarters when Admiral Dewey was obliged to drive
the *Irene* from Subig bay and stop German interference at that point with the insurgents. On the
other hand were the insurgents themselves, massed
round Manila, and inflated by the victories won and
the prisoners captured from outlying Spanish forces.
It was the 15th of July when Aguinaldo, destitute of
either loyalty or gratitude, forgetting the hand which
had raised him up, and swelling with a sense of his
own importance, felt it necessary to establish a government, of which he duly apprised Admiral Dewey. The
government consisted simply of himself as dictator, but
he showed his Latin blood by accompanying the fact
of his own dictatorship with high-sounding proclama-
tions, and a constitution in many paragraphs, which he
apparently made himself, and which was therefore certainly new, and to him probably satisfactory. The
cloud of words which he emitted was of little moment,
but the fact of his dictatorship and his assumption of
autocratic power added to the perils of the situation.
Altogether the conditions were menacing enough. In
the front was Spain, an open and public enemy, comparatively easy to deal with. On either hand were the

war-ships of unfriendly powers watching sullenly and eagerly for an error, for a sign of weakness, for the least excuse for interference. All around Manila were the insurgents, supporters in theory, but untrustworthy, treacherously led, and capable at any moment of actions which might endanger our relations with other powers, or of intriguing with those same powers against us.

So the days dragged by, the admiral, cool, firm, and vigilant, always ready, and making no mistakes, and then, two days after Aguinaldo's announcement of his own greatness, came a great and signal relief. On July 17 the second expedition, under General Greene, which had left San Francisco on June 25, arrived. General Greene came on the *China,* and the three other transports—the *Senator, Colon,* and *Zealandia*—came in soon after. They brought the First Nebraska, the First Colorado, the Tenth Pennsylvania, and the Utah artillery—all volunteers—eight companies of regulars, and a detachment of engineers, in all 158 officers and 3,428 enlisted men. This raised the total force at Manila to more than 6,000 men, and greatly strengthened the American position. The net about the Spaniards holding the Philippine capital was beginning to draw tighter.

This second expedition had stopped at Wake Island —a barren sand strip, but with possible value for future cables—had then looked in at Guam, and now, on a peaceful Sunday, rapidly disembarked on the shores of Manila bay. Thus re-enforced, the American troops were moved forward, and the camp established between the beach and the Manila road, about two miles from

Malate. This brought the lines very near the Spaniards and the Malate fort. There was a false alarm one night, produced by some Spanish shots at the insurgents, but, on the whole, the Spaniards kept quiet enough, having a proper respect, no doubt, for the war-ships frowning upon them from a very reasonable range. But events were moving faster now than in the long dreary time which followed the battle of May 1. The second expedition had scarcely time to settle down in their camps when, on July 25, General Merritt, one of the most distinguished officers in the army, arrived on the *Newport*. To him had been confided the command of all the American forces in the Philippines—both those already there and those which were still to come. He had intended to bring with him the third expedition, but, impatient of delay, had sailed with his staff on the *Newport*, on June 27, and pushed on alone at the highest speed attainable. When he arrived, he found General Anderson with headquarters at Cavité, and some troops holding the town, and General Greene encamped with his brigade near Paranaque. On the north flank General Greene was within 3,200 yards of the outer defences of Manila, which ran from old Fort San Antonio south of the Malate suburb, with more or less detached forts to the eastward, and to the swamps on the Spanish left. The queer feature of the situation was that between our lines and those of the Spaniards the insurgents, who had established scattered posts all about the city, had entrenched themselves within 800 yards of the old powder-magazine fort. Thus in the direct line of the American advance lay the forces of their would-be allies. In order to make that advance it was

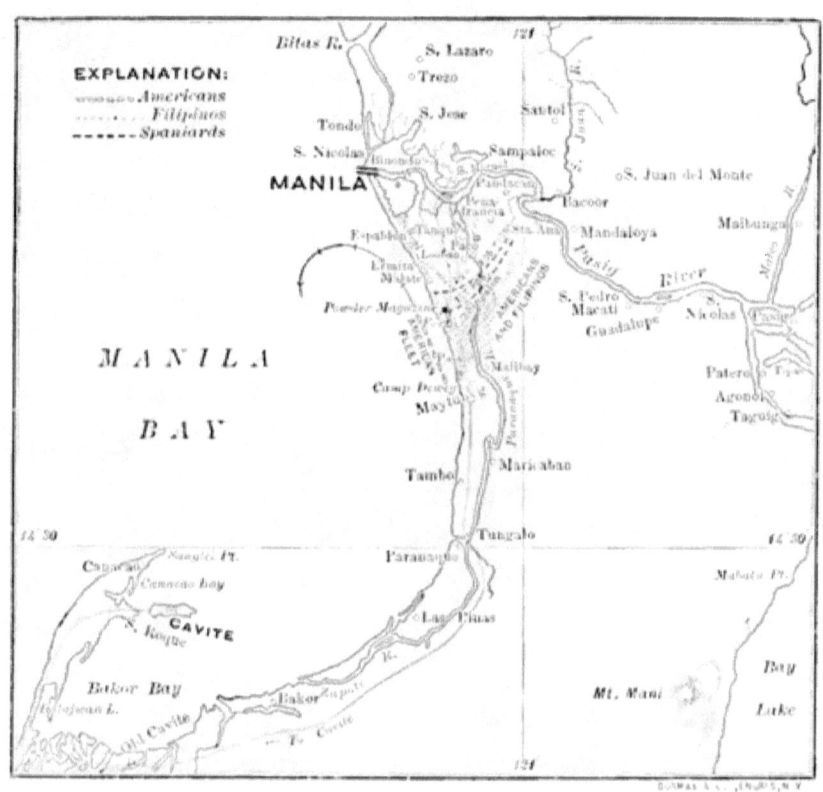

MAP OF THE BATTLE OF MANILA

necessary to get this intervening line out of the way. General Merritt, as clear on this point as Admiral Dewey, was wisely determined that he would recognize the insurgents in no way which could possibly involve the government of the United States. He was equally determined that he would have no military operations which depended in any degree upon them, and no joint military movements, the difficulties and perils of which he plainly foresaw. He therefore opened no communications with Aguinaldo, who had now reached such a point of pompous self-importance that he had not come to see the American commmander-in-chief upon the latter's arrival. This made it all the easier for General Merritt to ignore him, which was desirable, but did not clear the insurgent line away from the American front. The difficulty was solved by General Greene's inducing the insurgent brigade commander to move to the right, which did not commit us to anything, and gave us what we wanted—an unobstructed control of the roads necessary for the forward movement. With this point gained, General Greene, on July 29, advanced and took possession of the insurgent trenches with a battalion of regulars, another from the Colorado regiment, and a portion of the Utah battery. Finding the trenches weak and of bad construction, General Greene ordered another line constructed 100 yards further to the front, which was rapidly done during the night by the Colorado men. The line of intrenchments was short, not more than 270 yards in length, and on the right was protected only by some scattered barricades of the insurgents. Facing it, at close quarters now, were the stone fort, heavy intrenchments with seven guns, a block-house, which flanked the Americans on the right—all manned by regular soldiers, with abundant reserves in the city near at hand. The position was by no means a safe one, and the Spaniards, disturbed by the American advance, now beginning to press upon them, undertook to break up the intrenchments before they should be further strengthened or extended, and drive their approaching enemies back. They kept up a desultory firing upon our lines, as they had done with the insurgents, but it had been entirely harmless, and so long as our men kept under cover the bullets had spent themselves vainly against the earthworks or flown high and wide through the air. On the night of July 31, however, a serious and concerted effort was made to force our lines back. The night was intensely dark, a tropical storm was raging, and the rain was falling in torrents. In the blackness and noise of the storm it was almost impossible to know just what happened. The Tenth Pennsylvania was in the trenches, and when the Spanish fire increased in volume they began to reply to it, exposing themselves in doing so. Then their outposts came in with a report of a Spanish advance, and although the outposts of regulars staid where they were through the night, there can be little doubt that the enemy came forward, and also tried to flank us from the block-house and on our exposed right. No circumstances could be imagined more trying for new troops, with an unseen enemy firing heavily, an utter impossiblity of seeing or hearing anything, and a welter of confusion caused by storm and darkness. But the Pennsylvanians fired vigorously, and their reserves, brought up through the

zone of fire in rear of the firing line, suffered not a little. The Utah and regular artillery stood their ground undisturbed, served their guns steadily and efficiently, and held the Spaniards in check. Nothing could have been better than their behavior. General Greene, informed of what was occurring by some excited and not over-accurate messengers, sent forward to the trenches the California regiment and the Third artillery, supported by the First Colorado, who were to stop just out of range. The Californians and the artillery suffered in crossing the open ground in rear of the trenches, but went steadily forward, and by the time they reached the firing line the Spanish fire was slackening and the attack had been repulsed. The firing, which soon after ceased, was renewed in the morning about nine o'clock, but was without effect. In this night assault the American loss reached 10 killed and 43 wounded, but despite the most trying conditions, after the first excitement and confusion our men stood their ground coolly; and the heavy fire of the infantry, and especially of the Utah and regular artillery, proved too much for the Spaniards, whose attempt failed completely. Many Spanish dead and wounded were carried into Manila, but what their actual loss was it is impossible to determine, as even their wild official reports are lacking in this instance.

The Americans naturally held their line, but General Greene, feeling that the right flank could no longer be left as it was, weak and exposed, opened a new line of trenches, which were rapidly extended for 1,200 yards from the bay to the Pasay road. This was a strong line and well protected on both flanks, but the work both of making the trenches and of holding them was severe in the extreme. The incessant rain washed away the parapets, which could only be sustained by bags of earth. In the trenches themselves there were two feet of water, but the men worked away effectively and rapidly without complaint. They had also, as an accompaniment to their labors, constant firing from the Spanish lines. Sometimes it was heavy and concerted. At other times it was desultory, but any man working in the trenches who showed his head above the parapet was likely to be shot. When the firing became heavy the Utah battery would reply; and if it was thought that the Spaniards were coming out, the infantry would join in. The heaviest firing came on August 5, when the Spaniards opened at seven o'clock and kept it up until ten, and the Americans replied vigorously and effectively. Our loss was 3 killed and 7 wounded, but beyond this the whole of the Spanish firing was utterly futile. It was their appproved method of conducting war in Cuba, and, as it now seemed, everywhere else; but although it had no results, and was pitifully useless as a substitute for fighting, it was none the less annoying to men in trenches who were not yet ready to advance, because the commanders meant to take the city, if possible, without regular assault. So it was decided to put a stop to the Spanish firing, and word was sent, on August 7, that if there was not an end to it the ships would bombard. Thereupon silence fell upon the Spanish lines, and no more shots were fired in the American direction until the general and final advance began, a week later.

At no time would the Spaniards have failed to comply with any reasonable request backed by a suggestion

of bombardment, but now the threat had a deeper meaning than ever before. The third expedition, which followed General Merritt, arrived on July 31, the day of the fight at Malate, and brought nearly 5,000 officers and men—a powerful re-enforcement. But the arrival which was most impressive, and which at once changed the situation in a very important manner, occurred on August 4. The new-comer was eagerly expected, and every American was on the lookout for the arrival which meant so much. Officers in the yard of the arsenal at Cavité heard the men on the walls cry out: "There she comes!" "There's the *Monterey!*" Hastily climbing up, they looked forth toward the harbor entrance, and it was true—there indeed was the *Monterey.* Leaving San Diego on June 11 she had toiled across the Pacific slowly, not being built for such wide seafaring, and here she was at last safe and sound. Lying low in the water, she was not very fair to see; but she was clad in armor, and four 12-inch guns looked out from her turrets, altogether a very formidable ship for the smooth waters of Manila bay. To Admiral Dewey, facing armored ships with nothing but unarmored cruisers, and quite prepared to give a good account of himself against any odds, the coming of the *Monterey* was worth many regiments, and the balance of naval power began to come down toward his side. The meaning of the *Monterey* was easily understood—and by others than the Americans. The morning after her arrival, officers looking at the line of foreign war-ships thought there had been some change. They counted, and found that in truth there had been a change, for one or two of them had slipped off in the night. So they gradually departed until only a proper force for observation remained, and the German squadron, with its interference and ill-concealed threats and insolence, was reduced to suitable proportions. The *Monterey* had demonstrated once more Nelson's famous saying— that his fighting-ships were the best negotiators in Europe.

With all danger of foreign meddling gone, with more than ten thousand soldiers on shore, and with the *Monterey* lying low and menacing alongside the American cruisers, Admiral Dewey and General Merritt felt that the time had come to bring matters to a conclusion and take possession of the city, which had been won on the 1st of May. On August 7 the American commanders notified the Spanish general-in-chief that after the expiration of forty-eight hours they might attack the defences of Manila, and that they sent the notice in order to enable non-combatants to leave the city. Augustin the truculent, the maker of the proclamation which described Dewey and his men as the "excrescences of civilization" who were about to cast down altars and carry off wives and virgins, had slipped away under orders from Madrid, it is said, when the decisive moment drew near; with German aid getting safely off, and leaving General Jaudenes to face the inevitable. That officer now replied to the American communication, expressing his thanks, but declaring that he was unable, owing to the presence of the insurrectionary forces, to find a place of refuge for the women and children under his care. It was a manly letter, not without a note of pathos hidden under the polite and ceremonious words. His opponents were quite as anxious as he to avoid extremi-

WESLEY MERRITT

ties if they could; and so, two days later, they again
wrote to General Jaudenes, asking for the surrender of
Manila. They pointed out the hopelessness of his situation which made surrender consistent with honor,
the useless sacrifice of life which an attack and bombardment would cause, and expressed the earnest desire to spare the women and children and the wounded
from all the perils which might ensue. The Governor-
General, who, it is reported, had been appointed because Augustin wanted to surrender unconditionally,
replied with a refusal of the American demands, and
then asked for time to consult his government. This
General Merritt and Admiral Dewey very properly refused. Through the Belgian consul they sent a message that if the heavy batteries along the water-front
kept silent they would not shell the city, but Manila
they meant to have. It was also clear that the Spaniards were really ready to surrender, but that their
honor or their politics or something demanded a fight
and a show of force. They so clung to shams and so
shrank from realities that, although they meant to surrender, they were determined to have an attack made
upon them; and the American general, equally determined to have an end to the business, ordered an attack
on August 13.

The ships left their anchorage at Cavité early in the
morning. As they got under way and the *Olympia*
moved off, the English band on the *Immortalité* struck
up "See, the Conquering Hero Comes," and then, as
the battle-flags broke out on the fighting fleet, the English band played the "Star-Spangled Banner," and the
cheers of the American seamen rang strong and clear

across the water. As the American ships drew away, the English followed them a little further out, and when they came to their old anchorage near the Pasig river, the French and Germans got under way too. The German flag-ship steamed down behind the *Concord*, so that a high shot from Manila aimed at the latter might easily have struck her, and thereupon the *Immortalité* came in between the German and the American, and stopped. The hint was not lost. The Germans and French remained near Manila, while the English and Japanese were grouped on the American side; and with this arrangement the closing act of the drama went forward.

It was after nine o'clock when the *Olympia*, followed by the *Petrel* and *Raleigh*, and with the *Callao* near in, opened on the Malate forts. For the first few minutes the shots fell short. Then the squalls of mist and rain passed away, the range, which was now seen to be erroneous, was readjusted, and what General Merritt called "a hot and accurate fire of heavy shells and rapid-fire projectiles" was poured upon the forts. The Utah battery also opened, and at half past ten the ships, on signal, ceased firing, the infantry were let loose, and the skirmish-line of General Greene's brigade rushed into the powder-magazine fort and the trenches, which they found deserted. Up went the American flag, and, as the troops went forward, they were met by a second line of defence and a sharp fire. The Americans replied with volleys, subduing the Spanish fire, and then advanced steadily through the streets of Malate, with only some straggling shots from the direction of Paco. Passing through Malate and then Er-

RESISTANCE FROM THE HOUSES IN MALATE

mita, they emerged on the open space at the Luneta, to see the white flag over the walled city. As General Greene rode forward under a heavy fire he came upon a thousand Spanish troops—those who had been shooting from the Paco road, but had now stopped. Detaining their commander, General Greene sent the Spanish soldiers into the walled city, and then halted his men in such a position that, if there were any more fighting, he might be in a position to rush the gates.

Meantime General MacArthur, advancing along the Pasay road, had encountered a sharper resistance and met with a more serious loss; for the Spaniards there, well out of range of the ships, made a better stand. After an artillery engagement which silenced two Spanish guns in the Spanish battery, and hearing the cheers of Greene's men on the left, the brigade advanced and had a sharp action at the village of Singalon, where the enemy vigorously defended a blockhouse. The ground was difficult and the advance slow; but the men were well handled and fought well, so that at the end of an hour and a half the Spanish, yielding before the steady pressure, retreated; the Americans followed, and, passing through the Paco district, entered the city.

In this advance of the two brigades upon the city General Greene lost 1 killed and 6 wounded, and General MacArthur 4 killed and 37 wounded. What loss their opposition suffered does not appear to have been ascertained or reported. But the price paid was not a heavy one for the great city which fell into the hands of the Americans and which the Spanish would not yield without an actual attack. It is obvious, from the fig-

ures, that the resistance was neither serious nor pro-
longed, and there is no doubt that it might have been
both. The Spanish had 13,000 good troops, nearly all
regulars, and 22,000 stand of arms. Their intrenchments, supported by block-houses and forts, were excellent and formidable, while in front of the old city and
on the Luneta they are said to have had more than seventy heavy modern rifled guns. Here was abundant
material for a desperate defence, which, if made, would
have cost the Americans many lives and the utter destruction of the city.

No such defence was attempted, and the reasons are
obvious. In the first place, the Spaniards had been deprived of any hope of final escape by the victory of May
1, and by the manner in which Admiral Dewey firmly
held and controlled the bay, thus cutting them off from
all prospect of assistance. In the second place, they
were well aware that if they forced the final test the
American fleet, now strengthened by the *Monterey*,
would wreck and destroy the city, and that under those
conditions the American troops could not be withstood.
They might kill many of their foes, they would lose
many themselves, and the end would always be the
same. But there was another and still more convincing
reason than any of these. The long years of tyranny,
oppression, and torture were ready at last to exact their
compensation. All about Manila were the insurgent
bands, with bitter wrongs to avenge, half-civilized people raised now into very deadly activity by the coming
of the new conqueror, and watching eagerly for the opportunity to settle certain long outstanding accounts.
These native people wanted to kill and plunder. A de-

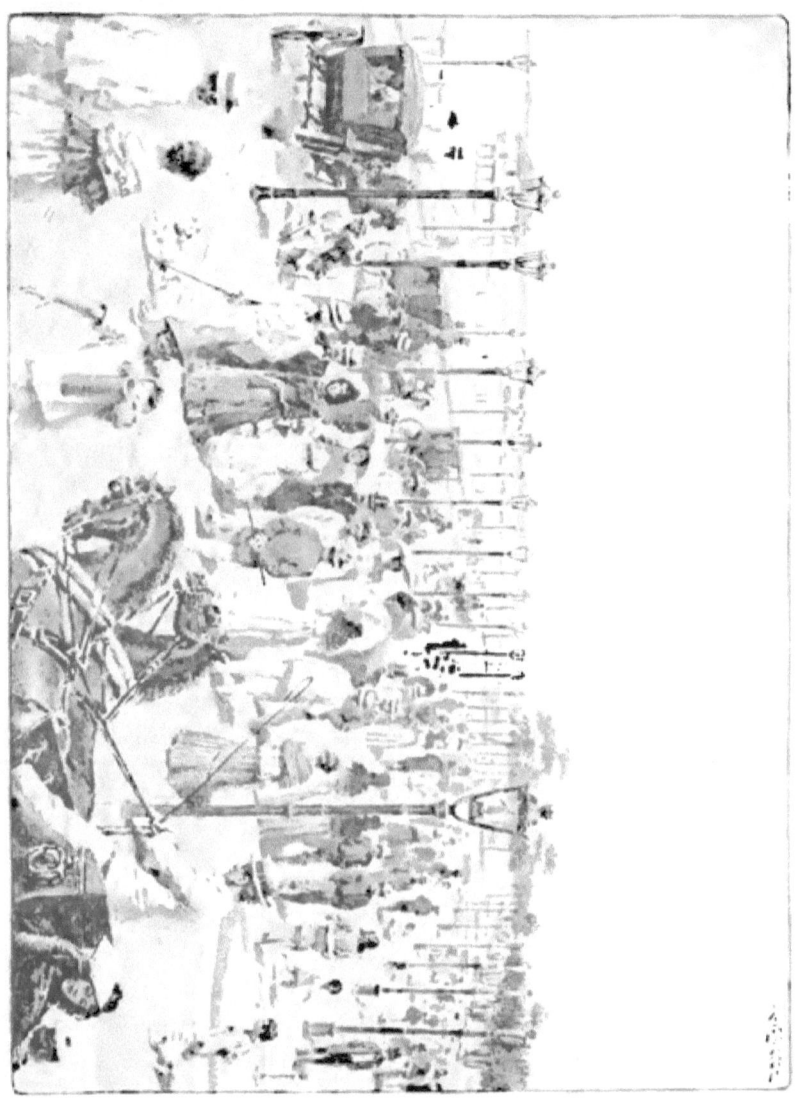

termined resistance meant a bombardment with a fierce
assault by the American troops, and when they rushed
in, there behind them, uncontrollable in the confusion
of a stormed and shattered city, would come the insurgents with pillage, bloodshed, and fire in their train.
The Spaniards shrank from such a prospect, for they
knew the insurgents, and they also knew what they
had done to these people now in arms. The only escape was through the Americans, who would protect
them and the city and curb the insurgents. So the
white flag went up soon after the naval fire ceased, and
then Lieutenant Brumby, representing the admiral, and
Colonel Whittier, representing the general, went in and
held a conference. General Greene went in also at the
head of his troops, and General Merritt came ashore.
They passed through the plaza, crowded with Spanish soldiers, found General Jaudenes in a chapel of the
cathedral, and there the capitulation was signed and the
city surrendered. The Oregon troops brought up by
water from Cavité landed through the surf and
marched up the Luenta. While they were advancing,
Lieutenant Brumby and his men hauled down the Spanish standard from the big flag-staff in front of the walls.
As the great banner came down, the Americans were
silent and the crowd looked on wondering, some of
the Spaniards among them shedding tears. Then there
rose in its place a flag brought from the *Olympia*. Up
it went, and then broke out before the breeze, the sun
coming through a rift in the clouds and shining bright
upon it. The marching Oregon troops saw it, their
cheers rang out, and their band sent the strains of "The
Star-Spangled Banner" floating down the promenade.

The ships saw it too, and the national salute pealed out from the guns of the *Olympia*. The emblem of what had been done was at last in place. Meantime, the realities were going on elsewhere in the surrounded city, where General Merritt, in the palace of a long line of Spanish governors, was taking possession of the treasure and the arms, and preparing the way for the government of Manila. Other realities were the entrance of Greene's and MacArthur's men through streets lined with Spanish soldiers, neither sullen nor revengeful, but glad that it was all finished, and that the days of useless fighting and of wasted lives were over. Still other realities were the American troops posted at the bridges and approaches to the city, holding back the insurgents, forbidding their entrance entirely, determined that there should be no pillage, no slaughter, no burning, nothing to dim or sully the fine record which had run on without fleck or stain from the May day of the victory. It was all very simple. There was very little pomp and parade. The navy of the United States were masters of the great bay. The soldiers of the United States—the highly trained regulars, the hardy volunteers from the States of the West and Northwest where half a century ago was only wilderness—held the city. Their general was in the palace, their flag fluttered on the Luenta. That was all. Yet under the simple facts were many meanings. The empire which Magellan had found for Spain in the East had passed away forever. Unfit to rule, she had been expelled at last from the Western Hemisphere. Unfit to rule, the war which she had drawn down upon her own head had driven her also from the East, and a new flag and

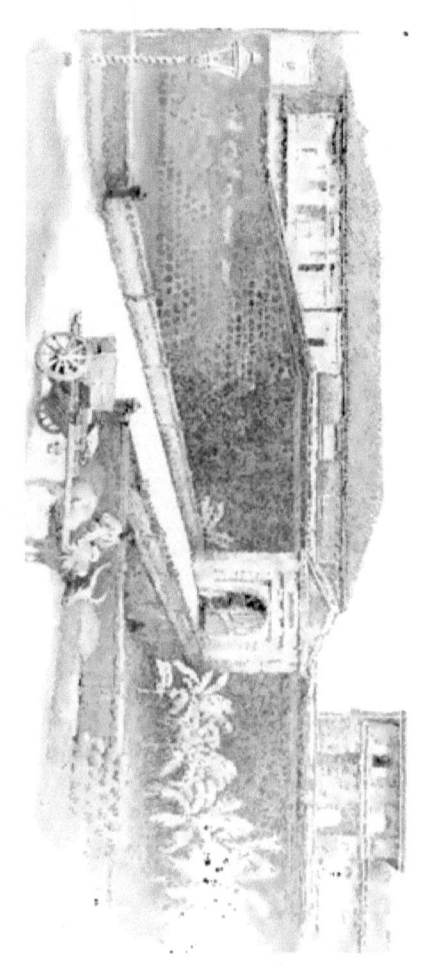

a new power in their onward march had risen up in
the Orient. The youngest of nations had come again
to the edge of that marvelous region, the cradle of the
race, whence the Aryans had moved westward so very
long ago.

CHAPTER XI

How peace came

More fortunate than the generals and the troops of Puerto Rico, Admiral Dewey and General Merritt, thanks to distance and a severed cable, were able to complete their work and set the final crown upon their labors by taking Manila before the order reached them to cease hostilities. That order, when it came, found them masters of the great Eastern city they had fought to win. In Puerto Rico the news stayed Schwan's cavalry in pursuit of the Spaniards, Brooke's gunners with the lanyards in their hands, and halted the other columns in their march over the island. In Cuba it saved Manzanillo, just falling before the guns of Goodrich and his little squadron, and checked the movements which were bringing port after port into American possession. It stopped also the departure of a fleet which, by its existence and intention, was a potent cause of the coming of peace. Even before the battle of the 3d of July the department at Washington was making ready to send a fleet consisting of the *Iowa*, *Oregon*, *Yankee*, *Yosemite*, and *Dixie*, under Commodore Watson in the flag-ship *Newark*, direct to Spain, primarily to fight the fleet of Admiral Camara, which had wandered helplessly across the Mediterranean with vague outgivings about going to Manila, but which merely went through

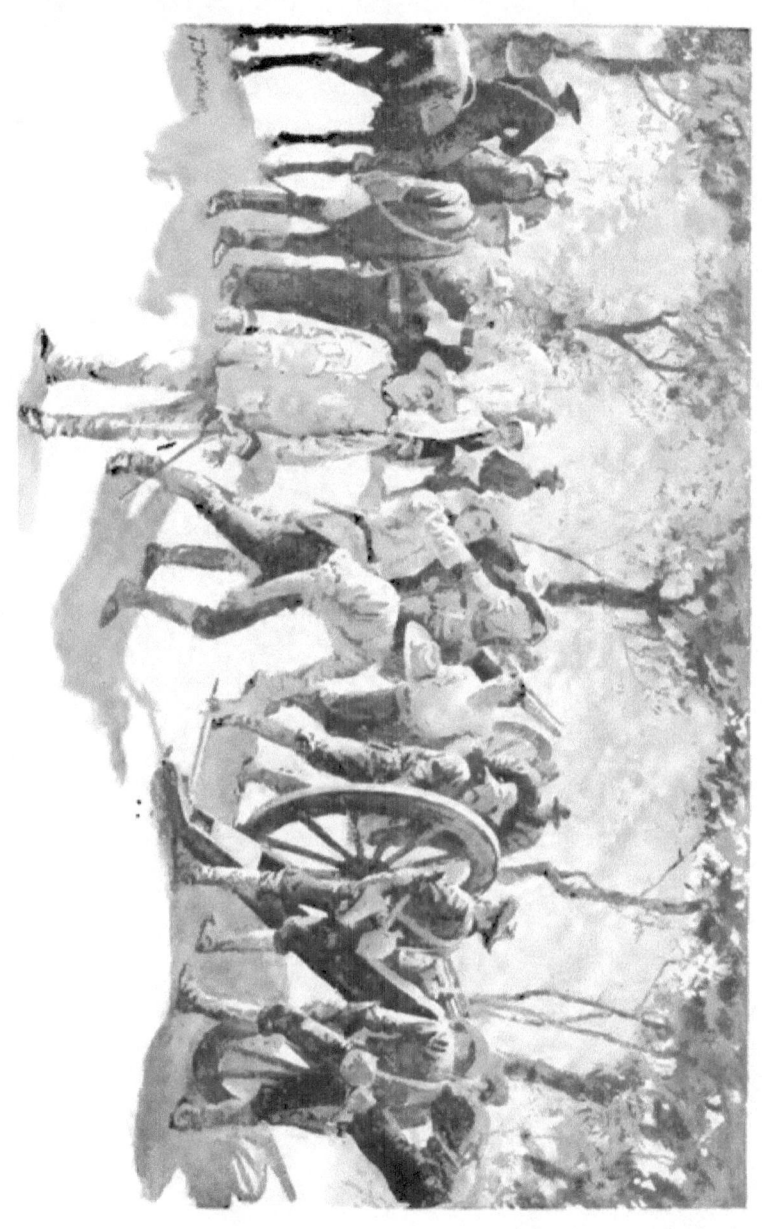

the Suez Canal, and then turned round and came back again. But after the battle of July 3 the preparations of Commodore Watson's squadron were pushed more energetically than ever, re-enforcements were prepared, and it was known that it was to cross the Atlantic in any event, and carry war to the very doors of Spain's coast cities. This fact was soon as well known in Europe as in America. Presently it became clear that Watson's fleet was no pretence, but a very grim reality; that it was nearly in readiness; and finally that it was on the very eve of departure. What American ships and seamen could do had just been shown at Manila and Santiago, and there was no reason to suppose that they would be less effective on the Spanish coast. Spain did not like the prospect, and some of her neighbors were as averse as she to the sound of American guns in the Mediterranean, not heard in those waters now for nearly a century. It would be something new, something which might disturb concerts and Bunds and other excellent arrangements, and must not be permitted. It became clear to the diplomatic mind that Spain must make peace and make it at once, on any terms. Hence arose what is politely called pressure, although poor Spain did not need much pressing. The war which she had forced—no one knows exactly for what reason—for what she called her pride or her point of honor, had resulted in a series of rapid, crushing, and unbroken defeats. She had expected, perhaps, to make a stand, to win a fight, somewhere; but her whole system, her entire body politic, was rottener than any one dreamed, and the whole fabric went to pieces like an egg-shell when struck by the hand of a vigorous, enterprising enemy. Her sea power was shattered and entirely gone in the Pacific and in American waters. Manila bay was in the hands of Dewey, and the surrender of the city waited only for his demand. Cuba could not be relieved; Santiago province was in American hands, and the rest of the island would go the same way as fast as the United States could land troops and capture ports. Puerto Rico was half gone, and the American columns were marching as rapidly as possible to complete conquest of the island. And then there in the background was Watson's fleet, very imminent now, and likely to be off Cadiz or Barcelona in a fortnight.

Clearly it was high time for peace, and on July 22 the Duke of Almodovar del Rio, Minister of State, transmitted through M. Cambon a letter to the President, asking if it were not possible to terminate hostilities, and confessing to the defeats which Spain had suffered, and the unequal character of the struggle in which she was engaged. This letter reached the President on July 26, and four days later Mr. Day, Secretary of State, made reply. He said that the President was anxious to end the war, and disposed to deal most generously with a brave adversary. He then laid down the American conditions, which were absolutely essential by their preliminary acceptance to any negotiations for a peace. These terms were—first, relinquishment by Spain of all claim of sovereignty over Cuba, and the immediate evacuation of that island; second—the President, in a spirit of generosity, not wishing to demand any pecuniary indemnity—the immediate cession to the United States of Puerto Rico, all other West Indian islands, and an island in the Ladrones to be selected by

the United States; third, that the United States should
hold and occupy the city and bay of Manila pending
the conclusion of a treaty of peace which should determine "the control, disposition, and government of the
Philippines." On August 7 the Duke of Almodovar
del Rio replied, accepting with many words, but still
accepting, the first two conditions, and answering the
third demand in a manner which might be taken as an
acceptance or not, but which was evidently designed to
open up discussion and controversy. But Mr. Day had
had recently a thorough if brief schooling in Spanish
diplomatic correspondence, and he had no idea of involving himself or his government in further debate of
any kind. Spain was to accept our demands or war
was to go on. The day of words, of phrases, and of
language generally had passed away in the smoke of
war, and now, if war was to cease, it was to be Yes or
No. So, with admirable decision and great cleverness
and ability, Mr. Day decided that the Spanish note
was a plain acceptance of our terms, and nothing else.
He accordingly wrote to M. Cambon, on August 10,
and to this effect, added that any lack of explic-
itness in the Duke's note being due undoubtedly,
to errors in transmission, or in the translation of
the cipher, he proposed to end all doubts and avoid
all misunderstandings by inviting M. Cambon to
sign, on behalf of Spain, a protocol embodying
in precise terms the three demands of the letter
of July 30, and three other articles providing for
the method of evacuating Cuba and Puerto Rico, for
the appointment of commissioners to negotiate a treaty
of peace, and for the cessation of hostilities on the sign-

ing of the protocol. No room any more for explanations and notes and arguments. War or the protocol, that was the choice. Spain at last had been brought, by her refusal to admit truth, face to face with an ugly reality from which there was no escape. Shams and falsehoods and large language were of no use here before the fact which could not be hidden any longer, and she authorized M. Cambon to sign the protocol. The signing took place at Washington, on August, 12, and hostilities ceased.

This was the practical end of active war, but it was only a truce or an armistice. The war was not ended or over, and could not be until a treaty was concluded. For this work, under the provisions of the protocol, the President appointed Mr. Day, who resigned the Secretaryship of State, Senator Davis of Minnesota, Senator Frye of Maine, Senator Gray of Delaware, and the Honorable Whitelaw Reid commissioners on the part of the United States, to negotiate a treaty of peace at Paris. The Spanish government appointed a like commission, headed by Don Eugenio Montero Rios, the president of the Senate, and a very learned and able lawyer of high distinction. The commissioners of both governments met in Paris on October 1, and exchanged their powers. The negotiations then began, and lasted until December 10, when the treaty was signed. The Spaniards struggled hard and resisted stoutly. All Europe was with them in sympathy, and especially France and Germany. The Americans were doing their work in a hostile atmosphere, with no friendly nation near except England, and they did it in a way which added another triumph to the annals of American diplomacy.

JULES CAMBON

The French Ambassador who signed the peace protocol on behalf of Spain

They were all men of the highest distinction, of experience, and tried ability, and they not only met the Spanish arguments strongly and thoroughly, but they conducted their difficult task without stumbling or error. There was a contest over the Cuban and other debts, which called forth much discussion, and a most successful parrying of all the Spanish efforts to secure for those debts some recognition or some acceptance by the United States. There was also discussion on some minor points, but the question upon which the real conflict turned, and which soon overshadowed everything else, was the Philippines. Dewey's victory had come with the shock of a great surprise as well as the splendor of a great glory. No one had dreamed that the war meant the entrance of the United States into the Orient. But there the flag was, there it fluttered victorious, and the stream of events, so much more powerful than human plannings when they are the outcome of world forces, moved relentlessly on. Dewey must be supported and relieved. So a ship and some troops went to him. Then it was clear that they were inadequate, and more ships and more troops followed across the Pacific. They could not be there for nothing. Manila must be taken, and so it was taken before news of the protocol could reach that distant place with its cut cable. Hostilities ceased, and we held Manila in our grasp. No one would have consented to give up that city and its noble harbor—the prize and pearl of the East. But if we were to retain Manila, the scene of Dewey's victory, which the American people would never surrender, were we to hold it alone and nothing else, surrounded by territory in other hands, with all the burdens and perils which such a situation implied. We must hold Manila, and if Manila, then the only possible thing was to hold the island of Luzon as well. That was as far as the President or the mass of the American people had gone when the commissioners sailed for Paris in September. Some members of the commission were utterly opposed to the retention of the Philippines or any considerable portion of any one of them. But when they settled down to work, when the inexorable demand for action came upon them, when they could no longer speculate upon possibilities without responsibility, as their fellow-citizens at home could do, then the question broadened and deepened, and began to settle itself and burn away all doubts, as great questions have a way of doing. The stream of events was running on in the same inevitable fashion. Those who had rejoiced in the rush of the current, and those who tried to stem it, alike went with it. The forces which had been let loose by the Spanish war were world forces, and they presented their arguments with the grim silence and the unforgiving certainty of fate. Will you go away and leave the Filipinos to Spain, they asked, leave them to a tyranny and oppression tenfold worse than that in Cuba which carried you into the war? Clearly impossible. Will you force Spain out of the islands, and then, having destroyed the only government and the only sovereignty which have ever existed there, will you depart yourselves and leave the islands to anarchy and bloodshed, to sanguinary dictatorship, and to the quick seizure of European powers and a possible world-wide war over the spoils? Again clearly impossible. Again no thoroughfare.

PUERTA DE ESPAÑA, FROM THE CHURCH OF SANTO DOMINGO

Again a proposition which no strong, high-spirited people could entertain. Will you, then, call in the other powers of the earth to help you settle the question of these islands, determine their destiny, and establish a government for their people? Once more, no. Such a solution is incompatible with decent pride and honest self-respect, and could lead only to mischief and confusion, to wars and rumors of wars. What then will you do? Is there aught you can do but replace the sovereignty you have dashed down, and with your own sovereignty meet the responsibilities which have come to you in the evolution of the time, and take yourselves the islands you have won? Quite clearly now the answer comes that no other course is possible. The American commissioners heard in all this, as the great master of music heard in the first bars of his immortal symphony, "the hand of fate knocking at the door." Some of them had always believed in this outcome, some had not, but all became absolutely convinced that there was but one road possible, and so they demanded all the Philippines from Spain, and made the demand an ultimatum. The Spaniards struggled hard. They disputed our right to make the demand under the terms of the protocol; they argued and resisted; they threatened to break off the negotiations; and then they yielded, because they could do nothing else. This done, the treaty was soon made, and it was an admirable instrument, a masterpiece in every respect. No loop-hole was left for any claim for debts or aught else; no words could be found which could be strained to bind the United States in any way in the future. The American commissioners came home with a triumphant treaty, a very fit result of an entirely victorious war.

Much dispute and opposition have arisen among people successful in war in times past, and will rise again, over treaties of peace, but such opposition has always proceeded on the ground that the victor nation received too little. The treaty of the United States with Spain, signed in Paris on December 10, 1898, has the unique distinction of having excited opposition and attack among the victors because it secured too much and was too triumphant. An organization called by the strange name of the Anti-Imperialist League was formed in the Eastern States. Some men who had once been eminent in politics gave their names to its support, and others who felt that they ought to be eminent in politics gave it their services. A vigorous crusade was begun, but the popular response in the way of the easily signed petition was surprisingly small for the good sense of the American people made two points clear to them. One was that a peace treaty ought to be ratified, the other that they had won these new possessions, and had no doubt that they could trust themselves to deal with them honestly, ably, and for their own truest and best interests, as well as for those of the people of all the islands. A failure in the field of popular discussion before the people and in the newspapers, the fight against the treaty was transferred to the Senate of the United States.

The constitutional provision which requires a vote of two-thirds of the Senate to ratify a treaty simplifies the work of opposition to ratification. It seemed incredible at first that a treaty of peace could possibly

MOUTH OF THE PASIG RIVER, FROM THE CHURCH OF SANTO DOMINGO

be defeated. Party lines were not drawn on the question, and it was at first supposed that resistance to the ratification of the treaty would be confined to a very few Senators, who had been opposed to the movement in favor of the Cubans, as well as to the entrance into war, and were now consistently opposed to its results. But as time went on the necessities of factions in the Democratic party developed an opposition which included a majority of the Democratic Senators, and this made the minority formidably large—nearly one-third of the Senate, if not in excess of it. It is not needful to trace in detail the course of the debate, which from the side of opposition proceeded on three lines—lack of constitutional power to acquire and hold the Philippines, the violation of the principles of the Declaration of Independence involved in doing so, and sympathy and admiration for the Filipinos, feelings as profound as they were rapid in growth. The friends of ratification took the very simple ground that the treaty committed the United States to no policy, but left them free to do exactly as seemed best with all the islands, that the American people could be safely intrusted with this grave responsibility, and that patriotism and common-sense alike demanded the end of war and the re-establishment of peace, which could only be effected by the adoption of the treaty. The contest was earnest and bitter, the canvass energetic to a degree never seen in the Senate, and the result close. When the Senate went into executive session on Monday, February 6, with the time for the vote fixed for three o'clock, the treaty had only 58 sure votes, 60 being needed for ratification; the opposition had 29 sure votes, and the remaining 3 were doubtful. At half past two one of the doubtful voters was declared to be for the treaty, making 59. Just before three o'clock another vote was promised, and the third doubtful vote was given to the treaty after the roll had been called. The final vote stood 57 to 27—including the pairs, 61 to 29, just two-thirds and one vote to spare. It had been a heated struggle. Opinion as to the outcome had fluctuated, even among those best informed, down to the last moment. Yet as one looks back when all is done, it seems clear that no other result was possible. The responsibility which had come to the American people with the flash of Dewey's guns on May 1 could not be avoided, and the American people were too strong, too high-spirited, too confident, to run away from it. The hand of fate was knocking at the door of the Senate as it had knocked at the door of the American commissioners in Paris. To that knock all doors fly open, and to the stern visitant without but one answer could be given.

Nothing remained after the end of the conflict in the Senate but the exchange of ratifications, which took place on April 11, 1899, and so the war ended. Its causes lie far back in the history and character of nations. Its immediate results were as striking as they were important and full of meaning. What the more distant outcome of these results will be in the future years no man can tell. We can only say with certainty that they will be far reaching and momentous. The war was brief, but it served to let loose forces which had long been gathering strength, and to complete movements which had been going on for centuries. For

THE CATHEDRAL, MANILA

three hundred years the conflict between the English-speaking people on the one side, and the French and Spanish on the other, for the control of the New World, had been in progress. France went down in 1760, the last vestige of Spanish power was swept away by the war of 1898. The result was inevitable, and the English-speaking people owned at last one-half of the New World, and had shut out Europe from all control in the other half or in the great islands of the West Indies.*

Thus were the immediate object and purpose of the war achieved in fulfilment of the irresponsible conflict of centuries between races, systems, and beliefs inherently antagonistic. But war is a fire, and when it begins no one can tell where it will stop or what it will burn away. The only thing we can be quite sure of is that war, once entered upon, cannot be limited, and may produce results of which no man dreamed at the outset. This war, merely as such, was not only short, but was far from being a large or extensive one. Yet it suddenly made clear many things not realized before, and brought forth unimagined results. For thirty years the people of the United States had been binding up the wounds and trying to efface the scars of their great and terrible Civil War. They knew that they had done much, they felt that the old passions had softened and were dying. The war came, and in the twinkling of an eye, in a flash of burning, living light, they suddenly saw that the long task was done, that the land was really one again without rent or seam, and men

---

*The remaining Danish, Dutch, and French possessions are too small to constitute an exception to the general proposition.

rejoiced mightily in their hearts with this knowledge which the new war had brought.

For thirty years the people of the United States had been absorbed in the development of their great heritage. They had been finishing the conquest of their continent, and binding all parts of it together with the tracks and highways of commerce. Once this work was complete, it was certain that the virile, ambitious, enterprising race which had done it would look abroad beyond their boundaries and seek to guard and extend their interests in other parts of the world. The work was done, but they did not realize it. Even the Venezuela intervention, a pure manifestation of the new spirit and the new time, did not make it clear to them. Then the war note rang through the land, and with dazzled eyes at first, and then with ever clearer and steadier gaze, they saw that in the years of isolation and self-absorption they had built up a great world power, that they must return to the ocean which they had temporarily abandoned, and have their share in the trade of every country and the commerce of every sea. Suddenly came the awakening to the great fact that they had founded an empire on their Western coasts, that they held one side of the Pacific, and could not longer be indifferent to the fate of the other side in the remote East. Now they read with instructed vision the prophecy of Seward, which foretold that the future course of trade and empire would lie in the Pacific. They knew at last that the stream of Eastern trade, which for centuries had flowed to the West, building up great cities and enriching nations as it passed from Byzantium to Venice, from Venice to Portugal, and from Portugal to Hol-

ESCOLLA, MANILA

land and to London, was now to be divided, and in part, at least, to pour eastward over the Pacific. Now men saw that the long connection, ever growing closer, with the Hawaiian Islands had not been chance; that the culmination of the annexation movement in the very year of the Spanish War was not accident, but that it all came from the instinct of the race, which paused in California only to learn that its course was still westward, and that Americans, and no one else, must be masters of the cross-roads of the Pacific.

But while the United States had moved so slowly for half a century toward Hawaii, the work of one May morning carried them on to the Philippines and made them an Eastern power. Whatever the final disposition of the islands, whether we hold and govern much or little, our flag is there, our footing has been made, and in the East we shall remain, because we are entitled to, and will surely have, our share of the great commerce with the millions of China, from whom we shall refuse to be shut out.

One other great result of the war, like the last a world result. We found in the trial of war who were our enemies in Europe, and we saw that they were many. We also found who our friend was, not as a matter of sentiment or community of speech and thought, but on the firm and solid ground of common interests. In the brief crash of the short-lived Spanish war the English-speaking people came together. In the light of those eager, hurrying days we saw that the English fleets made any attack on Dewey, even by combined Europe, impossible; and England saw that so long as the United States was her friend her base on the

Atlantic was secure, her food-supply safe, and that all Europe in arms could not harm her. Very plain also did it become to all men that in the East, where England had been so long, and where we had just entered, the interests of both nations were identical in preserving China for equal trade to all.

All these things the war made clear and certain. What these new conditions may come to mean in the future no one now can safely say. But if that future is to bring the struggle which many men peering into the darkness foresee—a conflict between the Slav and so much of Europe as he can drag with him on the one side, and the English-speaking man on the other; between the military socialism of Russia and Germany and the individualism and freedom of the United States and England; between the power of the land and the sea power—then the future historian will date the opening of this new epoch and of this mighty conflict, at once economic and social, military and naval, from the war of 1898, which in three months overthrew the empire of Spain in the Antilles and the Philippines.

APPENDIX A

Joint resolution for the recognition of the independence of the people of Cuba, demanding that the Government of Spain relinquish its authority and government in the island of Cuba, and to withdraw its land
and naval forces from Cuba and Cuban waters, and directing the President of the United States to use the
land and naval forces of the United States to carry
these resolutions into effect.

Whereas the abhorrent conditions which have existed for more than three years in the island of Cuba, so
near our own borders, have shocked the moral sense of
the people of the United States, have been a disgrace
to Christian civilization, culminating as they have, in
the destruction of a United States battle ship, with two
hundred and sixty-six of its officers and crew, while on
a friendly visit in the harbor of Havana, and can not
longer be endured, as has been set forth by the President of the United States in his message to Congress
of April eleventh, eighteen hundred and ninety-eight,
upon which the action of Congress was invited: Therefore,

*Resolved by the Senate and House of Representatives
of the United States of America in Congress assembled,*

237

First. That the people of the island of Cuba are, and of right ought to be, free and independent.

Second. That it is the duty of the United States to demand, and the Government of the United States does hereby demand, that the Government of Spain at once relinquish its authority and government in the island of Cuba and withdraw its land and naval forces from Cuba and Cuban waters.

Third. That the President of the United States be, and he hereby is, directed and empowered to use the entire land and naval forces of the United States, and to call into the actual service of the United States the militia of the several States, to such extent as may be necessary to carry these resolutions into effect.

Fourth. That the United States hereby disclaims any disposition or intention to exercise sovereignty, jurisdiction, or control over said island except for the pacification thereof, and asserts its determination, when that is accomplished, to leave the government and control of the island to its people.

Approved, April 20, 1898.

DECLARATION OF WAR.

CHAP. 189.—An Act Declaring that war exists between the United States of America and the Kingdom of Spain.

Be it enacted by the Senate and House of Representatives of the United States of America in Congress assembled, First. That war be, and the same is hereby, declared to exist, and that war has existed since the twenty-first day of April, anno Domini eighteen hundred and ninety-eight, including said day, between the United States of America and the Kingdom of Spain.

Second. That the President of the United States be, and he hereby is, directed and empowered to use the entire land and naval forces of the United States, and to call into the actual service of the United States the militia of the several States, to such extent as may be necessary to carry this act into effect.

Approved, April 25, 1898.

APPENDIX B

PROCLAMATION OF THE PRESIDENT

By the President of the United States of America.

A PROCLAMATION.

Whereas, by a joint resolution passed by the Congress and approved April 20, 1898, and communicated to the Government of Spain, it was demanded that said Government at once relinquish its authority and government in the island of Cuba, and withdraw its land and naval forces from Cuba and Cuban waters; and the President of the United States was directed and empowered to use the entire land and naval forces of the United States, and to call into the actual service of the United States the militia of the several States to such extent as might be necessary to carry said resolution into effect; and

Whereas, in carrying into effect said resolution, the President of the United States deems it necessary to set on foot and maintain a blockade of the north coast of Cuba, including all ports on said coast between Cardenas and Bahia Honda and the port of Cienfuegos on the south coast of Cuba:

Now, therefore, I, William McKinley, President of the United States, in order to enforce the said resolution, do hereby declare and proclaim that the United

States of America have instituted, and will maintain a blockade of the north coast of Cuba, including ports on said coast between Cardenas and Bahia Honda and the port of Cienfuegos on the south coast of Cuba, aforesaid, in pursuance of the laws of the United States and the law of nations applicable to such cases. An efficient force will be posted so as to prevent the entrance and exit of vessels from the ports aforesaid. Any neutral vessel approaching any of said ports, or attempting to leave the same, without notice or knowledge of the establishment of such blockade, will be duly warned by the commander of the blockading forces, who will endorse on her register the fact, and the date, of such warning, where such endorsement was made; and if the same vessel shall again attempt to enter any blockaded port, she will be captured and sent to the nearest convenient port for such proceeding against her and her cargo as prize, as may be deemed advisable.

Neutral vessels lying in any of said ports at the time of the establishment of such blockade will be allowed thirty days to issue therefrom.

In witness whereof, I have hereunto set my hand and caused the seal of the United States to be affixed.

Done at the City of Washington, this 22d day of April, A. D. 1898, and of the Independence [SEAL] of the United States, the one hundred and twenty-second.

WILLIAM McKINLEY.

By the President:

JOHN SHERMAN,
Secretary of State.

[No. 5.]

By the President of the United States,

A PROCLAMATION.

Whereas a joint resolution of Congress was approved on the twentieth day of April, 1898, entitled "Joint Resolution For the recognition of the independ-"ence of the people of Cuba, demanding that the Gov-"ernment of Spain relinquish its authority and govern-"ment in the island of Cuba, and to withdraw its land "and naval forces from Cuba and Cuban waters, and "directing the President of the United States to use the "land and naval forces of the United States to carry "these resolutions into effect," and

Whereas, by an act of Congress entitled "An Act to "provide for temporarily Increasing the Military Es-"tablishment of the United States in time of war and "for other purposes," approved April 22, 1898; the President is authorized, in order to raise a volunteer army, to issue his proclamation calling for volunteers to serve in the army of the United States.

Now, therefore, I, William McKinley, President of the United States, by virtue of the power vested in me by the Constitution and the laws, and deeming sufficient occasion to exist, have thought fit to call forth and hereby do call forth, volunteers to the aggregate number of 125,000, in order to carry into effect the purpose of the said Resolution: the same to be apportioned, as far as practicable, among the several States and Territories and the District of Columbia, according to population, and to serve for two years, unless sooner discharged. The details for this object will be immediately communicated to the proper authorities through the War Department.

In witness whereof I have hereunto set my hand and caused the seal of the United States to be affixed.

Done at the City of Washington, this twenty-third day of April, A. D., 1898, and of the Independence of the United States the one hundred and twenty-second.

[SEAL]

WILLIAM McKINLEY.

By the President:
    JOHN SHERMAN,
        Secretary of State.

[No. 6.]

By the President of the United States of America,

A PROCLAMATION.

Whereas by an Act of Congress approved April 25, 1898, it is declared that war exists and that war has existed since the 21st day of April, A. D. 1898, including said day, between the United States of America and the Kingdom of Spain; and

Whereas, it being desirable that such war should be conducted upon principles in harmony with the present views of nations and sanctioned by their recent practice, it has already been announced that the policy of this Government will be not to resort to privateering, but to adhere to the rules of the Declaration of Paris;

Now, Therefore, I, William McKinley, President of

the United States of America, by virtue of the power vested in me by the Constitution and the laws, do hereby declare and proclaim:

1. The neutral flag covers enemy's goods, with the exception of contraband of war.

2. Neutral goods, not contraband of war, are not liable to confiscation under the enemy's flag.

3. Blockades in order to be binding must be effective.

4. Spanish merchant vessels, in any ports or places within the United States, shall be allowed till May 21, 1898, inclusive, for loading their cargoes and departing from such ports or places; and such Spanish merchant vessels, if met at sea by any United States ship, shall be permitted to continue their voyage, if, on examination of their papers, it shall appear that their cargoes were taken on board before the expiration of the above term; Provided, that nothing herein contained shall apply to Spanish vessels having on board any officer in the military or naval service of the enemy, or any coal (except such as may be necessary for their voyage), or any other article prohibited or contraband of war, or any despatch of or to the Spanish Government.

5. Any Spanish merchant vessel which, prior to April 21, 1898, shall have sailed from any foreign port bound for any port or place in the United States, shall be permitted to enter such port or place, and to discharge her cargo, and afterward forthwith to depart without molestation; and any such vessel, if met at sea by any United States ship, shall be permitted to continue her voyage to any port not blockaded.

6. The right of search is to be exercised with strict regard for the rights of neutrals, and the voyages of mail steamers are not to be interfered with except on the clearest grounds of suspicion of a violation of law in respect of contraband or blockade.

In witness whereof, I have hereunto set my hand and caused the seal of the United States to be affixed.

Done at the City of Washington, on the twenty-sixth day of April, in the year of our Lord one thousand eight hundred and ninety-eight, [SEAL] and of the Independence of the United States the one hundred and twenty-second.

WILLIAM MCKINLEY.

By the President:

ALVEY A. ADEE,
Acting Secretary of State.

By the President of the United States,

A PROCLAMATION.

Whereas an Act of Congress was approved on the twenty-fifth day of April, 1898, entitled "An Act Declaring that war exists between the United States of America and the Kingdom of Spain," and

Whereas, by an Act of Congress entitled "An Act to provide for temporarily increasing the Military Establishment of the United States in time of war and for other purposes," approved April 22, 1898; the President is authorized, in order to raise a volunteer army, to issue his proclamation calling for volunteers to serve in the army of the United States.

Now, Therefore, I, William McKinley, President of the United States, by virtue of the power vested in me by the Constitution and the laws, and deeming sufficient occasion to exist, have thought fit to call forth and hereby do call forth, volunteers to the aggregate number of 75,000 in addition to the volunteers called forth by my proclamation of the twenty-third of April, in the present year; the same to be apportioned, as far as practicable, among the several States and Territories and the District of Columbia, according to population, and to serve for two years, unless sooner discharged. The proportion of each arm and the details of enlistment and organization will be made known through the War Department.

In witness whereof I have hereunto set my hand and caused the seal of the United States to be affixed.

Done at the City of Washington, this twenty-fifth day of May, in the year of our Lord one thousand eight hundred and ninety-eight, [SEAL] and of the Independence of the United States the one hundred and twenty-second.

WILLIAM McKINLEY.

By the President:

WILLIAM R. DAY,
Secretary of State.

By the President of the United States of America,

A PROCLAMATION.

Whereas, for the reasons set forth in my Proclamation of April 22, 1898, a blockade of the ports on the northern coast of Cuba, from Cardenas to Bahia Honda, inclusive, and of the port of Cienfuegos, on the south coast of Cuba, was declared to have been instituted; and

Whereas, it has become desirable to extend the blockade to other Spanish ports:

Now, Therefore, I, William McKinley, President of the United States, do hereby declare and proclaim that, in addition to the blockade of the ports specified in my Proclamation of April 22, 1898, the United States of America has instituted and will maintain an effective blockade of all the ports on the south coast of Cuba, from Cape Frances to Cape Cruz, inclusive, and also of the port of San Juan, in the island of Porto Rico.

Neutral vessels lying in any of the ports to which the blockade is by the present Proclamation extended, will be allowed thirty days to issue therefrom, with cargo.

In witness whereof, I have hereunto set my hand, and caused the seal of the United States to be affixed.

Done at the City of Washington, this twenty-seventh day of June, A. D., 1898, and of the Independence of the United States the one hundred and twenty-second.

[SEAL]

WILLIAM MCKINLEY.

By the President:

J. B. MOORE,
Acting Secretary of State.

APPENDIX C

MESSAGE

OF THE

GOVERNMENT OF H. M. THE QUEEN REGENT OF
SPAIN, SUBMITTED BY H. EXC. MR. J. CAMBON,
AMBASSADOR OF THE FRENCH REPUBLIC, TO WIL-
LIAM McKINLEY, PRESIDENT OF THE UNITED
STATES OF AMERICA.

MADRID, *July 22, 1898.*

MR. PRESIDENT:

Since three months the American people and the
Spanish nation are at war because Spain did not consent to grant independence to Cuba and to withdraw
her troops therefrom.

Spain faced with resignation such uneven strife, and
only endeavored to defend her possessions with no
other hope than to oppose, in the measure of her
strength, the undertaking of the United States, and to
protect her honor.

Neither the trials which adversity has made us en-
dure nor the realization that but faint hope is left us
could deter us from struggling till the exhaustion of
our very last resources. This stout purpose, however,

248

does not blind us, and we are fully aware of the responsibilities which would weigh upon both nations in the eyes of the civilized world were this war to be continued.

This war not only inflicts upon the two peoples who wage it the hardships inseparable from all armed conflict, but also dooms to useless suffering and unjust sacrifices the inhabitants of a territory to which Spain is bound by secular ties that can be forgotten by no nation either of the old or of the new world.

To end calamities already so great and to avert evils still greater, our countries might naturally endeavor to find upon which conditions the present struggle could be determined otherwise than by force of arms.

Spain believes this understanding possible, and hopes that this view is also harbored by the Government of the United States. All true friends of both nations share no doubt the same hopes.

Spain wishes to show again that in this war, as well as in the one she carried on against the Cuban insurgents, she had but one object: the vindication of her prestige, her honor, her name. During the war of insurrection it was her desire to spare the great island from the dangers of premature independence; in the present war she has been actuated by sentiments inspired rather by ties of blood than by her interests and by the rights belonging to her as mother country.

Spain is prepared to spare Cuba from the continuation of the horrors of war if the United States are, on their part, likewise disposed.

The President of the United States and the American people may now learn from this message the true thought, desire, and intention of the Spanish nation.

And so do we wish to learn from the President of the United States upon which basis might be established a political status in Cuba and might be terminated a strife which would continue without reason should both Governments agree upon the means of pacifying the island.

In the name of the Government of H. M. the Queen Regent I have the honor to address this message to your excellency, with the expression of my highest consideration.

Duc d'Almodovar del rio,
Ministre d'Etat.

Department of State,
Washington, *July 30, 1898.*

Excellency:

The President received on the afternoon of Tuesday, the 26th instant, from the hand of his excellency the Ambassador of France, representing for this purpose the Government of Spain, the message signed by your excellency as minister of state in behalf of the Government of Her Majesty the Queen Regent of Spain, and dated the 22d instant, as to the possibility of terminating the war now existing between the United States and Spain.

The President received with satisfaction the suggestion that the two countries might mutually endeavor to ascertain the conditions on which the pending struggle may be brought to an end, as well as the expression of Spain's belief that an understanding on the subject is possible.

During the protracted negotiations that preceded the outbreak of hostilities the President earnestly labored to avert a conflict, in the hope that Spain, in consideration of her own interests, as well as those of the Spanish Antilles and the United States, would find a way of removing the conditions which had, for half a century, constantly disturbed the peace of the Western Hemisphere and on numerous occasions brought the two nations to the verge of war.

The President witnessed with profound disappointment the frustration of his peaceful efforts by events which forced upon the people of the United States the unalterable conviction that nothing short of the relinquishment by Spain of a claim of sovereignty over Cuba which she was unable to enforce would relieve a situation that had become unendurable.

For years the Government of the United States, out of regard for the susceptibilities of Spain, had by the exercise of its power and the expenditure of its treasure preserved the obligations of neutrality. But a point was at length reached at which, as Spain had often been forewarned, this attitude could no longer be maintained. The spectacle at our very doors of a fertile territory wasted by fire and sword, and given over to desolation and famine, was one to which our people could not be indifferent. Yielding, therefore, to the demands of humanity, they determined to remove the causes in the effects of which they had become so deeply involved.

To this end the President, with the authority of Congress, presented to Spain a demand for the withdrawal of her land and naval forces from Cuba, in order that the people of the island might be enabled to form a government of their own. To this demand Spain replied by severing diplomatic relations with the United States, and by declaring that she considered the action of this Government as creating a state of war between the two countries.

The President could not but feel sincere regret that the local question as to the peace and good government of Cuba should thus have been transformed and enlarged into a general conflict of arms between two great peoples. Nevertheless, having accepted the issue with all the hazards which it involved, he has, in the exercise of his duty, and of the rights which the state of war confers, prosecuted hostilities by land and sea, in order to secure at the earliest possible moment an honorable peace. In so doing he has been compelled to avail himself unsparingly of the lives and fortunes which his countrymen have placed at his command; and untold burdens and sacrifices, far transcending any material estimation, have been imposed upon them.

That as the result of the patriotic exertions of the people of the United States the strife has, as your excellency observes, proved unequal, inclines the President to offer a brave adversary generous terms of peace.

The President therefore responding to your excellency's request, will state the terms of peace which will be accepted by him at the present time, subject to the approval of the Senate of the United States hereafter.

Your excellency in discussing the question of Cuba intimates that Spain has desired to spare the island the dangers of premature independence. The Government of the United States has not shared the apprehensions of Spain in this regard, but it recognizes the fact that in the distracted and prostrate condition of the island, aid and guidance will be necessary, and these it is prepared to give.

The United States will require:

First. The relinquishment by Spain of all claim of sovereignty over or title to Cuba and her immediate evacuation of the island.

Second. The President, desirous of exhibiting signal generosity, will not now put forward any demand for pecuniary indemnity. Nevertheless he cannot be insensible to the losses and expenses of the United States incident to the war or to the claims of our citizens for injuries to their persons and property during the late insurrection in Cuba. He must, therefore, require the cession to the United States and the immediate evacuation by Spain of the island of Porto Rico and other islands now under the sovereignty of Spain in the West Indies, and also the cession of an island in the Ladrones, to be selected by the United States.

Third. On similar grounds the United States is entitled to occupy and will hold the city, bay, and harbor of Manila, pending the conclusion of a treaty of peace which shall determine the control, disposition, and government of the Philippines.

If the terms hereby offered are accepted in their entirety commissioners will be named by the United States to meet similarly authorized commissioners on the part of Spain for the purpose of settling the details of the treaty of peace and signing and delivering it under the terms above indicated.

I avail myself of this occasion to offer to your excellency the assurances of my highest consideration.

WILLIAM R. DAY.

His Excellency the DUKE OF ALMODOVAR DEL RIO,
Minister of State, etc.

MESSAGE OF HIS EXCELLENCY THE DUKE OF ALMODOVAR DEL RIO, MINISTER OF STATE OF SPAIN, SUBMITTED BY HIS EXCELLENCY MR. J. CAMBON, AMBASSADOR OF THE FRENCH REPUBLIC, TO HONORABLE WILLIAM R. DAY, SECRETARY OF STATE OF THE UNITED STATES.

[Translation.]

MADRID, *August 7th, 1898.*

MR. SECRETARY OF STATE:

The French ambassador at Washington, whose good offices have enabled the Spanish Government to address a message to the President of the United States, has forwarded by cable your excellency's reply to this document.

In examining the arguments used as a preamble to the specification of the terms upon which peace may be restored between Spain and the United States, it behooves the Spanish Government to deduct from the order of events that the severance of diplomatic relations with the United States had no other purpose than to decline the acceptance of an ultimatum which Spain could only consider as an attempt against her rightful sovereignty over Cuba.

Spain did not declare war; she met it because it was the only means of defending her rights in the Greater Antilles. Thus did the Queen and the United States see fit to transform and enlarge the purely local question of Cuba.

From this fact your excellency draws the conclusion that the question at stake is no longer only the one which relates to the territory of Cuba, but also that the losses of American lives and fortunes incident to the war should in some manner be compensated.

As to the first condition, relating to the future of Cuba, the two Governments reach similar conclusions in regard to the natural inability of its people to establish an independent government; be it by reason of inadequate development, as we believe, or on account of the present distracted and prostrate condition of the island, as your excellency states, the fact remains that Cuba needs guidance. The American people are willing to assume the responsibility of giving this guidance by substituting themselves to the Spanish nation, whose right to keep the island is indisputable; to this intimation we have nothing to oppose. The necessity of withdrawing from the territory of Cuba being imperative, the nation assuming Spain's place must, as long as this territory shall not have fully reached the conditions required to take rank among other sovereign powers, provide for rules which will insure order and protect against all risks the Spanish residents, as well as the Cuban natives still loyal to the mother country.

In the name of the nation the Spanish Government hereby relinquishes all claim of sovereignty over or title to Cuba, and engages to the irremeable evacuation of the island, subject to the approval of the Cortes —a reserve which we likewise make with regard to the other proffered terms—just as these terms will have to be ultimately approved by the Senate of the United States.

The United States require, as an indemnity for or an equivalent to the sacrifices they have borne during this short war, the cession of Porto Rico and of the other islands now under the sovereignty of Spain in the West Indies, and also the cession of an island in the Ladrones, to be selected by the Federal Government.

This demand strips us of the very last memory of a glorious past, and expels us at once from the prosperous island of Porto Rico and from the Western Hemisphere, which became peopled and civilized through the proud deeds of our ancestors. It might, perhaps, have been possible to compensate by some other cession for the injuries sustained by the United States. However, the inflexibility of the demand obliges us to cede, and we shall cede, the island of Porto Rico and the other islands belonging to the Crown of Spain in the West Indies, together with one of the islands of the archipelago of the Ladrones, to be selected by the American Government.

The terms relating to the Philippines seem, to our understanding, to be quite indefinite. On the one hand, the ground on which the United States believe themselves entitled to occupy the bay, the harbor, and the city of Manila, pending the conclusion of a treaty of peace, can not be that of conquest, since in spite of the blockade maintained on sea by the American fleet, in spite of the siege established on land by a native supported and provided for by the American admiral, Manila still holds its own, and the Spanish standard still waves over the city. On the other hand, the whole archipelago of the Philippines is in the power and under the sovereignty of Spain. Therefore the Government of Spain thinks that the temporary occupation of Manila should constitute a guaranty. It is stated that the treaty of peace shall determine the control, disposition, and government of the Philippines; but as the intentions of the Federal Government by regression remain veiled, therefore the Spanish Government must declare that, while accepting the third condition, they do not a priori renounce the sovereignty of Spain over the archipelago, leaving it to the negotiators to agree as to such reforms which the condition of these possessions and the level of culture of their natives may render desirable.

The Government of Her Majesty accepts the third condition, with the above mentioned declarations.

Such are the statements and observations which the Spanish Government has the honor to submit in reply to your excellency's communication. They accept the proffered terms, subject to the approval of the Cortes of the Kingdom, as required by their constitutional duties.

The agreement between the two Governments implies the irremeable suspension of hostilities and the designation of commissioners for the purpose of settling the details of the treaty of peace and of signing it, under the terms above indicated.

I avail myself of this occasion to offer to your excellency the assurances of my highest consideration.

ALMODOVAR DEL RIO.

DEPARTMENT OF STATE,
WASHINGTON, *August 10, 1898.*

EXCELLENCY:

Although it is your understanding that the note of the Duke of Almodovar, which you left with the President on yesterday afternoon, is intended to convey an acceptance by the Spanish Government of the terms set forth in my note of the 30th ultimo as the basis on which the President would appoint commissioners to negotiate and conclude with commissioners on the part of Spain a treaty of peace, I understand that we concur in the opinion that the Duke's note, doubtless owing to the various transformations which it has undergone in the course of its circuitous transmission by telegraph and in cipher, is not, in the form in which it has reached the hands of the President, entirely explicit.

Under these circumstances it is thought that the most direct and certain way of avoiding misunderstanding is to embody in a protocol, to be signed by us as the representatives, respectively, of the United States and Spain, the terms on which the negotiations for peace are to be undertaken.

I therefore inclose herewith a draft of such a protocol, in which you will find that I have embodied the precise terms tendered to Spain in my note of the 30th ultimo, together with appropriate stipulations for the appointment of commissioners to arrange the details of the immediate evacuation of Cuba, Porto Rico, and other islands under Spanish sovereignty in the West Indies, as well as for the appointment of commissioners to treat of peace.

Accept, excellency, the renewed assurances of my highest consideration.

WILLIAM R. DAY.

His Excellency M. JULES CAMBON, etc.

———

PROTOCOL.

William R. Day, Secretary of State of the United States, and His Excellency Jules Cambon, ambassador extraordinary and plenipotentiary of the Republic of France at Washington, respectively possessing for this purpose full authority from the Government of the United States and the Government of Spain, have concluded and signed the following articles, embodying the terms on which the two Governments have agreed in respect to the matters hereinafter set forth, having in view the establishment of peace between the two countries, that is to say:

ARTICLE 1. Spain will relinquish all claim of sovereignty over or title to Cuba.

ARTICLE 2. Spain will cede to the United States the island of Porto Rico and other islands now under Spanish sovereignty in the West Indies, and also an island in the Ladrones, to be selected by the United States.

ARTICLE 3. The United States will occupy and hold the city, bay, and harbor of Manila pending the conclusion of a treaty of peace which shall determine the control, disposition, and government of the Philippines.

ARTICLE 4. Spain will immediately evacuate Cuba, Porto Rico, and other islands under Spanish sovereignty in the West Indies; and to this end each Government will, within ten days after the signing of this protocol, appoint commissioners, and the commissioners so appointed shall, within thirty days after the signing of this protocol, meet at Havana for the purpose of arranging and carrying out the details of the aforesaid evacuation of Cuba and the adjacent Spanish islands; and each Government will, within ten days after the signing of this protocol, also appoint other commissioners, who shall, within thirty days after the signing of this protocol, meet at San Juan, in Porto Rico, for the purpose of arranging and carrying out the details of the aforesaid evacuation of Porto Rico and other islands under Spanish sovereignty in the West Indies.

ARTICLE 5. The United States and Spain will each appoint not more than five commissioners to treat of peace, and the commissioners so appointed shall meet at Paris not later than October 1, 1898, and proceed to the negotiation and conclusion of a treaty of peace, which treaty shall be subject to ratification according to the respective constitutional forms of the two countries.

ARTICLE 6. Upon the conclusion and signing of this protocol hostilities between the two countries shall be suspended, and notice to that effect shall be given as soon as possible by each Government to the commanders of its military and naval forces.

[Signed at Washington, August 12, 1898.]

DEPARTMENT OF STATE,
WASHINGTON, *August 10, 1898*

EXCELLENCY:

I have the honor to say, as I assured you orally this morning, that upon the suspension of hostilities between the United States and Spain, as the result of the signing and sealing of the protocol upon the terms of which we have agreed, it is the purpose of this Government to take prompt and efficient means to aid the introduction of food supplies into the ports of Cuba.

Accept, excellency, the renewed assurances of my highest consideration.

WILLIAM R. DAY.

His Excellency Mr. JULES CAMBON, etc.

WILLIAM R. DAY,
        Secretary of State:

You are hereby authorized to sign, on the part of the United States, the protocol of this date embodying the terms on which the United States and Spain have agreed to treat of peace.

WILLIAM McKINLEY.

EXECUTIVE MANSION,
        WASHINGTON, *August 12, 1898.*

261

APPENDIX

[Translation.]

EMBASSY OF THE FRENCH REPUBLIC
IN THE UNITED STATES,
WASHINGTON, *August 12, 1898.*

MR. SECRETARY OF STATE: I have the honor to inform you that I have just received, through the intermediation of the department of foreign affairs at Paris, a telegram, dated Madrid, August 11, in which the Duke of Almodovar del Rio announces to me that, by order of Her Majesty the Queen Regent, the Spanish Government confers upon me full powers in order that I may sign, without other formality and without delay, the protocol whereof the terms have been drawn up by common accord between you and me. The instrument destined to make regular the powers which are thus given to me by telegraph will be subsequently addressed to me by the post.

His excellency the minister of state adds that in accepting this protocol and by reason of the suspension of hostilities which will be the immediate consequence of that acceptance, the Spanish Government has pleasure in hoping that the Government of the United States will take the necessary measures with a view to restrain (empecher) all aggression on the part of the Cuban separatist forces.

The Government of the Republic having, on the other hand, authorized me to accept the powers which are conferred upon me by the Spanish Government, I shall hold myself at your disposition to sign the protocol at the hour you may be pleased to designate.

Congratulating myself upon thus cooperating with you toward the restoration of peace between two nations, both friends of France, I beg you to accept, Mr. Secretary of State, the fresh assurances of my very high consideration.

JULES CAMBON.

Hon. WILLIAM R. DAY,
Secretary of State of the United States, etc., Washington.

No. 94.]   DEPARTMENT OF STATE,
                    WASHINGTON, *August 15, 1898.*

EXCELLENCY: I have the honor to make formal acknowledgement of the note you addressed to me, under date of the 12th instant, informing me of your receipt, through the medium of the department of foreign affairs at Paris, of a telegram, dated Madrid, August 11, in which the Duke of Almodovar del Rio, minister of state of Spain, by order of Her Majesty the Queen Regent, conferred upon you full powers to sign, without other formality and without delay, the protocol already drawn up by you and me, leaving the documentary confirmation of your said full powers to follow by mail; and adding that, the Government of the Republic having authorized you to accept the powers so conferred upon you by the Spanish Government, you were ready to sign the protocol at such time as I might designate.

The signing of the protocol on the afternoon of the 12th instant by you and me, in the presence of the President, followed by the immediate action of the President in issuing his proclamation suspending hostilities, in accordance with the appropriate stipulation of that protocol, testified in a most gratifying manner the full recognition by this Government of the powers conferred upon you, and, I am glad to believe, marked the first and most effective step toward the happy restoration of peace between the United States and Spain. It is especially gratifying to the President and to this Government that you, as the honored representative of the French Republic, allied to our American commonwealth by the unbroken ties of more than a century of close friendship and to the Kingdom of Spain by propinquity and intimate association, should have been thus instrumental in contributing to this auspicious result.

Referring to the observation contained in your note relative to the internal order of Cuba during the suspension of hostilities, I may remark that the forces of the United States, in proportion as they occupy Cuban territory in the course of the evacuation thereof by Spain and its delivery to the arms of the United States under the terms of the protocol, will, it is believed, be adequate to preserve peace and order, and no doubt is entertained of their ability to restrain any possible injury to the inhabitants of the island in the country which shall by degrees come under their control.

Be pleased, Mr. Ambassador, to accept the renewed assurances of my highest consideration.

WILLIAM R. DAY.

[Translation.]

The French ambassador, referring to his communication of the 12th instant, has the honor to inform the

Secretary of State of the United States, that he has just received, through the department of foreign affairs at Paris, the full powers which had been conferred upon him, in the name of the King of Spain, by Her Majesty the Queen Regent, to enable him to sign the preliminary protocol of the negotiations for the establishment of peace between Spain and the United States.

Mr. J. Cambon requests the Hon. William R. Day to please to find inclosed the said document, and avails himself of the occasion to renew the assurances of his highest consideration.

Washington, *August 30, 1898.*

Hon. Wm. R. Day,
Secretary of State of the United States, etc., Washington.

[Translation.]

DON ALFONSO XIII

BY THE GRACE OF GOD AND THE CONSTITUTION, KING OF SPAIN, AND IN HIS NAME AND DURING HIS MINORITY,

DONA MARIA CRISTINA,

QUEEN REGENT OF THE KINGDOM.

Whereas it has become necessary to negotiate and sign at Washington a protocol in which the preliminaries of peace between Spain and the United States of America shall be settled, and as it is necessary for me to empower for that purpose a person possessing the

requisite qualifications: Therefore, I have decided to
select, after procuring the consent of His Excellency
the President of the French Republic, you, Don Julio
Cambon, ambassador extraordinary and plenipotentiary
of the French Republic in the United States of America, as I do, by these presents, select and appoint you
to proceed, invested with the character of my plenipotentiary to negotiate and sign with the plenipotentiary
whom His Excellency the President of the United
States of America may designate for that purpose the
aforesaid protocol. And I declare, from the present
moment, all that you may agree upon, negotiate,
and sign in the execution of this commission ac-
ceptable and valid, and I will observe it and execute it, and will cause it to be observed and executed as if it had been done by myself, for which
I give you my whole full powers in the most ample form required by law. In witness whereof I
have caused these presents to be issued, signed by my
hand, duly sealed and countersigned by the undersigned, my minister of state. Given in the palace at
Madrid, August 11, 1898.

[L. S.]   MARIA CRISTINA.

JUAN MANUEL SANCHEZ Y GUTIERREZ DE CASTRO
Minister of State.

APPENDIX D

THE TREATY OF PEACE

THE UNITED STATES OF AMERICA AND HER MAJ-ESTY THE QUEEN REGENT OF SPAIN, IN THE NAME OF HER AUGUST SON DON ALFONSO XIII, desiring to end the state of war now existing between the two countries, have for that purpose appointed as Plenipotentiaries:

THE PRESIDENT OF THE UNITED STATES,

WILLIAM R. DAY, CUSHMAN K. DAVIS, WILLIAM P. FRYE, GEORGE GRAY, and WHITELAW REID, citizens of the United States;

AND HER MAJESTY THE QUEEN REGENT OF SPAIN,

DON EUGENIO MONTERO RIOS, President of the Senate, DON BUENAVENTURA DE ABARZUZA, Senator of the Kingdom and ex-Minister of the Crown, DON JOSE DE GARNICA, Deputy to the Cortes and Associate Justice of the Supreme Court, DON WENCESLAO RAMIREZ DE VILLA-URRUTIA, Envoy Extraordinary and Minister Plenipotentiary at Brussels, and DON RAFAEL CERERO, General of Division:

Who, having assembled in Paris, and having exchanged their full powers, which were found to be in due and proper form, have, after discussion of the matters before them, agreed upon the following articles:

APPENDIX

ARTICLE I

Spain relinquishes all claim of sovereignty over and title to Cuba.

And as the island is, upon its evacuation by Spain, to be occupied by the United States, the United States will, so long as such occupation shall last, assume and discharge the obligations that may under international law result from the fact of its occupation, for the protection of life and property.

ARTICLE II

Spain cedes to the United States the island of Porto Rico and other islands now under Spanish sovereignty in the West Indies, and the island of Guam in the Marianas or Ladrones.

ARTICLE III

Spain cedes to the United States the archipelago known as the Philippine islands, and comprehending the islands lying within the following line:

A line running from west to east along or near the twentieth parallel of north latitude, and through the middle of the navigable channel of Bachi, from the one hundred and eighteenth (118th) to the one hundred and twenty-seventh (127th) degree meridian of longitude east of Greenwich, thence along the one hundred and twenty-seventh (127th) degree meridian of longitude east of Greenwich to the parallel of four degrees and forty-five minutes (4° 45′) north latitude, thence along the parallel of four degrees and forty-five minutes (4° 45′) north latitude to its intersection with the meridian of longitude one hundred and nineteen degrees and thirty-five minutes (119° 35′) east of Greenwich, thence along the meridian of longitude one hundred and nineteen degrees and thirty-five minutes (119° 35′) east of Greenwich to the parallel of latitude seven degrees and forty minutes (7° 40′) north, thence along the parallel of latitude seven degrees and forty minutes (7° 40′) north to its intersection with the one hundred and sixteenth (116th) degree meridian of longitude east of Greenwich, thence by a direct line to the intersection of the tenth (10th) degree parallel of north latitude with the one hundred and eighteenth (118th) degree meridian of longitude east of Greenwich, and thence along the one hundred and eighteenth (118th) degree meridian of longitude east of Greenwich to the point of beginning.

The United States will pay to Spain the sum of twenty million dollars ($20,000,000), within three months after the exchange of the ratifications of the present treaty.

Article IV

The United States will, for the term of ten years from date of the exchange of the ratifications of the present treaty, admit Spanish ships and merchandise to the ports of the Philippine islands on the same terms as ships and merchandise of the United States.

Article V

The United States will, upon the signature of the present treaty, send back to Spain, at its own cost the Spanish soldiers taken as prisoners of war on the capture of Manila by the American forces. The arms of the soldiers in question shall be restored to them.

Spain will, upon the exchange of the ratifications of the present treaty, proceed to evacuate the Philippines, as well as the island of Guam, on terms similar to those agreed upon by the Commissioners appointed to arrange for the evacuation of Porto Rico and other islands in the West Indies, under the protocol of August 12, 1898, which is to continue in force till its provisions are completely executed.

The time within which the evacuation of the Philippine islands and Guam shall be completed shall be fixed by the two Governments. Stands of colors, uncaptured war vessels, small arms, guns of all calibres, with their carriages and accessories, powder, ammunition, livestock, and materials and supplies of all kinds, belonging to the land and naval forces of Spain in the Philippines and Guam, remain the property of Spain. Pieces of heavy ordnance, exclusive of field artillery, in the fortifications and coast defences, shall remain in their emplacements for the term of six months, to be reckoned from the exchange of ratifications of the treaty; and the United States may, in the meantime, purchase such material from Spain, if a satisfactory agreement between the two Governments on the subject shall be reached.

ARTICLE VI

Spain will, upon the signature of the present treaty, release all prisoners of war, and all persons detained or imprisoned for political offences, in connection with the insurrections in Cuba and the Philippines and the war with the United States.

Reciprocally, the United States will release all persons made prisoners of war by the American forces, and will undertake to obtain the release of all Spanish prisoners in the hands of the insurgents in Cuba and the Philippines.

The Government of the United States will at its own cost return to Spain and the Government of Spain will at its own cost return to the United States, Cuba, Porto Rico, and the Philippines, according to the situation of their respective homes, prisoners released or caused to be released by them, respectively, under this article.

Article VII

The United States and Spain mutually relinquish all claims for indemnity, national and individual, of every kind, of either Government, or of its citizens or subjects, against the other Government, that may have arisen since the beginning of the late insurrection in Cuba and prior to the exchange of ratifications of the present treaty, including all claims for indemnity for the cost of the war.

The United States will adjudicate and settle the claims of its citizens against Spain relinquished in this article.

Article VIII

In conformity with the provisions of Articles I, II, and III of this treaty, Spain relinquishes in Cuba, and cedes in Porto Rico and other islands in the West Indies, in the island of Guam, and in the Philippine Archipelago, all the buildings, wharves, barracks, forts, structures, public highways and other immovable property which, in conformity with law, belong to the public domain, and as such belong to the Crown of Spain.

And it is hereby declared that the relinquishment or

cession, as the case may be, to which the preceding paragraph refers, cannot in any respect impair the property or rights which by law belong to the peaceful possession of property of all kinds, of provinces, municipalities, public or private establishments, ecclesiastical or civic bodies, or any other associations having legal capacity to acquire and possess property in the aforesaid territories renounced or ceded, or of private individuals, of whatsoever nationality such individuals may be.

The aforesaid relinquishment or cession, as the case may be, includes all documents exclusively referring to the sovereignty relinquished or ceded that may exist in the archives of the Peninsula. Where any document in such archives only in part relates to said sovereignty, a copy of such part will be furnished whenever it shall be requested. Like rules shall be reciprocally observed in favor of Spain in respect of documents in the archives of the islands above referred to.

In the aforesaid relinquishment or cession, as the case may be, are also included such rights as the Crown of Spain and its authorities possess in respect of the official archives and records, executive as well as judicial, in the islands above referred to, which relate to said islands or the rights and property of their inhabitants. Such archives and records shall be carefully preserved, and private persons shall without distinction have the right to require, in accordance with law, authenticated copies of the contracts, wills and other instruments forming part of notarial protocols or files, or which may be contained in the executive or judicial archives, be the latter in Spain or in the islands aforesaid.

APPENDIX

ARTICLE IX

Spanish subjects, natives of the Peninsula, residing in the territory over which Spain by the present treaty relinquishes or cedes her sovereignty, may remain in such territory or may remove therefrom, retaining in either event all their rights of property, including the right to sell or dispose of such property or of its proceeds; and they shall also have the right to carry on their industry, commerce and professions, being subject in respect thereof to such laws as are applicable to other foreigners. In case they remain in the territory they may preserve their allegiance to the Crown of Spain by making, before a court of record, within a year from the date of the exchange of ratifications of this treaty, a declaration of their decision to preserve such allegiance; in default of which declaration they shall be held to have renounced it and to have adopted the nationality of the territory in which they may reside.

The civil rights and political status of the native inhabitants of the territories hereby ceded to the United States shall be determined by the Congress.

ARTICLE X

The inhabitants of the territories over which Spain relinquishes or cedes her sovereignty shall be secured in the free exercise of their religion.

ARTICLE XI

The Spaniards residing in the territories over which Spain by this treaty cedes or relinquishes her sovereignty shall be subject in matters civil as well as crim-

APPENDIX

inal to the jurisdiction of the courts of the country wherein they reside, pursuant to the ordinary laws governing the same; and they shall have the right to appear before such courts, and to pursue the same course as citizens of the country to which the courts belong.

ARTICLE XII

Judicial proceedings pending at the time of the exchange of ratifications of this treaty in the territories over which Spain relinquishes or cedes her sovereignty shall be determined according to the following rules:

1. Judgments rendered either in civil suits between private individuals, or in criminal matters, before the date mentioned, and with respect to which there is no recourse or right of review under the Spanish law, shall be deemed to be final, and shall be executed in due form by competent authority in the territory within which such judgments should be carried out.

2. Civil suits between private individuals which may on the date mentioned be undetermined shall be prosecuted to judgment before the court in which they may then be pending or in the court that may be substituted therefor.

3. Criminal actions pending on the date mentioned before the Supreme Court of Spain against citizens of the territory which by this treaty ceases to be Spanish shall continue under its jurisdiction until final judgment; but, such judgment having been rendered, the execution thereof shall be committed to the competent authority of the place in which the case arose.

APPENDIX

ARTICLE XIII

The rights of property secured by copyrights and patents acquired by Spaniards in the island of Cuba, and in Porto Rico, the Philippines and other ceded territories, at the time of the exchange of the ratifications of this treaty, shall continue to be respected. Spanish scientific, literary and artistic works, not subversive of public order in the territories in question, shall continue to be admitted free of duty into such territories, for the period of ten years, to be reckoned from the date of the exchange of the ratifications of this treaty.

ARTICLE XIV

Spain shall have the power to establish consular officers in the ports and places of the territories, the sovereignty over which has been either relinquished or ceded by the present treaty.

ARTICLE XV

The Government of each country will, for the term of ten years, accord to the merchant vessels of the other country the same treatment in respect of all port charges, including entrance and clearance dues, light dues, and tonnage duties, as it accords to its own merchant vessels, not engaged in the coastwise trade.

This article may at any time be terminated on six months' notice given by either Government to the other.

ARTICLE XVI

It is understood that any obligations assumed in this treaty by the United States with respect to Cuba are limited to the time of its occupancy thereof; but it will upon the termination of such occupancy, advise any Government established in the island to assume the same obligations.

ARTICLE XVII

The present treaty shall be ratified by the President of the United States, by and with the advice and consent of the Senate thereof, and by Her Majesty the Queen Regent of Spain; and the ratifications shall be exchanged at Washington within six months from the date thereof, or earlier if possible.

In faith whereof, we, the respective Plenipotentiaries, have signed this treaty and have hereunto affixed our seals.

Done in duplicate at Paris, the tenth day of December, in the year of Our Lord one thousand eight hundred and ninety-eight.

[SEAL]   WILLIAM R. DAY,
[SEAL]   CUSHMAN K. DAVIS,
[SEAL]   WILLIAM P. FRYE,
[SEAL]   GEO. GRAY,
[SEAL]   WHITELAW REID.

Hecho por duplicado en Paris á diez de Diciembre del ano mil ochocientos noventa y ocho.

[SEAL]   EUGENIO MONTERO RIOS,
[SEAL]   B. DE ABARZUZA,
[SEAL]   J. DE GARNICA,
[SEAL]   W. R. DE VILLA URRUTIA,
[SEAL]   RAFAEL CERERO.

www.ingramcontent.com/pod-product-compliance
Lightning Source LLC
Chambersburg PA
CBHW031059110726
47900CB00003B/990